MW00715441

STOP IT THERE, BACK IT UP!

50 YEARS OF HOCKEY WITH HOWIE MEEKER

HOWIE MEEKER

with

CHARLIE HODGE

FOREWORD BY DAVE HODGE

Copyright © 1999 by Howie Meeker and Charlie Hodge

All rights reserved. No part of this publication may be reproduced or transmitted in any form or by any means, electronic or mechanical, including photocopying, recording, or any information storage and retrieval system, without permission in writing from the publisher.

Published in 1999 by Stoddart Publishing Co. Limited
34 Lesmill Road, Toronto, Canada M3B 2T6

Distributed in Canada by General Distribution Services Limited
325 Humber College Blvd., Toronto, Ontario M9W 7C3
Tel. (416) 213-1919   Fax (416) 213-1917
Email Customer.Service@ccmailgw.genpub.com

Distributed in the U.S. by General Distribution Services Inc.
85 River Rock Drive, Suite 202, Buffalo, New York 14207
Toll-free tel. 1-800-805-1083 Toll-free fax 1-800-481-6207
Email gdsinc@genpub.com

03 02 01 00 99 1 2 3 4 5

Cataloguing in Publication Data

Meeker, Howie
Stop it there, back it up!: 50 years of hockey with Howie Meeker

ISBN 0-7737-3203-9

1. National Hockey League — History. 2. Hockey — History.
3. Hockey players. I. Hodge, Charlie , 1955–   II. Title.

GV847.8.N3M43 1999   796.962'64
C-99-931448-3

Jacket design: Bill Douglas @ The Bang
Design and typesetting: Kinetics Design & Illustration

Every reasonable effort has been made to obtain reprint permissions. The publisher will gladly receive any information that will help rectify, in subsequent editions, any inadvertent omissions.

THE CANADA COUNCIL | LE CONSEIL DES ARTS
FOR THE ARTS | DU CANADA
SINCE 1957 | DEPUIS 1957

We acknowledge for their financial support of our publishing program the Canada Council, the Ontario Arts Council, and the Government of Canada through the Book Publishing Industry Development Program (BPIDP).

Printed and bound in Canada

CONTENTS

■ ■ ■

FOREWORD

■ ■ ■

Introducing Howie Meeker on television was one thing. "Here's Howie with the highlights," usually sufficed. He would take it from there.

Introducing Howie Meeker in this form is something entirely different. Golly gee — where do I start?

Most Canadians know something about him, but chances are they don't know everything when they hear him described as a small-town Ontario lad who grew up fishing and hunting and skating on frozen ponds and went on to become a war veteran, federal politician, four-time Stanley Cup winner, member of the Hockey Hall of Fame, and everybody's favourite between-periods TV commentator.

Canada is the only place in the world you could hope to discover someone like Howie, because in no other country, and in no other person, can you find such passion for hockey, and such dedication to the teachings of the game.

Howie Meeker skated for the first time at the age of three. He's liable to skate for the last time at or about the age of 93. (He'll wonder why I would suggest he might have less than 20 years left on those skates of his.) But maybe he'll need to conserve his energy so he can continue to refine plans for Howie Meeker Hockey School clinics of the future. Funny thing is, the original Meeker doctrines can apply to present and future players, because the day will never come when the sport of hockey has fully digested his most basic thoughts.

A Howie Meeker book could be about many things — war, politics, Canada, personal dedication and commitment to tasks at hand, and his life's work — but it's not a Howie Meeker book if it's not about hockey, for hockey has been his life before and after everything else.

Howie spent his early days as a junior star in Kitchener and Stratford, Ontario. Later, he returned from war duty overseas to begin an NHL career with the Toronto Maple Leafs. And what a beginning! He won the Calder Trophy as the NHL's top rookie, and left behind a rookie record that still stands when he scored five goals in one game. He won his first of four Stanley Cups in that first season.

Eight years later, a back injury brought an end to his playing career, but just as a serious war injury caused by an exploding grenade merely slowed him down a little, his injury on ice couldn't finish his hockey career. In many ways, he was just starting to make his mark on the game.

He became a coach with Pittsburgh of the American Hockey League, and then with the very team he had helped to achieve Stanley Cup glory — the Toronto Maple Leafs. He remains well known for his short stint as Leafs' general manager, when he punched the boss's son in the nose.

Newfoundlanders might still wonder how that ever happened, because the Howie Meeker they inherited was the boss, the creator of an entire hockey training system for St. John's and the surrounding area. He was hardly a fighter, but rather a lover of the game and of those who wanted to learn to play it.

In 1968, Meeker was on a business trip to Montreal when Ted

Darling spotted him in a hotel lobby and wondered if he would be interested in providing some guest commentary for *Hockey Night in Canada*, alongside Danny Gallivan and Dick Irvin. Ted might as well have invited a chocolate lover to visit Hershey. The only thing that Howie liked more than a hockey game was a hockey game on television, specifically during its intermissions.

The game stood still for Meeker in more ways than one, when he'd say "stop it right there," and he made it come alive again whenever he issued the instructions to "back it up and let 'er go!"

Just as Foster Hewitt described hockey goals for all time with his simplicity of "He shoots, he scores!" Howie Meeker developed a hockey language for watching televised replays. For that and many other reasons, it was fitting that Howie received the Foster Hewitt Memorial Award upon his induction into the Hockey Hall of Fame in 1998.

Meeker has spent more than 50 years in and around the game of hockey. Thus, there was more than enough personal material to fill the pages of his biography, *Golly Gee, It's Me! — The Howie Meeker Story*.

But just as an intermission ultimately gave way to another period-opening face-off, cutting off Howie before he had a chance to finish talking, that book ended without allowing Howie the opportunity to talk about hockey itself, and the many friends and characters he's met along the way.

Here, you will find his thoughts on the greatest teams and players of the past, and on the state of the game and what should be done to make it better.

I'm thrilled he's written down his experiences, if only for my benefit. I spent 16 years beside him in the *Hockey Night in Canada* television studio, and I was having too much fun to learn much of anything from him then.

Here, again, for all of us, is "Howie with the highlights."

DAVE HODGE, JULY 1999

ACKNOWLEDGMENTS

■ ■ ■

Thanks to editors Jim Gifford, Don Bastian, Wendy Thomas, Ron Wight, Lloyd Davis, and Sharon Hodge. Also many thanks to Don Tamboline, Ron Elliot, Maxine Carpenter, John Spalding, TSN, Leah Meeker, Mike Meeker, Brett, Shauna, and Chelsea Fagan, Dan Diamond, Jimmi McDonald, Mike Keenan, Craig Hodge, Grace Meeker, Kitty Stolar, *The Hockey News*, Rob Sayce, Billy, *Inside Sports*, Pastor Dan Thiessen, Peter Hanlon (Calgary Flames), Jim Krahn, Lars Larson, Butch O'Brien, Ralph Krehbiel, Ted "Teeder" Kennedy, Vic Lynn, Mayor Julia MacDonald and Parksville City Council and staff, The Hockey Legends, Bill Snaychuk, the Vancouver Canucks, Don Skoyan, Muggy, the Canadian Hockey Hall of Fame, Bob MacPherson, Tom Deir, Bucky, and Bruce Bennett. (When Charlie was a youngster, Bruce was the corner butcher in Kelowna, B.C., and gave him all his hockey magazines and issues of *The Hockey News* when he was finished with them. Thank goodness Charlie is a pack rat.)

HOWIE MEEKER AND CHARLIE HODGE

P A R T

■ ■ ■

The Game

1
For the
"Older" Kids

■ ■ ■

I was playing defence and was the first man back deep in our end. I picked up the puck in the corner, shook my head and shoulders as I beat the first forechecker, and then turned to pass the puck to an open forward I hoped was somewhere behind our blueline. Instead, all I saw were three of my guys, skating full-speed through the centre ice area, waving their sticks for a pass.

"No way. I'll give it to my defence partner and let him do whatever," I thought — but I couldn't find him. He wasn't behind or in front of the net, not in the corner, or the face-off spot.

Where the hell did he go?

Finally I spotted him. He was also skating under a full head of steam over our blueline, hollering, "Howie, Howie!" In the meantime I was up to my waist in alligators with opposition checkers all over me, so I did the only sensible thing and bounced the puck off the boards into the centre ice area.

Later, on the bench, I advised both my wingers to go to the hash marks on the face-off circle when I got the puck and to stay there, and I'd get them the puck. If and when they ran into trouble, they should either pass it back to me or a teammate or put the puck against the boards and out. Never, never, never in the middle!

So I got the puck, beat a forechecker, took one stride toward the opposition winger who came to me, and gave my now open winger the puck. He took two strides with it, saw the pinching defenceman, and passed the puck *into the middle*, right on to the opposing centre's stick — tape to tape.

Our centre was gone, the far winger with him at centre ice looking over his shoulder for a pass, my defence partner was on his way out of our zone, and it was five red jerseys against me and the goaltender.

That's when I awoke and sat bolt upright in bed, beads of sweat rolling off my face. When I switched on the light to straighten out the wet sheets, cover them with a towel, and change my pyjama top, Grace woke up; our two schnauzers, Tara and Sam, woke up begrudgingly at the foot of the bed.

"Bad dream?" Grace asked, knowing the answer. I used to have them regularly when I was coaching for a living. I hadn't had one for 10 years and had forgotten how it used to spoil our days and nights.

"My, oh my, Gracey, if I ever come and tell you I am going to play Old-timers hockey, hit me right between the eyes with a sledge-hammer, burn my equipment, and hide the car keys," I begged.

■ ■ ■

How old is old?

I'm a fairly healthy 76-year-old and consider nothing old except my short-term memory. I can still find my way home from the Comox ski mountain, traverse the route to the Parksville arena for my occasional hockey games, and remember my new wife, Leah's, birthday. But there are times, I admit, when I forget just what or why it is I am doing something. Sometimes I even forget how I got involved in Old-timers hockey. But making notes for this book brought it all back.

It was one day back in 1985, just before I'd had that frightening dream. I was sharing a couple of neat double scotches with a great Parksville fishing buddy, Bill Stanton, an ex-RCMP officer, and he suggested I try playing Old-timers hockey. "How about joining us old boys on Monday, Wednesday, and Friday mornings at the rink? Come give it a try, Howie."

Right away my mind flashed back to the ponds, rivers, and backyard rinks, those cold, crisp winter days when the top priority was to have fun. I realized right then that it had been 50 years since I played a game of hockey where the score wasn't important; where checking, hitting, and excessive stickwork was frowned upon; and scoring goals came miles ahead of defence. I longed for a game where the enjoyment of playing came ahead of winning.

"Golly gee — do you think, maybe, the 60-and-over gang could become kids again? Nah!"

During my first four years playing in the National Hockey League, I constantly worried about losing my job. Years later, when I was coach of the Leafs, we had one win and two ties in 12 games in November 1956. I later found out that if owner Conn Smythe didn't want it, and hadn't planned it that way, I'd have been fired right then. Soon after, Hap Day was fired by Conn so that son Stafford could run the hockey club. Months later, when the die was well cast, I was given the boot.

A little later, I wound up taking a third-rate hockey system in Newfoundland hopefully to better things by coaching junior high and senior high school hockey teams, and also a junior and a senior team in two extremely competitive six-team city leagues.

More often than not, those St. John's junior or senior team competitions were religious wars. Every game, high school to senior hockey, was played in a sold-out stadium and it was pure mayhem. Truly a religious war within an arena. And out in the hinterlands, geeze, did the "bayman" ever love to clobber the "townie," which more often than not they did.

Finally, in Lotus Land, for 10 years the only hockey for me was the hockey school, as well as my *Hockey Night in Canada* job on CBC, covering BCTV Canuck games, and doing guest appearances on NBC and TSN.

Play hockey again? For *fun*? The concept seemed foreign.

Old-timers hockey, yes or no?

Well . . . maybe.

When I ran the idea past Grace, she said, "You're nuts! For 30 years I've had to listen to you rant and rave about players who won't or can't think on your hockey teams. For the last 10 it's been quiet and peaceful. You bitch when the wind blows because it keeps you off the water, you bitch when the fishing is poor, or the road to Mount Washington ski hill is closed, but that I can put up with.

"No, you're not going down there with those old farts and then come home and spoil my days and nights. I've had enough of that rubbish."

And I knew she was right.

But . . . maybe. Maybe those old farts, many of whom had successful marriages, had raised a family, had grandchildren, and were in tough physical and mental competition all their lives — maybe they could be just like I hoped for . . . able to think, and learn skills, and still have fun.

I continued to rationalize the possibilities. After all, many of them had been successful financially, and showed a willingness to change by moving, like me, from the frozen tundra of central or eastern Canada to Lotus Land, B.C. That showed flexibility.

But what about on the ice, inside the arena?

Out of curiosity I had to find the answer to that question.

Surely it wouldn't spoil their day if someone scored a goal against them and they lost the morning fun game? Hey, holy cow, they wouldn't keep score, would they? Golly gee, if they were up by five or six goals, they wouldn't take a shot away from the opposition, would they? I felt I had to at least find out.

A few days later, however, I yet again conceded a point to Grace and agreed with her earlier suggestions.

"You're right, dear, things are just too good. No wind, sunny days, calm water which makes great winter fishing, and steelhead fishing in the Englishman River. (Neighbour) Jim Kingsley and I can catch the odd beauty. And there's the wonderful spring salmon fishing in the chuck out front of the house, or the tremendous downhill skiing at Mount Washington. That gives me lots to do on the three or four days I'm home every week."

What had changed my mind against playing?

Two things, actually. In 20 years of coaching amateur hockey, I'd been relatively successful. My teams had been in the finals of every age group more than my fair share, and more often than not we'd picked up a gold medal. Except on rare occasions, I did it with sound goaltending, hard work, checking, discipline, and system. I can look back at the 40 years and I don't think I had 15 good offensive players; surely never three at once on any one of the many teams I coached — even the Leafs. Clearly, to try to teach offensive skills in hockey to anyone over 12 years of age was a waste of time.

Mainly we scored on the other team's mistakes, the power play, and one or two guys getting together for a great offensive effort. By the time I left Newfoundland, I had had enough of constantly teaching defence and checking skills and didn't want any more.

The second reason was that dream.

It really shook me up and temporarily put the nail in the coffin of my Old-timers hockey temptation. I remember that it truly was a "dark and stormy night," all dreary and rainy, around 4 a.m. when I woke from that horrible hockey nightmare and swore off ever playing or coaching the game again.

But the only thing for sure in life, besides death and taxes, is that nothing is for sure.

So, it was a few months after Bill suggested I become involved in Old-timers hockey and I was down at the local arena making reservations for my hockey school when I glanced out the office window and saw 15 or 20 old farts playing hockey. On closer look, I counted 18 of them butchering the game. But holy smokes, that slim grey-haired old geezer playing centre was amazing.

I pinched myself to make sure it wasn't another dream.

I'd seen some great ones handle the puck: Billy Taylor, Edgar Laprade, Max and Doug Bentley, Jean Beliveau, Bill Cowley, Wayne Gretzky, Mario Lemieux, and more, but that old guy had as much feel and grace as anybody. On top of that, the old fart on his right wing, who just skated from the top of his circle half-speed to the top of the opponents' circle, handling the puck three or four times, was also pretty good. Geeze, they both had played quality hockey.

Then some little devil inside me said, "Wouldn't it be fun to play with those two!"

I broke into a smile, then a scowl. "Leave, right now, stupid," I muttered to myself. But I was hooked.

After finishing my business with Terri Bedwell, I went inside the arena, sat high in the far corner, and thoroughly enjoyed the display of mental and physical skills those two experienced wizards put on. There were also two younger guys (Eddie Taylor and Alex Chern) in their early 50s in the other group who'd likely played the game at a high level.

"No, get out," I again scolded myself, getting up from my seat. Before leaving, I asked Marilyn Newstead, another young lady in the arena office who helps keep my hockey school full, "How often do these old geezers play?"

"Monday, Wednesday, and Friday, 7:45 to 9:15."

What I did in the next few days boggles my mind. It boggled Grace's too.

Nobody anywhere has had a better life than I have: two happy marriages — first to Grace, and now to Leah — good family, no debts, reasonable financial security, earning a wage for something I'd have paid them to let me do. Leah and I spend a month each winter in California golfing, soaking up the sun, doing a little writing, a lot of walking and sight-seeing, and challenging my computer at bridge. In my time at home besides spending time with Leah, boating, fishing, skiing, and a lot more golf, I put in many happy hours among my plants, hedges, flowers, and six big raised garden beds. I make time to take my two dogs on their 4 p.m. and late night walks along the beach. In the afternoon walk, we venture to the French Creek store for the *Globe and Mail*. I smoke my one cigar a day on the evening walk up to the mall. I have a good life.

Sometimes I visit my old fishing buddy, Bill Stanton, who'd invited me earlier to join him playing Old-timers — he doesn't live too far from my home. Not long after my visit to the arena, the dogs and I dropped over to see Bill one afternoon. He and I settled in the shade of his garden and we talked boats and fishing for a while. Then in a lull I asked, "Bill, who is that grey-haired old smoothy playing centre on your Old-timers team?"

"Baz 'Bomber' Doran."

The lightbulb went on. No, it couldn't be! Not the same Baz Doran who for six years terrorized the American Hockey League both on and off the ice as a star player in Syracuse. Mentally and skilfully, for over 10 years, he was as good as or better than most quality puck-handlers in the NHL. He was tough and talented.

Doran's winger on the local Old-timers team was Roy Jardine, a top junior A player and semi-pro back in the old Michigan-Ontario league. As the dogs and I left later that afternoon, Bill repeated the offer, "Come and join us."

That night I set the alarm clock for 7 a.m. Grace hollered, "No, you're not!"

"No, dear, I'm not playing. I'm going down to watch a genius in action. This guy Baz is a legend, honey, with more stories about his off-ice antics than his on-ice, where there were none better," I assured her.

So at 7:45 a.m. the dogs and I, with a large coffee thermos, were huddled top row, far corner of the Parksville Arena, when the players started coming onto the ice one at a time. Finally Baz arrived, took no more than two strides, and had a puck, another stride, and zippo — 85 feet across the ice right on Roy Jardine's stick blade. From 150 feet away, I could see the smile on Roy's face and the big grin on Baz's. Roy didn't break or speed up his stride. Hell, he could have put his stick on the ice and closed his eyes and Baz still would have put the puck dead centre on his blade.

Fifteen or 20 minutes later, the 20 to 24 guys split into two teams and away they went. After the glow of the brilliant hockey demonstration by Doran (a ballet performer on skates and a Gretzky with the puck) subsided a little, the skills of Roy Jardine became apparent.

I couldn't help thinking, "Geeze, that might be fun after all, playing with those guys." Nevertheless, I tried to find reasons to stop my growing temptation. I soon noticed that when a player went off the ice for a rest, he was liable to be there for five or 10 minutes. Most of the guys wound up taking their rests standing still or coasting on the ice while the play went on. They just wouldn't come off the ice.

Of the 20 players, five or six were good, five or six average, and the remaining 10 or 12 were weak. It seemed that the average shift would see three weak and two average players against three good, one average, and one weak. The downfall was that the weaker players never touched the puck, and the second they did, they'd give it to the opposition 98 out of 100 times.

Part of the problem was ego. It seems every adult player thinks he's a good or average player, even when he is not. He's highly insulted if or when he's designated to play on the average or weak shift. Because of that, it's a steady diet of a good player sooner or later making a pass to a weak player — who immediately gives the puck to the other team.

As I watched the seniors, it hit me like a ton of bricks. Just like the present-day minor hockey system, the adults are just as dumb as the kids are. I'd been here before.

Between 1985 and 1990, we developed a system at our hockey schools to help overcome that very problem. We'd use two pucks at the same time and also play half-ice, five-a-side, for the development of the players' skills. By handling the puck much more often, the weaker player soon became more competitive with the other weak or average players. It was amazing how two separate games would develop at once, with the weaker players seeking each other out on the ice and the same with the more skilled players. It worked like a charm.

The seniors I was observing that morning, however, appeared content to play with mismatched players on the ice, resulting in the puck being turned over constantly to the opposition. I shuddered. There it was, happening right in front of me with the Old-timers. Nothing had changed.

"Yeah but . . ." the inner voice continued in an attempt to justify my temptation, "a few of the skilled guys on each team are getting their jollies by making a couple of very good offensive plays to each other."

I furthered the bluff, suggesting to myself that the weaker players, as well as most others, were getting their jollies by checking New Jersey, Philadelphia, Dallas, or Florida style. In reality, when a weaker player finally did control the puck, all five guys (good and bad) on the other team simply attacked him, like a pack of lions on a wounded water buffalo.

No sir, nobody was going to get a shot on net, let alone a goal.

I shook my head in disappointment.

For the rest of the day and that evening, I wrestled with my decision not to play Old-timers hockey. But jeepers, wouldn't it be fun to play with Baz and Roy for a shift or two, even against little or no opposition? As for the overall checking philosophy of the seniors' game, well, maybe I could change it a little.

Later that day, as I sat in our Sea Room in my favourite chair looking out over the Strait of Georgia, with my feet up and a cold beer in my hand, I closed my eyes and daydreamed. I visualized making a pass to an open spot, with Baz on his way there, having it picked up, then heading for a spot presently occupied by an opposition checker, who soon would be chasing Baz. I saw myself arriving there in perfect time to receive a return pass, head for the defenceman, take him wide, and then look up to see Baz's and Roy's sticks on the ice, heading for open space that I had created. I gently passed the puck between the legs of a checker, over a stick blade, and when it landed in front of the net, either linemate could have put it in.

When a play like that actually happens in hockey it is heaven. You just don't get that same feeling from getting a birdie playing golf, landing a 35-pound salmon or a 20-pound steelhead, or even going through the Mount Washington moguls at medium speed.

Right then I realized I was close to changing my mind again.

There was one other nagging memory I was missing, only found in hockey. That camaraderie among teammates in the dressing room before and after a game, practice, or pickup scrimmage.

My mind whirled back to the previous winter when I'd attended a couple of practices before a fund-raising game. I was up at 6:30 a.m. and I could tell Grace was thinking, "Dummy." The dogs, one on my leather chair, the other on Grace's favourite chair, each opened one eye, shook their heads, rolled over, and went back to sleep. While the coffee perked, I ran downstairs and packed my hockey equipment. After three cups of coffee, it was 7:15 and as soon as I turned out the kitchen lights, both dogs were up and out of the chairs like a shot, standing at the front door waiting to go out into the cold wet morning.

Five minutes later I made the left turn off the main highway to the arena. There were two cars ahead of me and two or three lined up behind, all stuffed with hockey players and gear, waiting to turn on to the road leading into the parking lot. As soon as I hauled my equipment out of the car, the greetings and banter between friends began. Throughout the parking lot all the way to the old, damp dressing room, the chatter continued. For the next three-quarters of an hour, the gossip, teasing, funny stories, plans for fishing, golf replays, ski trips, jock talk, rumours, and just plain out-and-out lies continued.

I liked that friendship and bonding, that camaraderie. Always did, always will . . . and I missed it. Old-timers hockey offered that again.

That little voice inside said, "Go on, stupid, give it a try!"

When I told Grace, she smiled and said, "I'd have been disappointed and quite upset if you didn't try it. Go and have fun."

Next morning I had the alarm set for 6:30, but I was wide awake at 6. The night before, I'd put my clothes in the hallway so as not to disturb Grace in the morning. Still yawning, I raised the thermostat, put on the coffee, and turned to go to the Sea Room until the coffee was ready, and there sat my two dogs. Sam gave me his "rroof," which means "breakfast for two," so I got their large bone, broke it into eight or 10 small pieces, and fed it to them as I drank my first cup of coffee. After breakfast, they usually "rruuf" for a bathroom run outdoors and then Sam scrambles into Grace's chair, and Tara into mine, and go back to sleep until they hear Grace get out of bed.

But not that morning. They both went and lay side by side by the front door, even though I was still in my pyjamas. After another coffee, I ran downstairs to get my equipment, ran back up to get dressed, grabbed the car keys, filled up my thermos, turned off the lights, put on a jacket, and stepped out the door into the cold, wet, miserable, wonderful morning — two excited dogs and all.

I had just started to roll out the driveway when that little guy inside my head said, "Time out — this has to cost money. Get your wallet."

Shit, it's in the house, but where?

As I backed up to the front door, the two dogs looked at each other and I swear that Tara, with one ear up and the other one down, growled to Sam, "Same old stupidity, he hasn't once jumped into the car and gone straight somewhere in the last 10 tries."

Five minutes later I still couldn't find my wallet when the voice inside said, "Did you look in your hockey bag?"

Back outside to the van I went, raised the rear door, turned on the inside car light, and there it was tucked in the corner. I had put it there the night before — so I wouldn't forget it.

Back behind the wheel I drove up the driveway past Jim Kingsley's and stepped on the brakes. "Aw heck, what day is this, Sam? Can't be Wednesday morning — garbage day, but it must be because Jim has his usual two-and-a-half very large cans right beside the road. And I can't miss today because my cans are over-flowing," I grumbled to the adorable but disgruntled mutts.

Once again I knew what the dogs were thinking. Tara looked pleadingly at Sam as if to say, "Come on, Sam, let's go back to bed. This turkey ain't going nowhere."

I turned on the CD (to some good dog music), put the heater on high and the car in park. No way I was going to back up again. "Be right back, boys," I said, jumping out of the car and into the pissing-down rain. I ran back to the garage, carried the garbage cans to the top of the driveway, and made a beeline for my van. I have four leather captain's chairs in the van, and when Grace isn't along, Sam rides shotgun. I knew he was miffed at me when I jumped back into the van because he was fast asleep in the second row.

Now I was in a bit of a hurry because I didn't want to be late on the ice the first day. A hundred yards out of my driveway I had to make a sharp left turn. It was 7:30 in the morning and since no one else was stupid enough to be on the road that early I took the turn a little too fast . . . and sharp. I heard a thud, crash, tinkle, tinkle.

What was that?

One hundred more yards up the road and another sharp left turn was ahead. Halfway through it, that voice inside my head blurted out, "Coffee! Ah shit, it was on the roof!"

I'd put it there when I opened the front car door. For a moment I thought, "Do I stop and back up?"

No way, I decided. The dogs would never let me live it down.

Somehow I figured the dogs would find a way to tell Grace about my absent-minded accident. So I decided I'd fool the little buggers and go around the block to pick up the trashed mug. I drove a quarter-mile and took a sharp right, another quarter-mile and a sharp right turn again, another 100 yards and yet another right turn. I was halfway through the third right turn when I heard a quick, concerned "rrrruff." Sam left the comfort and warmth of his leather chair to come to the co-pilot's seat, obviously attempting to give me directions. The bark had been Sam telling me, "Dummy, you just missed the left turn that would take us to the rink." He sat there, looked at me, tilted his head like I was daft, and then impatiently repeated himself, "Rrruffff! (You missed a turn.)"

"In a minute," I replied.

After stopping and retrieving my insulated (and now noticeably banged-up) coffee mug, we made it to the arena without any further problems.

■ ■ ■

Normally when I stop at the rink, I park in the small lot right in front of the building, the dogs leap out, cross the road, and wait for me at the front door. I leave my attaché case on the desk and then rain or shine, take the dogs on their 10-minute jaunt through the park.

At 7:30, still dark and raining, with hockey bag and stick in hand, I opened the arena front door. Before I could take one step inside, both dogs scooted by me into the lobby. When I arrived, both were sitting there waiting for me; Sam was near the doors leading to the ice surface, while Tara was sitting in front of the meeting room, which is our instructors' room during hockey schools. When I brought the dogs to the rink, Tara liked to stay in the warmth and comfort of the meeting room, having once shivered through a morning of practice with Sam, who preferred to wait for me in the arena, in the high corner seats, my usual perch. So on the first day of my Old-timers initiation, when I opened the doors to the stands and ice surface, Sam scrambled to his designated seat, Row E seat six. He leaned against the wall, sat himself down, and waited for the show to begin. One of the staff took Tara into the meeting room.

When I picked up my hockey stick and that duffel bag full of gear, all of a sudden I felt tired. Already it seemed like a 12-hour day: lost wallet, garbage, the dented coffee mug rescue, Sam and Tara settled, and now . . . having to go into a room full of strangers. As I opened the dressing-room door, the sound of Bill Stanton's voice telling his morning joke burst through.

I looked around the room. Have you ever gone shopping for a dog in a pet store or SPCA, where every animal was bright-eyed, sleekly groomed, bushy tail wagging, with eyes that promised great enjoyment? That look was on every face in the room. It was the look of little kids getting ready for sport's greatest treat.

Scattered all over the floor about the room were hockey bags, skates, and sticks, and a large freezer chest in the middle of the room.

Along with the sights and sounds of a hockey dressing room came a very familiar and comforting odour, which had hit my nostrils the second I'd opened the door. Leather, heat liniment, hockey tape, steamy showers, and a dank arena smell permeated the air. As I took two deep breaths, I could almost taste the game. Ahhh, yes sirree, that's hockey.

Before the laughter fully subsided from Bill's joke I introduced myself and shook hands with Jim, Tom, Gerry, Bill, and others. I spied an opening between two guys for a small ass and quickly sat down, then emptied my duffel bag.

As I put on my gear I looked around the room. Geeze, what a change in equipment from my days as a junior and pro player. The shoulder pads have protection down to the navel front and back (someone went back to medieval times to dream those things up), and the shin pads and elbow pads give protection from the wrist to the shoulder both front and back. Amazing stuff.

Even though no one in the room could break a pane of glass with their shot, the newfangled gear the guys put on could stop a cannon ball. I began to think I was about to play in the wrong game, that I was in the wrong room and maybe this was the Aussie football team on skates I was with. Looking at those guys I felt like I was wearing zilch — and I was.

The equipment show went on . . . not hockey pants but kidney protection chest high, and charley horse protection down to the knee! I hadn't bought a piece of hockey equipment, including skates, in 30 years. Other than at hockey school, I hadn't had my equipment out in 10 years. My gloves are a pair I resurrected and reconstructed with skate laces and esnolite 20 years ago after son Andy threw them out.

When I opened my equipment bag, those trusty, mouldy gloves were on top. I always placed them on top of the other gear so I could put my skate blades on them and wouldn't cut the bag. When I set them aside on the floor, some brave soul piped up, "Great gloves, Howie," to a howl of laughter from the crew.

I'm too cheap to buy new ones. The last ones I priced were $125, so I just laced the wrists and the tops of the wrist protection together with an old skate-lace so they wouldn't fall apart. I took them to a cobbler to get new palms sewn in. When he quoted a price of $85 I said, "How about just fingers, eight of them, only three inches each from the top of the finger down toward the palm. How much would that be?" I thought he'd say $40, but there was no way I'd pay that much. He must have known that because he said it would be $25. He had a deal.

My shin pads are from 1976, my Woolco days, when they featured a line of equipment that I designed. The thing about the shin pads was that they grew with the kid. The concept was to buy a pair when the boy was around eight and as he grew, you loosened the screws, pulled the shin-bone protection to the right size, then tightened the screws again, and you had an new pair with a perfect fit. Fifteen or 20 years ago when my oldest grandchild had pitched out his set, I found them, extended the shin protection to the limit, glued on some ensolite around the knee pad, and I had the lightest and best pair of shin pads in the game.

By now the early birds were dressed and on their way to the newly resurfaced ice. From watching the two previous scrimmages, I knew that Baz wore a dark jersey, so naturally I put my white one on first, then my elbow pads, then my dark blue sweatshirt. I picked up my stick and headed for the Promised Land.

I wasn't on the ice five seconds, on my way to take a warm-up skate or two around the rink, stick on the ice, when this puck gently hit dead centre on the blade. I looked across the ice and there along the boards going the other way was Baz. When our eyes locked, we both smiled and he raised his stick in a welcome gesture.

Fifteen minutes passed while everyone warmed up their goalies and fooled around with one of the many pucks on the ice. Finally someone said, "Let's play a game." It took 10 minutes to decide who should start and who should sit. I got smart early for a change and volunteered to play defence. We had two lines of forwards, six total, and three defencemen — which meant I got more ice time.

During my eight years as a player with the Toronto Maple Leafs, I can remember the minute details of a few goals I scored, a couple of key goals by teammates, and, yes, a few scored by the likes of Howe, Richard, Schmidt, and the Bentley brothers. I also recall some super saves by folks like Broda, Durnan, Brimsek, and Sawchuk. My first 30 seconds of Old-timers hockey, played at age 62 back on that morning in 1985, now has a spot in my hockey memory bank as well.

At the centre ice face-off circle, Baz looked over his shoulder and winked, then drew the puck right on my blade. I skated toward centre ice, then faded to the boards. Roy Jardine was on right wing 10 feet away, moving at very slow speed and I hit him with a pass. Baz, after giving me the puck, read the play, and in his velvety smooth, long, gracious stride went in a big circle, and as soon as I hit Roy, he floated wide open up through centre ice, took the pass from Roy at the red line, went straight for the defenceman, took him wide, and dropped the puck to me. I was home free as the birds, so I headed for the other D-man, took him and the goalie with me wide the other way, and without looking threw the puck to the top of the opposite circle where I knew Roy would be standing, stick on the ice. He was and had three options: shoot the puck into the open net, pass it to Baz who was home free, or give it to our left winger, 73-year-old Dot Robertson. As I knew he would, Baz gave it to Dot, who shot and somehow missed. Yahoo, now that's hockey and that's great fun!

When I was on the ice with Baz and Roy, I thought I'd died and gone to heaven. I'd often heard of a soft pass or hard pass, and concluded one was slow, the other fast. In baseball, there are slow ball pitchers and fast ball pitchers, but some players throw what's called a heavy ball. When it explodes in your glove, it shakes your hand and arm right up to the shoulder. I soon discovered Baz's passes, slow or very, very fast, settled on the blade of your stick like a butterfly. No going to meet the high, hard one, rolling the wrist as you drew back to lighten the contact and maintain control. If his pass had pace on it, you could just watch the puck draw to the centre of the blade, roll the wrist just a teeny-weenie bit, and zappo, like two space capsules coming together to dock, the puck was on your stick waiting for further direction. No artist ever had more skill with the brush than Baz Doran had with his hockey stick and a puck.

As the morning game proceeded, a number of negative "yeah buts" began to surface, but not enough to destroy my wonderful new world of personal hockey enjoyment. Still, enough little things were going on to keep all the players from experiencing the highs that Baz, Roy, and I were enjoying, and that bothered me.

When Baz and I were on the ice, we'd tip-toe through the tulips with the puck two or three times, and when we'd had our fun, creating and going to open ice, passing slow or fast in-the-air passes to each other, we'd pass to a teammate who would give it to the other side.

By watching and playing with Baz in the following few years, I learned so much, and five or six times every scrub game I had more fun than even in the days back on the river and pond, when it had been mostly a physical game and not mental.

Over a period of 40 years, I'd had many great physical and mental hockey partners but rarely was I their equal. Finally I was in tune, in complete harmony with a hockey Einstein who headed for holes like a scared gopher, who created open ice like a giant ice breaker, who read my mind better than Grace, and whose every pass was the right pace and dead centre on my stick.

No wonder those great players play well into their 40s. Suddenly I understood the easier side, and the smarter side to the game.

One day Baz didn't show up, but he explained at the next practice that he'd had a doctor's appointment. Over the next weeks, I gradually realized that Baz wasn't Baz. His shifts got shorter, he lost some jump, and the passes were not right on. He began to miss the occasional morning.

When I finally mentioned it to Roy, he said, "Haven't you heard? Baz has cancer."

My oh my, how that hurt. I never did get close to the old guy socially, but for many months, three mornings a week, we were one and the same, in hockey mind and soul.

Eighteen months later Baz got his chance to play in the big Arena of Dreams. And I still miss him.

■ ■ ■

Hockey to me had always been damn hard work. I always played with an ache, pain, cut, break, bruise, missing teeth, or a black eye. I had at least one of each, at all times, every year from October to April, for very little money. But because of that price paid, I enjoyed some team success and championships and was thankful for it every second.

With my newfound pleasure in having such a bright hockey partner as Baz, I became determined to make sure that others could learn to enjoy the game of hockey at a higher mental level as well. The feeling was akin, I suppose, to the fanaticism and euphoria of finding religion or quitting smoking. Even during that first contest, the not-so-smart part of me began to think, "How can you make this better for the group?" But the smart part said, "Shut up and enjoy yourself. Have your shower and go home."

After that first game, we headed to the dressing room, pooped and sweating, where the teasing began again regarding the saves made, goals scored . . . Best of all, as he opened the cooler in the middle of the room, a player announced that a cold beer was just two dollars. Folks, beer was made to be consumed in a hockey dressing room with 15 other guys who have just completed a game or practice. You don't know the taste or true pleasure of beer until you've had one in similar circumstances.

After a quick shower in the tiny cubicle, it was back to my seat at the wind tunnel. I put on my sweater and sat there in complete satisfaction finishing my beer, all the time enjoying the small talk of men in complete harmony. The guys began to drift out and so with a "Thanks fellows, had a great time. Probably be here Friday morning," I left the dressing room, picked up Tara in the lobby (Sam had already found me), and returned home to a very inquisitive Grace.

"How did it go?" she asked.

I babbled happily, trying to explain what a thrilling experience it was to head for a spot you know is developing, put your stick on the ice, and like magic and as gentle as a hummingbird landing on a flower, the puck nestles onto the blade. It was a whole new game. It was the game I'd discovered doing my TV hockey work, but I never dreamed I'd ever take part in it.

"What about the dogs? You didn't leave them in the car?"

"No, Tara slept in the meeting room and Sam was the only non-paying spectator. He sat and watched the action from my seat and then sneaked into our dressing room afterwards."

"Going back Friday morning?" she asked, full well knowing the answer.

"Wild horses couldn't keep me away," I replied, but that little voice inside my head said, "But a scheduled NHL broadcast game in Pittsburgh will."

Sure as heck on the daily calendar on the fridge door — "Saturday game, Pittsburgh in Toronto. Friday 7 a.m. Nanaimo airport to Vancouver, then Vancouver to Toronto. Arrive in Hogtown around 4 p.m. Fri. night."

"Shucks. But I'll make it back on the ice Monday morning."

■ ■ ■

Friday morning, after a couple of hours of homework on the Vancouver to Toronto lap of my plane journey, I got to thinking again about the Old-timers game. I wanted to figure out a way to build in more enjoyment for everyone playing.

As I sit here writing these notes more than a dozen years later, at age 76, I look back and wonder why I didn't have enough sense to serve my own personal pleasure, and let sleeping dogs lie.

Too soon old, too late smart.

I really couldn't have slept at night, though, without having tried to open that door to the enormous pleasures one gets from being able to "think" (even a teeny-weenie bit) while playing the game of hockey. I had to try to open that door to new hockey thrills. "All the guys are intelligent and smart thinkers," I rationalized, as I talked myself into how to make the game pleasurable for all the players, no matter their level or abilities.

The first thing to do was to set up a system to change lines, guaranteeing equal ice time and regular shifts for all the players. After about the third session, over a beer, I made the suggestion, and everyone thought it was a good idea. I used my hockey school bell and set it to ring every two minutes to signal a line change. Super!

The next problem was how to divide the teams up to be balanced. If 20 players showed up, the trick was to split the talent as evenly as possible — 10 on each side. Then split the ten into two five-man A and B units with the best five on the A and the others on B. The A lines played against one another and then the B lines.

Deciding who should split up the teams was tough. When I was there it was not a problem — I was handed the job. I always played with the B team and we usually had the four least skilled players on our side. Most of the time I played an A shift as well because very seldom did we have four defencemen.

The split wasn't hard from a mathematical point of view, only from an ego perspective. The four good players stood out like sore thumbs, likewise the four poorest. The problems were usually with the remaining two both on the same team, both thinking they were A players and one highly insulted when asked to perform for the B squad.

We also had an age variance. The verbal rules said Old-timers were 50 years and over, but often we had a couple of mid-40-year-olds show up to play. On the other end, we had regular players like Frank Robertson in his late '70s and wife, Dot, in her early '70s.

When I showed up to play, we usually stuck to the philosophy and split into five-unit shifts. When I wasn't there, no one else was willing to be the asshole who decided the B player.

My major complaint of my Old-timers hockey experiences was that despite trying to even up the shifts, it couldn't be done effectively. It would break my heart to see the most skilled players use all their energy and toughness to take the puck away from the less skilled player before he or she could even carry it a few strides and pass or shoot the puck. No fun there, boys.

I created some pretty hard feelings trying to get the talented players to let the other guys enjoy the game. I suggested they should let the others try to be creative with the puck, and let them learn. I argued that without the eight to 10 B guys, us A guys couldn't make out.

Not too many listened. Three or four years later, the over-65 group and some younger B guys got their own ice time and moved on. The early-morning group dropped down to seven or eight players a side, but in recent years it has increased again.

Eventually, with the addition of some Nanaimo and Comox players, we had teams of 65 and older players, many of whom wanted to play other communities and attend the big March Old-timers tournament in Victoria. I was very reluctant to get involved. Been there, done that.

During my 70 years of hockey, I'd probably lost more games

than I'd won, so losing didn't bother me any more. I'd learned that you try your best, try to play smart, and let the chips fall where they may. But I didn't want to be embarrassed.

The lack of physical skills found in the average Old-timer doesn't bother me at all. So what if he can't skate, can't handle the puck, can't give or take a pass, shoot, or even think? Because he loves the game, all of those problems I can accept. I think it's super that he gets involved. But, if and when he wants to play competitive Old-timers hockey, he has to be willing to play a simple, behind-the-blueline system. In order to compete, he must be disciplined and willing to think just that little bit.

Getting beat 6–4, 8–6, or 12–9 is not a problem. Members of both teams have likely been creative, handled the puck, and had scoring chances — lots of fun. Getting bombed 10–0 or 12–1 tells me the losers were probably all non-thinkers with little or no physical skill. With or without the puck, they couldn't think their way out the Zamboni door.

The only saving factor is that more times than not both teams play the same type of game. The score is usually 3–2 or 4–3 with both teams giving the puck to the opposition at least 100 times a game. That's 33 times a period, which is under the average of most games I've researched over the years.

I remember vividly a lesson learned at age 11, back around 1934, on the big skating pond in the park in Kitchener, Ontario. Hundreds of kids and adults skated to music in a tight inner circle while on the outer fringes kids from ages 6 to 16 had a dozen or two hockey games going. At age 10 I'd worked my way up to the best group of 12- and 13-year-olds' second or third line. I was on the black team of about eight players. In the middle of play one of our best players, Bobby Schnurr, called time, came over to me, and said, "Hey kid, what team you on?"

"Yours," I replied nervously.

"Well, we're mostly wearing black shirts, the other guys all have light or bright colours on, right?"

I nodded my head.

"Well then, how come when you get rid of the puck you mostly give it to the other team? Keep doing that and you can get your ass out of here. We work like a dog to get control of the puck, give it to you, and you give it back to them. Something's wrong with that picture, right?"

"Y-y-y-yes sir. I'll try not to do it again." What a great hockey lesson from a 13-year-old and his group, who without the help of adults, had figured out and solved the major problem that most Old-timer hockey players and every division of minor hockey have today.

■   ■   ■

When word got around that Parksville had a 60-years-and-older team, we began to get invitations to play from other Island and B.C. mainland communities and on occasion I was home and able to play. At one tournament, during the warm-up I glanced at the other team and thought, "Jiminy Cricket, they've got some great looking 60-year-olds."

The game started first shift and their guys were as slow and cumbersome as our shift; we had a slight edge in talent. Second shift, I was thinking, "Holy cow, these guys backcheck and will they ever run out of legs." When our third shift went against their first shift, we were in trouble from whistle to whistle. Heck, when our third line played their second, it was still no contest.

In most friendly games, the opponents had six, seven, or eight players within the age bracket agreed upon. The remainder were way under-age, and when we were foolish enough (and most of us were) to try to keep up, the next few days of aches, pains, and sore muscles made us ask if it was worth it. Recently, more and more 50-plus people have started to play the game, and the under-age problem has almost been eliminated.

From 1986 to 1989, I played fairly regularly. When work permitted I played Monday, Wednesday, and Friday from 7:45 to 9 a.m. On Tuesdays the senior hockey players usually skied at Mount Washington, leaving home at 7 a.m., and were on the ski-lift, ready to go, by 8:45 a.m.

During those years I was a perfect asshole, I'm sure, spoiling many a player's morning game by asking, requesting, suggesting, insisting, and finally demanding that when I got the puck the wingers went to the hatch marks and stayed there until I gave them the puck, or went by them with the puck. And that when they had the puck they never, never passed it into the middle. The basic rule was "When in trouble, put the puck against the fence and out, and with it always 'go wide.'"

You'd think I'd asked them to explain Einstein's Theory of Relativity, or how to build the atom bomb. Again, we had a wide range of skill levels, mental and physical, represented on the club, but few of the teachable level. They just couldn't see the picture.

Early on in my new Old-timers hockey adventure, I decided two things: that I would never score a goal, and that I would never, ever take the puck away from an opponent. I would never stop him from shooting or passing the puck. I decided I would never at any time attack the puck carrier's stick.

A dozen years later most of the originals of 1985 weren't playing or had joined with that special group of 70 years and older. Most of the new players who replaced them were not aware that I would not take any offensive move away from them. When caught out of position, I'd skate, for the exercise, to catch the puck carrier, get beside him, and not let him improve his physical position. However he had the complete freedom, for as long as he wished, to make a play, pass the puck to a teammate, or take a shot on goal.

My other rule was when an opponent did make a good play, I'd let him have the shot, then I usually stood six feet in front and six feet beside the net, waiting for a loose puck or someone on the other team to give it to me, and they usually did. I never took away the shot.

I always consulted with my goalies and asked if they wanted a few shots. Most of the time they agreed.

I had some pretty competitive players on my side over the years in Old-timers, who even kept score shift by shift. On occasion I'm sure they got mad at me when I wouldn't check the puck carrier. I still do that in the few tournaments or charity games I play in now, and I don't try to score a goal. Once in a while when a goalie cheated (and played the pass receiver and not the puck carrier), I'd put the puck in the net, but in 15 years I scored maybe 15 goals. Five hundred assists, yes, but very few goals.

Patience and timing are two very important hockey skills both on offence and defence, with thinking, discipline, game sense, and team work next in line. These are by far the most rewarding pleasures a player can have in hockey, and 95 percent of those playing beer league and Old-timers hockey don't know what I am talking about. They will never get to fully appreciate the world's finest team sport.

Parksville had a very talented 35-and-over club in the early '90s and when two of their best, John Moore and Lyle Denninson, turned 50, they occasionally came to our morning games. Moore was another defenceman originally from Ontario and had a feel for the game that also made him an excellent referee. He played the game almost as well as he called it. So, with Les Mitchell, a very talented and very mean 65-year-old and yours truly on defence, we had three guys who could shake, rattle, and roll. The other newcomer, Dennison, was the Eddie Shack or Davey Keon kind with unlimited energy. Lyle would skate like mad for the full shift but always with a purpose. My, oh my, could he play the game and what a smart centre ice man.

Naturally I made sure both newcomers played with my team, the black one. With Mitchell, Moore, and myself, we had three D men with two forwards, Dennison and Roy Reiber up front — all who could play the game with great skill, both mentally and physically.

Sooner or later, however, the puck would go to the fifth fellow (the missing third talented forward), the fellow without a clue on our team, and everything would come to a screeching halt.

But one day a redheaded, freckled-faced guy with a brush cut stuck his head into the dressing room door and said, "Gentleman, I am John Koppa. Can I join you?"

After the warm-up, John was put on the second shift and away the first line went. Lyle to me, to John Moore, to Roy going across the opponents' blueline, to Lyle driving between the two D-men, home free to our left winger to put it in the net — and he missed the same by three feet. I stayed on for the second shift with Les

Mitchell. The puck came to him from the face-off, to me on the bottom far circle. I started out and soon the checking winger and centre were chasing me from right to left, and I headed for the defenceman on Les's side of the rink. Just before I was about to put the puck against the fence and out, I saw Koppa standing on the hatch marks. I couldn't believe it. The odds against that happening seemed 100 to 1. So I went as far as I could and with three checkers on my tail, I dropped the puck to Koppa. When he started out, no one was within 50 feet of him and he wasn't challenged until he hit the opposing blueline. Needless to say next shift he was on our line. For the rest of that morning and for about seven or eight other outings I never enjoyed hockey more at any level.

When we were kids back on the river, pond, or back yard rink, I usually had the most skills, and none of us knew about the philosophy or thinking part of the game. In the NHL my brain couldn't keep up to my feet, but in later years as my feet slowed, my brain became active. At best, even in the pros, you had two other guys on your shift that had reasonable physical and mental skills, and yet even that was great fun. I've always envied the skilled players and groups of players who could or can create things, or generate excitement in our great game: Lach, Richard and Blake; Bauer, Schmidt, and Dumart; Mikita, Hull, and Wharram; Orr, Hodge, Esposito, and Cashman; Lemieux, Jagr, and Francis; Gretzky with any of about six Oilers, and dozens and dozens more. Geeze, how can you take money for having so much fun?

With John Koppa on our unit, we finally had five guys, all with great physical and mental skills . . . incredible. Hundreds of thousands of Canadians at every age play this great game every year, yet less than 10 percent have good physical skills, and less than 5 percent understand that patience, timing, and mental skills even exist. To get a shift of five guys with both skills is very rare. Even in the NHL it doesn't happen too often. Three, sometimes four guys but five? Unless you were the Oilers of the 1980s or Detroit in the mid and late 1990s, forget it.

■ ■ ■

When the practice ended, I was showering with Koppa and complimented him on his skills and grasp of the game. When I asked where he played his hockey my mouth fell open in amazement when he replied, "Nowhere really. I never had the time, played a little beer league hockey over in Port Alberni but that's all."

Time! Stop it there, back it up!

"Naw, you're pulling my leg. You mean you're telling me that no one taught you the physical skills, and you've never had any coach tell you how to play the game?"

"That's right," he replied.

"Man oh man, you're a rare and very lucky dude. I've been in the game at every level for almost 65 years and I have probably seen 20 players who were born with all or most of the physical and mental skills. Anyhow, thanks very much for showing up. You made my day and I am sure the other guys' as well," I told him.

I'd finally experienced the ultimate in the game of hockey, equal to or better than making the Toronto Maple Leafs, winning the rookie award, scoring an overtime goal in the playoffs, and winning the Stanley Cup.

Although it was at a much-reduced speed, to finally be able to combine physical and mental skills with four other talented performers was, I guess, the good Lord's reward for the work I'd been doing in the game all my life.

The last couple of years from 1993 to 1996, I finally got smart, played just twice a week, and mostly kept my big mouth shut. We'd have a 65-and-over and a 70-years-and-older team practice on Tuesdays from 10 to 11:30 a.m., then pick a good bar and go for lunch.

I usually play one tournament in the over-70 division in Victoria in March, and it's fun. We have 10 very good players (when all are healthy), good goaltending, and are "in" most games right down to the final whistle.

Over the years in Old-timers, I played with at least a dozen players who were absolutely a pleasure to play with or against. (It's almost as much fun to watch and play against a 'thinker' as it is with him). Fellas such as Ed Taylor, Jack McRae, Bob Murrant,

Chuck Chestnut, Jack Harlow, Alex Chern, and special sorts like Les Mitchell, John Moore, Roy Reiber, Wilf Seaker, Lyle Dennison, and John Koppa were great fun and very inspirational. But none of them ever touched Baz Doran in that first couple of years.

For one reason or another, I lost interest in playing in 1996–97. During the fall of 1996 into late November, the weather was excellent and being an outdoor man I was just too busy. Then in mid-November to Christmas I was away a lot promoting my book *Golly Gee — It's Me*. In late January I left Parksville for San Diego and then Palm Springs for February. By the time I got home, it was yard and garden time so Old-timers hockey was never the high priority.

At the beginning of the 1997–98 season, I hung up my skates from regular play and retired the stick. I decided in October of 1997 to take up golf with one main purpose in mind: to be able to challenge little brother Tom, who plays in the upper 70s. (It's one of those brother things.) In 1998, I lost Grace and I spent six months completely lost. That was when Charlie and I started banging out another book (the one you hold right now); I kissed away the winter of 1998–99 because there was little time for much else. Luckily I met Leah during that same time.

In early 1999, I spent a weekend playing in my favourite Old-timers tourney in Victoria (as well as a lot of golf with Leah and the hockey gang). It was a good tournament, and I had a lot of fun.

I will likely only play once in a blue moon in charity events or whatever, but for now, aside from hockey schools, my skating and shooting days are done.

I doubt I will miss playing the game much. What I know I will miss is the unique friendship found in hockey. I'll miss the guys I've spent the last 12 years playing with. For me it's the camaraderie of the game that really made hockey special. I think that always was the real hook of the game. Skill level played no role in that sort of feeling, that kinship.

■ ■ ■

Old-timers hockey may be a lot of fun for the old farts on the ice, but I'd be the first to admit it's not exactly the most exciting example of the game. As an action-packed spectator sport, it ranks right up there with tiddlywinks and watching the lawn grow. An Old-timers Hockey Jamboree in Victoria a few years ago was testimony to that thought.

The tournament organizers asked me to be their special guest that year, which of course meant attending most of the games, having a beer with the boys in the dressing room and hospitality room afterwards, attending all the special events, and being guest speaker at the awards banquet. I figured I may as well have my dessert with the full meal, and enrolled to play as well in the 70-and-older division. Most senior hockey players want their wives to attend the game and some insist that they do. (Jeepers, they've got to be mad at them and want to get even — and the wives have to be nuts to sit on a cold hard bench in a miserable, poorly lit, cold arena to watch 30 old guys butcher the game of hockey.)

I was in Victoria for five full days for the tournament, and Grace decided to drive down for our final day of games and the banquet. She arrived at the start of the second period of my final game and sat with the other wives directly behind our bench. Two shifts later I noticed she wasn't there.

After the game I found her sitting reading a book in the very comfortable hospitality room, sipping a glass of wine. When I inquired why she left the game, she replied, "Ahh, come on, Howie. What's going on out there really isn't a spectator sport."

Good ole Grace, bang on the mark once again.

Later on that day, in the same hospitality room, we were having a drink with three of the wives of some players on the ice, when a fourth wife came bursting into the room all excited.

"Phyllis, Phyllis," she beckoned all aflap, "your husband just scored."

Quick as a wink, Phyllis grinned and replied, "Good thing he can still score somewhere."

Old-timers hockey has been very good to me. I made some new and very good friends. I met players with hockey genius, Baz and others, and several times played with a five-man unit all on the mental level of Kennedy, Lach, Schmidt, Laprade, Gretzky, and Lemieux.

I couldn't have asked or expected anything better.

Well maybe, I could.

Since 1953, I've been a teacher of individual and team hockey skills. I'm pretty good at it actually, but when I look at the results of my halfhearted effort for 10 years in Parksville I get to thinking, "Smart ass, you've still got a lot to learn."

I found out over more than 30 years of working with 7-to-12-year-old boys and girls that there was a 90 percent chance of improving their physical skills, and about a 50 percent chance of sharpening their thinking skills.

However, after close to 16 years of Old-timers hockey, I can honestly say that with most Old-timers you have absolutely no chance of improving physical or mental skills. Zilch!

What you see is what you get, and if you can take it, it's wonderful. Give it a try.

FOR THE
KIDS

■ ■ ■

Dinner is done. Leah has lovingly immersed herself in another creation on canvas, and I decide to seek some quiet moments as well in a favourite chair in the Sea Room, which looks out over the spectacular panoramic vista of the Strait of Georgia. It's been a crazy week; the one coming up is even busier. For an old guy I sure am busy.

I seek the comfort of the room, dim the lamplight, and gaze out over the ocean. I'm bushed and the slowly unfurling sunset over the water, soft music, and sip of London Dock make a nice touch to the day.

But the mind doesn't take a break.

Instead, THE BOOK returns . . . and I ponder it all. It's been a lot of work. A lot of names, and numbers, and facts, and thoughts, and stuff. I've agonized, analyzed, and guessed about things I've been a part of, watched, or recorded for hockey history. And most of it has been about adults.

But as I sit here, and the sky shifts slowly to purple with streaks of gold and splatters of pink, I remember once again what really matters about hockey. What really counts. Kids.

It's that youthful joy of chasing a puck with a stick, and chasing our dreams just as quickly. It is the joy of scoring the greatest goal ever, or at least within that hour, on the local pond, lake, river, dam or even . . . an indoor community rink. Hockey is the joy of listening to Foster on the radio or TV and then running outside and replaying the goals in a rousing round of road hockey with siblings, friends, neighbours, and maybe even Dad.

Hockey is about kids having fun, getting exercise, playing together, and chasing dreams. But somewhere along the line we lose the fun, excitement, and dreaming. That, folks, is a real shame. Far too many kids leave the game too soon. Hockey is a game we could and should play for most of our life.

My philosophy about hockey, and minor hockey in particular, is very simple. Every teenage girl or boy should have the opportunity to play the game of hockey, at their skill level, and in a non-violent atmosphere, at least twice a week. And on the way to becoming a teenager, they should be provided the opportunity to learn the physical and mental skills of the game.

But it ain't happening. Not even close. And Canadian hockey is dying because of it.

My theories about making hockey work are the result of operating a 102-team league with players ages 8 to 18 in two, then later three, arenas, for 10 years in St. John's, Newfoundland. They were also developed and adjusted from years working at maritime (St. Andrew's, N.S.) hockey schools; hearing about students' problems; studying how to teach physical and mental skills; four years of producing the *Howie Meeker Hockey School* films with CBC; two years of helping create *Pro Tips* for *Hockey Night in Canada*; along with 30 years of active TV broadcasting in the NHL. All of that, plus eight years of playing the game myself at the top level coaching at every level — from community minor leagues (tykes to midgets, ages 8 to 16), junior and senior hockey at high levels, minor pro in Pittsburgh, and the Toronto Maple Leafs — helped me to greatly appreciate and understand the skills and sacrifices each NHL performer must make to get there. I saw their efforts first-hand and I learned a great deal and realized how much of the game there is to learn.

All of that knowledge has simply reinforced my deep concern for where we are going with our hockey programs — or should I say where we *aren't* going.

I've been expressing my concern about hockey and its lack of proper skill training programs since the 1960s. With the 1999–2000 season upon us, absolutely zilch has taken place to improve the situation. How dumb are we?

Quite simply, we have to change our approach to minor hockey throughout the country by making it fun for all those participating. Fun can't exist when 85 percent of the players still in the game drop out between age 12 and 16. Minor hockey should be fun for everyone, and also has to be a skill-teaching experience. It's the duty of the adult instructors to create an on-ice atmosphere where boys and girls can improve their skills, without the fear of being constantly under attack, physically or mentally.

Sadly, there's little or no skill-teaching going on in this country. If the kids had the adequate skills, they wouldn't be dropping out nearly as much because they'd be having too much fun.

What happens and what doesn't happen in the hundreds of arenas across Canada involved in our minor hockey system has a profound effect on what we see on TV and how we perform in the various international hockey events.

Soon after the entertaining but eye-opening 1972 Canada-Soviet series, I expressed the view (and continue to do so) that Canada's hockey supremacy would come to a crashing halt in 15 to 20 years if we didn't get our act together. It's taken longer, but it's happened!

Remarkably, the '72 Series was just the tip of the iceberg in the sinking of Canadian hockey supremacy. We kept getting hammered but we just wouldn't open our eyes or face the facts.

In January 1974, the OHA's major junior A Peterborough Petes took part in a junior tourney in Leningrad, and the Soviets kicked the tar out of them 9–0. I figured the loss at the junior level, on top of our recent senior and pro level embarrassments, would finally be enough. But it wasn't.

A few weeks later, a touring Soviet midget hockey team ran around Canada thumping our kids; I saw them whump an Oshawa club 16–6. The key was found at the Soviet club's high-energy practice session earlier that day. Leapin' lizards, what a show that was. They never stopped skating for the full 70 minutes, literally, and practised game situations, five different drills with full player movement all the time. Amazing.

Afterwards I told the press, "There's no bloody way our spoiled, pampered, Canadian kids could have survived such a workout. A teenage team from Canada could not get through a warm-up practice like the Ruskies did without being down on their knees, winded. To Russian kids, performing skills is as easy as talking or breathing, but we don't provide that same opportunity for our kids to learn the game."

I went on to berate our level of fitness, emphasizing how out of shape we were compared to Soviet players, how they were much stronger on the skates, and from the waist down, than Canadian or American kids.

"They perform the skills and handle the stick like a toothpick because of their upper body strength. Their moves are so quick and so sure. They make sure they have a proper grip on their stick at all times, and this gives them better control of the puck. They control the puck better than we do. There isn't a team in the NHL that passes the puck as well as those 16-year-olds," I scolded.

Well, the shit hit the fan, again, and I was about as popular as a fox in a henhouse, but it was the truth. However, the great minds that run Hockey Canada and our national and minor hockey programs did nothing effective to change the situation. A slim win in the 1976 Canada Cup once again satisfied the egos of Canada's hockey gurus, along with the nation's many armchair hockey experts. And along came the 1979 Challenge Cup.

No more surprises for our pros. We were ready (again) this time and it was time to "really kick some Ruskie butt," in a three-game hockey series. So, once again we sent our best to meet theirs. And *they* kicked *our* butt — but good.

The Soviets hammered the pro team from the NHL 6–0 in the

final game of the three-game Challenge Cup series. The headline from the *Globe and Mail* read "Russians rout pros" while the *Toronto Sun* headline simply read "OUCH!" In 96-point type.

Under that headline *Sun* writer John Iaboni wasted no time hitting the nail on the head. "Hockey is no longer our game. It belongs to the Soviet Union," his article began.

Coach Scotty Bowman reflected later, "They have a program that has accelerated since they played us in '72 and collectively we're going to have to take a long look at the game they're playing. I have no idea how they organize their younger players. . . . We certainly don't know as much about them as they know about us."

Bowman's comments, read today, are even more indicative of the problems. The Soviets hockey program had in fact accelerated long before 1972, which is why we got thumped back then. Bowman's later comments are even more revealing. Not only did Bowman have no idea how the Soviets organized their hockey programs, *nobody* in Canada had bothered to find out.

Why? Because we arrogantly continued to keep our hockey heads stuffed up our lazy butts. We never bothered to see what anyone else did because that would be admitting we had something to learn — God forbid. What fools we are. The Canadian know-it-all attitude toward hockey is about as stubborn and stupid as the average male's attitude about asking for directions or reading a road map — it doesn't happen until we are really lost.

In the same issue of the *Sun*, George Gross also saw the glaring light as explained to him by assistant GM for the team, Cliff Fletcher.

"Whether we like it or not, we should realize that technically speaking the Soviets are better than we are. They skate better, pass better. . . . It all boils down to the fact that they work on their fundamentals from a very young age and never stop. They have a feeder system right down to the 10-year-olds and we've just seen the results," Fletcher said.

Fletcher also rightly nailed the junior program and system, explaining that extensive travel destroyed energy and practice time, and that the loss of junior sponsorship from pro teams hurt the game.

"People who own junior clubs make it their livelihood. They're not concerned with player development. They hire a coach and put him under the gun to win at all cost because a winning team will draw fans, and that spells money for the owners."

Well, it's been 20 years since the 1979 lesson, and sadly not a lot seems to have changed on the Canadian hockey frontier. During the 1999 World Championships, Canada was eliminated in the semi-finals (by a fairly talented Czech team) in yet another bizarre shoot-out scenario. (Sweden turned the same trick a few years before.) Canadian fans immediately grumbled about the sudden-death shoot-out system, and how stupid it was. The fact of the matter is that Canada never should have had to go that route in the first place. Some Canadians attempted to excuse the club saying the best Canadians were in the playoffs but that largely fell on deaf ears. The Czechs were without Jaromir Jagr (league scoring champ), Dominik Hasek, Martin Straka, and other strong players.

Clearly Canada no longer dominates the game of hockey. At any level.

And unless we change our skill-teaching programs (and there isn't a decent skill-teaching program in any Canadian minor system I know of), we are in deep, deep trouble. And unless we change our philosophy regarding kids' hockey, Canada will become a second-rate hockey country within 10 years. We will be dominated by Finland, Russia, Sweden, the Czech Republic, the United States, and Slovakia. Count on it.

You have to have your head stuffed very deep in your stinky equipment bag not to see the tremendous impact the skilled European players have had on the NHL. Once you get past Kariya, Lindros, Yzerman, and Gretzky, in recent years the number of Canadians dominating the game are pretty few.

In 1997–98 the top three rookies in the NHL were European. In the 1998–99 NHL regular season, only five of the top 14 scorers were Canadian and just eight of the top 21. In the 1999 junior NHL draft the top four were European (two Czech, two Swede) while only four Canadians made the top 10. The fifth pick was American Tim Connolly and finally, in sixth, a Canadian goalie named Brian Finley.

Of the top 18 picks in the draft, only six positions went to Canadians. Another 10 years of that (and it's been going on for five or six years already), and it will be impossible for us to maintain international standards. When Canada's international hockey opponents are producing 17 or 18 of the best 18-year-olds in the world, and Canada producing just nine, it doesn't cut the mustard.

More important is the number of players a nation places within the top 10 selections. Odds are good that six or seven of the top 10 chosen will sooner or later develop into All-Stars, or will help their team play over .500 hockey. There will be some players from selections 11 to 27 who will turn out better than some from spots one to 10, but the gravy is generally found in the first 10 at the draft banquet.

Canadian kids making the NHL draft today are (in the main) very big, very strong, tough, hard-working, disciplined, but average skaters and most have a feel for the game. Yet they have very few stick skills compared to the Europeans. They can't carry, pass, or receive the puck, can't back up and turn, and have very few offensive game skills. In fact, I'm having trouble thinking of many recent Canadian picks who could as junior draftees. (Sure, b'y, there are exceptions, I'm sure).

All the wonderful Canadian players who finally made it to the top of the pack made it there in spite of the hockey system, not because of it. They made it there largely on their own work and skill development, and I really admire them for that.

When I constantly can see 23-, 24-, or 25-year-old NHL players who still can't make or receive a pass, I think, "Geeze, if we taught skills like the Finns or the Swedes, wouldn't they be great players?" Canadians wouldn't have a worry in the hockey world and would dominate international competition. Every NHL game on TV would be a classic contest. Better still, there'd be at least 20 very competitive teams instead of six or eight.

William Houston's series of articles in the *Globe and Mail* in February 1998 were not far off the mark in analyzing the Canadian game, especially after the Olympic Games loss at Nagano. One article in particular stood out, "Olympics proof we are mediocre." In it Houston hit many points right on the mark.

The break-up of the Soviet Union in 1991 freed Eastern Europeans to join the NHL. In the old days, Canadians, through aggressiveness, could control, or at least contain, European players. But they are no longer intimidated. They are comfortable in the NHL and, because of their high skill level, they out-perform Canadians.

Europeans get the edge on Canadians early. They flourish in a youth-development system that stresses basic skills. Children are instructed by professional coaches and teachers. They learn fundamentals — skating, passing, and stickhandling.

In Canada, children are taught by volunteers, many of whom are inexperienced or incompetent, or both. Kids are thrown into games, as many as three or four a week, or 80 to 100 in a season. They rarely practice. The demand to win games takes precedence over having fun and developing skills. They are instructed to play defensively and encouraged to intimidate. Not surprisingly, kids start dropping out at the age of 12.

At the Canadian junior level, hockey is a business. Owners care little about developing players. Their priorities are winning games and producing revenue.

A junior in Canada might play as many as 90 games in a season, counting exhibition and playoff games. Although Canadian Hockey has set the minimum practice-to-game ratio at 3 to 1, it is no better than 2 to 1 in junior hockey. The European junior player, on the other hand, plays a 50-game schedule and has the advantage of four practices to each game. In addition, European federations begin a streaming process for youths when they reach their early teens.

Streaming identifies talented players, brings them together on teams and creates an environment in which they can reach their maximum potential. This system is exclusionary, but it has produced stars such as Peter Forsberg, Teemu Selanne, Jaromir Jagr, Pavel Bure, Mats Sundin, and Sergei Fedorov. Last year, USA Hockey started hot-housing its best junior players.

The Canadian major-junior leagues have gone in the other direction. In the past 17 years, they have expanded by 15 teams. Franchise fees have put money into the owners' pockets, but expansion has diluted the product and denied skilled players the opportunity to improve their game by playing with teammates of a similar level.

The Canadian system, starting with children at the age of 6 and concluding with the 20-year-old junior, produces players who are aggressive, hardworking and willing, but deficient in basic skills.

European hockey develops a player who is superior to a Canadian in skating, passing and creativity. He may not be as tough as his Canadian counterpart, but he'll probably learn to cope, especially if he spends a year or two in one of Canada's junior hockey leagues. For the Canadians, however, it's too late to learn skills that should have been taught to him when he was a child.

I immediately sent a fax to the *Globe*, praising the article and suggesting it be sent to every member of our federal and provincial governments, and every hockey program organiser, coach, executive member, and parent of kids registered in minor hockey.

A week or so later, even the *Globe and Mail*'s editorial writers saw the light with an editorial called "Hard Lives — Who Killed Canadian Hockey." The writer was dead on the mark, saying Canada lost in Nagano because it relied on a game using size and strength instead of skill and speed. He quoted Team Canada GM Bobby Clarke on why we lost at Nagano:

We are the grinders, clutchers, bangers, the no–name role players, the men with heart enough to make up for our shoddy skills. Yes this is what Canadian hockey is all about. Here in the Church of Don Cherry, blessed are the toothless muckers, for they shall inherit a National Hockey League contract. . . . The quality of Canadian hockey is not merely declining, it is in free fall. . . . They say the definition of stupidity is doing the same thing over and over again and expecting different results. Welcome to Canadian hockey.

The first step in treating the illness must be acknowledging that we have one. So here goes: Canadian hockey is sick. Now on to figuring out what the problem is and how to cure it. . . . This is our game. If we want it back, we are going to have to fight for it — with our hearts, but above all with our heads.

Awesome article. Right on.

So what are the problems, the lacking skills, and possible solutions? That's another whole book, but here's a micro look.

Many elements of hockey today drive youngsters out of the game far too early, and violence is a big part of it. Anybody who tells you differently is full of it. Either that or just plain macho and pigheaded.

I remember a quote from some time ago by then Hartford Whaler (now St. Louis) tough guy Kelly Chase. Kelly said about being an enforcer, "It's like when you've had somebody in school organize a fight for you. You know that at 3:30 you've got to go out and have that fight. That's how I feel every game, and probably how I've felt ever since junior hockey. Eventually that's what chases a lot of boys away from the game." Thanks, Kelly, well said.

I make a point of seeing at least one hockey tournament at every age level every year. Almost without exception, at bantam age and under, the two biggest, strongest, and toughest teams meet in the finals, and most of the time size decides the winner. Often the most physically and mentally skilled players are the smallest or of average size, and by game three in the tourney they are beat to a snot from being hooked, held, and knocked into the boards by opponents a foot taller and 50 pounds heavier.

In midget, juvenile, junior B hockey, and even Tier II junior A it's the same thing — size and strength and a bully or two eventually come out on top. If you think that scenario is simply an unplanned by-product of the game, think again. It is a calculated, intentional decision — and it is wrecking the Canadian game for millions of kids, past, present, and (though I hope not) likely the future.

For years our hockey system has been designed to drive the boy of average size, average skills, and average mental toughness out of the game by the time he's 13 or 14. That's because the coaches, like our educators, are not interested in the dregs or even the average, but only the elite. Somehow the adults seem to figure they gain status by being the coach and travelling around the country with the kids. They get the jobs because they can put in the time, but it is often a status symbol to most of them, and the quality of coaching at various levels is often horseshit, absolute horseshit.

That scenario leads to the biggest problem in Canadian hockey which is that we have people with no bloody idea which end of a net is up supposedly teaching kids the game.

When parents "decide" that Johnny is going to play the piano (and the parents can't play well themselves), they go to the pros. They hire a professional piano instructor. So why is it when Canadian parents "decide" Johnny is going to be a pro hockey player, they suddenly believe they can teach him how even though they have no skills?

It boggles the brain.

How can non-skilled parent-coaches teach anyone to play when they don't have a feeling for the game, and they can't skate, or pass the puck, or shoot? How can they teach unless they know how to sell and teach the student (and other parents) balance on skates, cutting the stick and why, explain the mechanics and techniques of passing and shooting?

Hockey is the greatest game in the world to play. However, moms and dads who wouldn't know a hockey stick from a garden hose are generally still controlling our minor hockey league systems. Many of them have already heard my ranting and raving, and they understandably feel attacked. Some hate my guts — but so be it. My concern is for kids and for the game, not for the adults involved.

I've come to the conclusion most hockey parents don't or won't understand or accept my philosophy about "every teenage girl or boy having the opportunity to play the game of hockey, at their skill level, and in a non-violent atmosphere." I could write a book on the problems of adult hockey in Canada, however, they pale in comparison to the problem of kids' hockey in this country.

The Canadian minor hockey philosophy, adopted by the parents who run nearly all the systems, is formed largely from what they see on TV. What they see they emulate, and what we get is a game of physical toughness over speed, skill, and finesse. Many of the youngsters are all too happy to accept that philosophy, especially if they're big, strong, and semi-skilled. It doesn't hurt that often their parents are on the executive or coaching staff, or are friends with someone who is. Those kids automatically make the team and get oodles of ice time.

A large number of kids who start in minor hockey are out of hockey by age 15, the majority by 13 or 14, which is a time when the game could be of real value. Kids ages 7 to 11 don't really need hockey; there are many other things going on in life and fascinating events to keep them hopping and busy. In my view, it's the "tweens" and teenagers who often desperately need something challenging and physical to do — and hockey could be part of the solution.

I'm convinced, and can prove, that a proper hockey system, designed from day one to teach skills and offer non-violent games through the developing years, will help keep kids involved in the game much of their lives and certainly into young adulthood. I also can guarantee a minuscule number of hockey dropouts, and I'm smug about this because over a 10-year period in St. John's we proved it. In addition, we offered very challenging programs for the skilled players, which were greatly utilized.

Some years ago, around 1993, a minor hockey tournament was held on the Vancouver Island peninsula and I was asked to contribute to their program. I sent this message:

Congratulations on being able to play the world's greatest game. To stay involved and 'have fun' during the teenage years, your mental skills are far more important than your physical hockey skills. Your wonderful hockey career will be very short, come crashing down at age 13, unless you and your teammates learn to use your heads (think) while playing the physical game. During the formative years, 8-13, insist, demand that the mental aspect of the game gets as much or more attention as the physical. These days, being small and skilled or big and strong, rough and tough, isn't enough. Without the 'smarts' you're on the outside looking in!

Seven or eight years later, I checked it out and there has been no change in their system or any organization on the Island. Amazingly apathetic.

My greatest concern is seeing very few teenagers playing the game and the source of that problem starts at the bottom, right in atoms, mites, and the littlest of tykes. Even though there's a (questionable) coaching certificate program, we still largely have unskilled dads, ingrained with local hockey philosophies, teaching something they know diddley-squat about. Unskilled parents can't teach skills or operate a league. Parents are terrific at running concessions, organizing tournaments, raising money, registering kids, getting publicity, or doing a zillion jobs connected with minor hockey, but to supply philosophy regarding skills, or running the game — no bloody way.

On the ice, the parents' or coaches' lack of training or their inability to teach skills is often quickly overcome with the famous old solution "Let's have a scrimmage," which they do in the majority of systems around the country. Most minor hockey systems totally waste a youngster's practice time, and let the kids simply play two or (if they're lucky) three games per week. Any dummy can count to five skaters plus a goalie, and during games that's about all the coaches do. There is no or very little effort made to correct team and/or individual mistakes during a game. They can't run a practice, teach a skill, or monitor and referee a game.

Minor hockey in Canada is largely a social club for most adults. In most communities, parents travel regularly on weekends all over with the kids in the guise of being all-star or rep parents; but for a significant number of them it's also a great big party. Some of those "wonderful" parents don't care for the game, don't care for their kids, and use the game and child's hockey star status for their own ego and social standing in the community. Most of the coaches and local executives are just as bad.

I recently heard from several gullible local parents who spent outrageous amounts of money on elite training camps and tournaments for their kids to the tune of thousands of dollars, and with absolutely, positively no chance of any benefit to the kid. A group of coaches and parents had got together and decided to form Island-wide novice (8 and 9) and atom (10 and 11) elite hockey teams. The coaches selected 30 or 40 players and sent out invitations to parents to attend tryouts in Victoria at a cost to participate of around $80 per player. They had to arrange their own travel and find their own food and accommodation. Sixteen kids from all over the Island, Port Hardy to Victoria, were chosen. Dollars to doughnuts a bunch of those 16 were pre-picked. The others likely wasted time and money. Those who made it then attended four tournaments in the summer. The families spent four days in Vancouver at the Vancouver Select Tournament, paid for ferries, car transportation, room and board, and entertainment. The entry fee was $80 per player, $950 per team.

One family I talked to spent seven days in Vancouver attending the Super Series for all age teams. (I'm talking 10- and 11-year-olds here.) The costs? About $1,100 per team, approximately $80 each, again, hotel or motel, food and entertainment for the family. . . . And at one of the tournaments each adult had to pay $20 to see their children play as well!

When I inquired about the approximate summer cost, the angry mother replied, "A minimum of $3,500." I was stunned.

Multiply that dollar amount times 12 players per team, times six teams in that division, times a minimum of six divisions equals big money. Add the cost of a normal minor hockey season to that and it easily is above $5,000. Trust me — a boy will not at age 10 or 11 ever improve his physical or mental skills one iota on full-ice tour-nament games under those circumstances.

I can understand the adults' or parents' foolishness, and also the occasional leeches who promote and own ice surfaces for rent, but I can't understand why national and provincial hockey gover-nance turns a blind eye to the folly that's going on. In order for these tournaments to exist, they must have the blessing of those hockey authorities. If they have given approval, they are as big a part of the sting as anybody.

Having all-star teams of boys from all over British Columbia — or any other province — at ages 7, 8, 9, 10, and 11 is criminal, asinine, and an absolute waste of time and money. Provincial-, area-, and community-funded skills and drills programs are super, but competitive games on full ice — no way. Playing full ice is the greatest deterrent to the development of hockey skills possible for young kids, especially at a cost of $3,500 per person. Shameful.

And stop it there, back it up . . . British Columbia is not alone. Check the North American continent, folks.

The CAHA, Hockey Canada, and most governments at all levels have stood idly by and watched not only our lead in top-level competition and teenage hockey fall behind other countries but the disintegration of structured hockey as well.

Many Canadians might say, "Stop it there, back it up, Howie. Haven't we won a Canadian junior title year after year?"

Sure, but we never win in the departments of speed, skill, and finesse. Time after time, when it's all over, it's the other kids who make the all-star teams, who are drafted ahead of ours and who go on to star in the NHL. But it's our goaltender who's the MVP and we've simply out-pummelled the opponents.

When I refer to teenagers not playing the game, I'm talking about the average kid who simply wants to have fun and enjoy the game at his level, not one that either aspires to or is being pushed toward NHL stardom. The hundreds and thousands of those teens in every community in this great country should be allowed and encouraged to continue to play the game at a recreational, fun level, if that is what they desire. Unfortunately, our governing bodies, national, provincial, and local, appear to be interested only in the elite kids, and so are most parents. There is little or no room for hockey as part of the school physical education or team-building programs. Absurd and insane.

What cuts me most is watching the parent who, after finally discovering that Johnny isn't going to make the local or provincial rep team, drops out of hockey or leaves the boy to fend for himself. I've seen it too many times.

"So stop it there, back it up, Howie! Haven't our governments spent millions of dollars and thousands of hours training the layman coach? Isn't it compulsory to have a level two or three before you can go on the ice and get behind the bench?"

Sure, b'y. As stupid as that rule is, you're right. And it means zip in many cases. Example: when I go into a rink and there's a game going on, any age, the first thing I look at is the length of the stick being used by the players. That tells me four things immediately: The knowledge and dedication of the coach, the personality of the student, the intelligence and knowledge of the parent, and the effectiveness of the training programs in the province or country.

Most players in the NHL, when on skates, have a stick that is three to five inches below their chin when it's stood on end. For most, it's the only way they can keep the full blade on the ice when carrying or passing the puck. It is by far the most important rule to puck control and passing. The student is not teachable and will never, ever become outstanding, good, or even competent with the puck unless his stick is cut in a similar manner.

When I run a team practice or hold my hockey school, I make sure everyone understands that the instructional time period belongs to me. I have a motto when it comes to teaching hockey. "The practice session is mine. The game belongs to the boys." At my schools or practices, during the first shift of the first day we check all the players' sticks and cut them off if they are too long. Those with very expensive aluminum sticks are given one day to replace them. On day two we cut them if they haven't been replaced.

Occasionally kids and parents say, "No way." If it's a practice, I simply respond that either the player leaves the ice or I will. I won't waste my time. If it's at my hockey school, I simply refund their money. You have to help make the student teachable. If he's not, why waste his time or mine, or the parents' money?

After watching two or three shifts of whatever is going on at a game or practice, I usually count about eight out of 10 players with sticks too long. Nine out of 10 coaches with coaching level patches from the wrist to the shoulder like military badges have the majority of players on their team, themselves included, with sticks too long, shafts too stiff, or blades too big.

Some teaching system!

To correct this simple problem takes *no skill* and *no feeling* for the game at all; it takes *no* teaching or game knowledge. You don't have to demonstrate and talk through the art of balance on skates, or how to position your hands on the stick to carry or pass the puck, or take a wrist shot or slap shot. You don't have to argue and demonstrate the advantage of a straight-bottom blade instead of a curved or rockered blade. Don't have to talk through and demonstrate five different kinds of passes. You don't even have to talk about how to *feel* the puck on the blade, how it feels to the hand and brain when it's on the heel, centre, or end of the blade. You don't have to teach the kids how to develop power when backing up, how to make a 180-degree turn and come out faster than you went in, or explain why you don't chase the puck carrier when you've turned him.

I could write another book (a very large one at that) on skills to teach and "how to," but when all is said and done, folks, the most important rule for the beginner to pro in hockey is simply "Cut the stick off well below the chin!"

However, amazingly, after more than 30 years of being told how wrong it is, our minor hockey (coaching certificates and all) still have eight out of 10 kids playing the game with sticks too long. And they think they have done a good job!

On those wonderful rare occasions when I find eight out of 10 players on a team with sticks the right length, I find out the coach's name and make an effort to contact him and congratulate him because he's something special. His task of keeping players with the right length of stick is very difficult for a couple of reasons. An example: As I said, at my first hockey schools, during the morning sessions we'd cut all the players' sticks. In the evening session I'd say to my son, Mike, "Geeze, boy, there's a dozen kids out there with sticks too long. How did we miss that many?"

"That's their second stick, Pop."

So we'd cut again.

We'd have what we called an NHL game at 7:30 p.m. with staff and students every evening. I'd watch some and still see kids and staff with sticks too long — geeze! Then I found out the kids had practice sticks and game (too long) sticks. We finally got smart. Now we cut *all* the players' sticks on the first day.

When I get involved with a local minor team, I know that all players have practice and game sticks, and I know what the brave coach is in for. If he's persistent, and unless the kid is the son of the league president, you've got him cornered. Once you've settled the stick issue with the kid, though, be ready for the big one. Young Johnny's gone home after practice and explained his problem to his parents. Dad, usually but not always, says, "Give it a try, son. The coach this time might be right."

Hockey Mom is quite often another kettle of fish.

"No way — what Johnny wants Johnny gets," like he has since day one. Super Hockey Mom dashes to the telephone and calls the coach, more than likely at dinner time.

"Coach Howie, this is Johnny Smith's mother. He tells me you want to cut off his hockey stick. Are you mad or what? You touch his stick and the rest of the parents will have you fired, replaced, and I'll see to it because the president of the league is my cousin's second husband's boss. And you won't get another coaching job in our league."

Think I'm kidding? I'm not. Then there's the incident that happened to my brother, Tom, who played top-class U.S. college hockey with St. Lawrence and won a national championship or two. An excellent teacher of individual and team skills, Tom had a very good peewee team in Ottawa. His philosophy was "I've got three shifts of five and everyone plays, despite the score or time in the game."

Well, his team won some tournaments and lost a couple as well. I know he lost a few in the finals or semi-finals because even during close games, with two minutes left, if it was the third shift's turn, Tom played them.

The parents had a meeting and suggested he change his tactics. When Tom said no, they insisted that the best players (11- and 12-year-old kids) play more than others.

My big brother believed so much in the game and the kids playing it that he got up and said, "Ladies and gentlemen, I guess you'll have to find yourselves another coach."

Yahoo, what a guy! But hockey and the kids were the real losers. A great teacher and coach with international experience and a feel for the game was driven out by overbearing parents.

So whenever I see a team with the majority of players having their sticks cut properly, I grin because I know they have got somebody special for a coach.

If the stick is too long in most cases there is a serious problem. It's either a very poor training program, a coach who doesn't understand stick skills, and/or parents who are just plain ignorant.

Still, you can talk till you're blue and few listen. Just this past winter, Leah and I attended a game that my grandson, Tyler, was playing in with his Parksville peewee house against Comox in a mid-term holiday tournament. Wouldn't you know, nine out of 10 kids had sticks too long. Rather than rant and rave in front of Leah, I tried to sit there and suffer quietly while pucks went under toe, under heel, and even under the middle of the blade of kids carrying the puck or receiving a pass with their cumbersome sticks. Finally, after watching black sweaters pass the puck to red sweaters and vice versa for 10 more minutes, I burst out, "Dammit, Leah, oops sorry, Jiminy Cricket, these kids have been in the system for four, five, and six years and no one has ever told them that you don't give the puck to the other team, that if you're wearing a red jersey you don't pass it to a black. What the hell are those three adults doing behind the bench? Geeze — give me strength. Why don't they teach the kids that you don't run ahead of the play coming out of your own zone, you don't ever pass from the boards to the middle, don't ever *force* the puck carrier to pass the puck?"

Suddenly I felt a tug on my arm, and Leah says, "Howie, don't get so excited. The boys are having fun. Besides, it's just house league and they are just babies."

I shut up for about 15 seconds, then said, "Leah, there are four, maybe five kids out there that have enough talent to make a competitive team three or four years down the road. But I want the 20 others to still be playing hockey at ages 14, 15, 16, and 17. At what level I don't care — recreational, non-contact — but with enough physical and mental skills to have fun, to be able to make a pass, receive a pass, carry and move the puck. Have some knowledge of how to play the game to be creative, not always, but once or twice a night beat the opposition with your head. That's what will keep kids playing. In most cases that one talented, big and strong kid will continue to play for a while. It's the other 24 we have to keep playing through the teenage years."

Leah nodded understandingly at my frustration. There was a look in her eye that said, "Perhaps you care *too* much for the game." Thank goodness someone understands my idiosyncrasies.

I've got CAHA and Hockey Canada instruction books three feet high in my basement, and from what I see on the ice all over British Columbia, except for the few very gifted players, 95 percent of our kids still have poor physical and mental game skills. Books, videos, and clinics haven't worked. From my experience working in the midget, bantam, and peewee divisions, most players have so few stick skills and by age 13 or 14 have developed such bad game skills they're almost unsalvageable. That leaps to 100 percent non-teachable if they are limited to one hour and 15 minutes of ice time per week, starting at 6 a.m. or even two games a week and the occasional tourney.

Another serious problem is that from whenever they start until around age 12, the best skaters have been able to pick up the puck and beat with a deke or skating one, two, or three checkers before running out of ice. When those players get to second-year peewee or first-year bantam, though, things change quickly. Suddenly everybody is as big, strong, tough, and skates and checks as well as he does. They also work as hard and are just as smart as he is, so it's almost impossible for the puck carrier to beat anyone one on one.

However, try to tell or show that hotshot that he can't (and never will again unless he creates a doubt in the checker's mind) beat somebody one on one — and he'll laugh in your face. Unless the kids are taught that early in their hockey life, they are in for a rude surprise and geeze, it's tough on them.

Even with the younger peewee players, quite often the two or three best players on the team have egos so big you can't get to them at practice or games. It's tough for a variety of reasons, including meddling parents and their "connected" friends, to bench a player for any length of time. Besides, it's not helping a player to sit on the bench, and it only becomes an adult power-trip for control. Great in war, not effective in minor hockey.

I have finally learned after many years that a whole lot of commando tactics do not cut the mustard with today's kids. Besides I just don't have the energy to yell and scream like I used to to get kids' attention. In the long run, it doesn't work that well anyway. The game and the learning of skills must be fun. That's not to say that discipline, concentration, and respect are not important, they are. It's just that the concepts must be transmitted in a different way.

Yes folks, some old dogs *can* learn a few new tricks, including even stubborn old cusses like myself. And like Howie Meeker, minor hockey has to evolve in order to survive and grow. To be the best it can be.

Today we are hurting the beginners. Youngsters ages 7 to 12 are missing out and it breaks my heart. That's when they can and should be taught skills: skating, stickhandling, passing, thinking, and timing. Today though, it's just not happening.

The best teaching practice I've seen in any arena on Vancouver Island involves about 50 skaters, ages 7 to 10. On the ice, they're broken into four or five groups, each with a course or drill to follow or do. The instructor quickly demonstrates the routine and then says to the player at the front of the line, "Get a puck and do what I just showed you. When you finish the drill, stand over there and wait."

And there the drill ends — wonderful.

Nine kids wait, daydreaming, talking, or shooting at the boards or goalie, while those on the course go from A to B, good or bad, right or wrong, completely unsupervised. Then those who complete the course once again stand around and talk, flick pucks around, and do nothing.

When I attend a provincial coaches clinic, I ask the instructors, "When Johnny goes from A to B and obviously can't perform the skill, what are the mechanics of teaching that skill — how do you teach him the skill?" I usually get a blank look or a glassy-eyed stare. Yikes, they're the ones running the clinics and supposedly teaching. What's wrong with this picture?

With 50 skaters, having just four or five instructors each with 10 kids you haven't got a chance. It can't work. At our hockey schools, we have 50 skaters with 12 or 13 instructors and at least seven counsellors in different phases of development. When we do a skating or puck-handling drill, the lead instructor is responsible for time spent on drill instruction, pylon placement, and position of teachers. We have 20 people spending time with the slower learners, teaching mental and physical skills. When a player is in trouble, you have to be one on one with the student, and work with him so that he first of all understands the drill, and then understands how to do the skill. It's great fun, and damn hard work. But it works!

Canadians could learn so much from others about skill improvement techniques such as skating and puck control. All we have to do is watch or ask. American players and coaches have progressed rapidly by being willing to watch and learn from others, including Europeans.

The European players stand out in stick and game skills, and I wondered why for some time. About 10 years ago, when I was broadcasting 40 games a season and the playoffs, I began to notice that one on one against the opposition in the corners or anywhere, it was usually the North American who went down. One day while broadcasting the Air Canada Midget Tournament in Calgary, I bumped into Dave King, the coach of our national team at the time.

"One on one, in power-skating skills, the European wins most physical battles. How come?" I asked.

"It comes from their soccer training. It also provides them with a great amount of other skills," King said. The lightbulb came on as he continued. "Here in Canada at age 14, 15, or 16, we start building and strengthening their upper body so that they are 5' 10" tall and look like Charles Atlas or Arnold Schwarzenegger — built like a boxer. However that really only harms their game because they've lost considerable puck handling skills because of the bulk, and worse still, they've heightened their centre of gravity. They've become top-heavy and are easily knocked down or off balance, and when they're finally balanced their feet are too wide apart to generate power.

"The European does it differently. Their emphasis is on strengthening the body from the waist down. Walk into any NHL room and you can pick out the Europeans by the size of their upper legs and thigh muscles. One very big advantage is they have lowered their centre of gravity, making it harder to be knocked off the puck, and that extra strength means more and longer power when needed."

It seemed so simple.

"Geeze, Dave," I asked, "why don't Canadians do the same?"

"We're trying. Our national training program is now directed more at the lower body, but many people think our game is all intimidation and upper body strength and it's hard to change their beliefs."

I realized I was not alone in my concern for our system, but also saddened by realizing that if people weren't going to listen to Dave King, coach of the national team, about our problems, then I was farting against thunder.

Europeans have a huge lead over us in stick and game skills. If we don't keep up with the new training practices, in the main developed and practised by Europeans, it's game over. We will have no one to blame but ourselves.

In 40 years of minor hockey I know that you *can* keep the teenager in the game. You can improve, greatly improve, everyone's physical and mental skills, enough that playing the game is fun.

There is no bigger thrill than making a creative play in a hockey game. By giving our big, strong, tough kids some real physical and mental skills, top spot in the hockey world would be ours a fair share of the time.

Is there a solution? Sure, but it will likely never happen.

My son, Mike, dreams about convincing minor hockey in Canada to let us demonstrate the Meeker Hockey System, a program of skills and drills that teach the teacher how to teach. It provides the potential to have kids and adults within their own communities learn and then teach the game and skills properly — hometown people employed in teaching a community-based hockey program to accommodate all facets of the community involved in playing the game. The program also provides the potential for co-ed hockey, especially for teens. Can you tell me a better way to get young male teenagers involved in the game of hockey again, in a fun, non-violent way, than by making co-ed fun leagues at night? Why not?

I'm convinced, however, that minor hockey will simply never learn and never be prepared to change or alter. Minor hockey has little hockey logic running the show. To work properly, having rotating parents in charge is not the answer. Nor does having bureaucrats involved in making the rules that game associations and training programs have to operate under.

Perhaps I'm burned out, but I suspect it is a much bigger problem than Howie versus minor hockey. I'd like to think that Mike and the many other very good, very dedicated hockey people out there who love the game and kids, just like I do, can turn the horses around. However, I can't help but feel that the horses are still headed for the cliff.

That fear is not lessened when I hear the likes of Canadian Amateur Hockey Association president Bob Nicholson, at the end of the 1999 season, beak off about how there will be a review of "how we do things in Canada regarding teaching of the game. We have to look inside and outside the game" — whatever that means. Nicholson made his comment, but absurdly added at the end that, "We're not doing it because we think that Canadian hockey is in desperate need." Talk about head in the sand and denying the blatant.

I firmly believe the key to properly securing Canada's place in the sport of hockey is for Canada to create a sports' college system attached to one of our universities, where our teachers of hockey, soccer, and other sports can go and acquire the needed skills. They've had such colleges in Europe and Russia for years.

In the case of hockey, we have to have a national philosophy geared toward keeping the youth in the game, not just producing NHL stars.

Hundreds, if not thousands, of young players in Canada can't quite make the pros but still want to remain in the game. Hundreds of young people taking physical education would be available as instructors. The graduates from such a sports university could go into the community, working with locals, and run the community hockey programs according to the philosophy of teaching the teacher how to teach. Programs could be constantly monitored as would be the on-ice activities.

Hockey could become a solid employer of young adults across the country, helping to teach in communities everywhere. Perhaps some creative economics in funding might encourage this shift. Such instructors could be jointly funded perhaps by federal, provincial, and municipal or regional governments.

Recognizing that North America is based on a democratic process, such a hockey vision will take significant buy-in from hockey folks across the land. Not all minor hockey folks and others concerned will be in a big hurry to join the shift; opposition will certainly exist. Incentives will be needed in order to promote the change in approach to how we teach and present the game.

Within three years, I guarantee that those who joined the program would be winning in every league and most tournament games. In fact, after five years the first-year team in every division would constantly win, and in some cases the second-year team could successfully play in the division above. In a very short time parents whose kids are not in the new system will be demanding their kid get the same training. Trust me.

Folks, what now passes for our national game is in dire straits. Professionals and bureaucrats at government and sports body levels, who have no feeling, or love, or understanding of the game, have been allowed to foster philosophy and programs that, once outside the university, or Ottawa, just can't work. Most of them simply talk big but inside just don't give a damn. "I'll hang on 'til pension time and get out." Shame!

If you want to change what's happening to our great game, let your voice be heard. Send a letter to Mr. Nicholson, the CAHA, the federal and provincial government reps in your area, local politicians, and minor hockey people and tell them your thoughts. Otherwise, you become part of the problem not the solution. And Lord knows we need a solution soon.

WHERE IS THE GAME GOING?

■ ■ ■

So, what's the future of the NHL, and hockey? Where is the game going?

The future of recreational, minor, junior, NHL, and worldwide hockey is dependent on a variety of factors; some are unique to the individual category and some are common to all of them, but they are all linked. I've already expressed my views on minor hockey and its relationship to hockey in general. Let me clarify, if need be, that despite the sad shape minor hockey is in, I still believe there is *tremendous* hope for it in Canada. However, Canadians must be willing to make changes in the system in order for that to happen.

I dearly hope the United States continues to learn from the European minor hockey training systems rather than the current Canadian methods.

Recreational hockey also has tremendous growth potential and anything that can help get teenagers and adults back in the game — well hot damn, let's do it! The benefits, both physical and social, would be tremendous. Again, that success will be dependent on the willingness of the politicians, educators, and public to make it work. It can be done and I believe there are enough people who care about the game and kids to make it happen.

What does the future hold for Canadian professional hockey players, and what influence will Canadians have on professional hockey five years down the road?

Twenty-five years ago I predicted that unless we changed our approach to the game at the community level (minor hockey), the Europeans and Americans would supply the players with colour and the offence, while Canada would supply the defence. It's pretty well happened that way. Take away Eric Lindros, Paul Kariya, and Joe Sakic, and the few remaining Canadian offensive players are in their mid-30s.

During the 1999 June draft, the top Canadian player was picked sixth overall, and he was a goalie. Is anyone listening yet?

There needs to be once again some sort of correlation or connection between the pro leagues, universities and colleges, and junior hockey leagues if we hope to truly create an atmosphere in which Canadian players can develop their skills. Junior hockey doesn't provide it and has become business, just like the NHL and any other pro league.

As I pointed out earlier, that scenario affects the decisions that coaches and general managers make about players. Do they slowly develop the younger player and his skills, or do they want to fill the stands? The guy holding the purse strings generally wouldn't know a puck from a Ping-Pong ball and couldn't care less. He only knows and cares about the profit margin. In his world, the red line is not good.

One of the famous Sutter brothers recently purchased the Red Deer Rustler junior club. A few years ago the team was bought for around $500,000. It was suggested that Sutter paid between $2 million and $4 million. What's really scary is that NHL expansion clubs in 1967–68 paid that same dollar for their franchises. How times have changed.

If good hockey people, like the Sutter clan, get involved in the Canadian junior leagues, there's some assurance of skill teaching and continued concern for the game and players. There is definitely room for a vibrant, profitable, and effective junior system in this country, yet once again it takes the right captains driving the damn boat.

Where is the NHL game going?

Unless the Canadian government comes up with some tax concessions for Canadian teams, similar to those of U.S. clubs, only Montreal, Toronto, and perhaps Vancouver will survive. Under current conditions, the NHL in Canada is going bye-bye. There is a movement afoot to find such solutions (as this book goes to press) and I hope common sense and not the almighty cents prevail. It wouldn't surprise me one bit if Vancouver's U.S. owners get tired of continuing their multimillion-dollar losses and take their basketball and hockey teams to greener pastures. In 10 years or less, the Habs and Leafs could be the only Canadian teams in the NHL.

Remember, hockey is no longer a sport; it's big business, and a very costly one at that.

Finding financial cures for NHL problems such as bankrupt teams, soaring player salaries, and tax snags will take some creative work and some hard decisions. But at least the NHL has watched other pro sports deal with the issues and has been down the road a few times itself. The reality is that players, owners, and league governors have to come to some rational compromises before the game out-prices itself completely.

There is also a new pressure present today in the NHL. The leaders of the financial conglomerates that now purchase NHL franchises are used to winners. In the United States (due to other financially successful enterprises that they control), some owners can write off substantial losses in other ventures, such as hockey, because they are not there for the money. Since it is prestige they truly want, the personal embarrassment of running a dog in a high-profile game like hockey riles them. They want to be a "somebody," and most will pay any price to be seen on TV and written about in the papers.

Only about six NHL teams of 27 in 1998–99 had a realistic chance of winning the Stanley Cup and possibly making money. With little or no chance of making money and winning a Stanley Cup, an owner has to be nuts to be involved. In 1998–99 playoffs, only Detroit, Colorado, Dallas, and New Jersey seemed like serious contenders although Ottawa, Philadelphia, Buffalo, and Toronto were pretty close.

With good leadership, a lopsided trade or two, and a gem of a draft pick, teams such as Anaheim, New York Rangers, Boston, Toronto, Florida, Washington, Montreal, Edmonton, and St. Louis might make it to the finals again within the next five years. The Mighty Ducks, even with Teemu Selanne and Paul Kariya (the best two offensive people in the league), are still three top-notch players away from going anywhere significant.

Even with similar good fortune, Tampa Bay, New York Islanders, Calgary, Nashville, Chicago, Vancouver, San Jose, or Los Angeles still couldn't make to the finals in 10 years, except by fluke. Only major trades, wise selections and training, and very costly moves could make that happen.

Where is the NHL game going?

It's going to lose owners and teams in the next 10 years because of rising salaries and costs.

There was a time when a hockey club's future could largely be decided at the draft and trade tables. That impact has diminished for two reasons in recent years: there aren't enough young quality junior players to satisfy the needs of all the pro teams, and (surprise, surprise) money.

Once past the number 10 pick, the chances of getting a player who will help your club play .500 hockey within five years is pretty slim. However, the odds have improved slightly since the Europeans and United States have upgraded their development even more.

Free agency and big dollar trade deals really count, and place the importance of the draft in proper perspective. Look at the deals Detroit made just before the March 1999 trading deadline. Those with the dollars and the player depth can make trades, pay the salaries, and take advantage of the unloading going on by teams who are hurting. In the year 2000, five or six NHL teams will be in dire straits financially and will likely unload a top middle-aged player, draft picks, or young borderline NHL talent to lighten their salary commitments. The teams in financial trouble are usually those getting the best draft picks but even if they strike oil three or four years after starting the well, they won't have enough money to get the black stuff to market. Will the Sedin twins still be in Vancouver in 2005? (Heck, will Vancouver be in the NHL in 2005?)

The owners, however, are largely to blame. First, they overpay their draft pick while he underperforms for three or four years, and when he finally comes close to returning performance for dollars paid, he becomes a restricted or totally free agent and goes on the open market. The owner then either loses the player or overpays him (again) to keep him. So money and a bunch of borderline NHLers become the key to winning. A very smart general manager helps too.

There will be a 30-team NHL by 2000–2001 after the Atlanta Thrashers join the league in 1999–2000 and the following season sees the arrival of the Columbus Blue Jackets and the Minnesota Wild. Under the existing format and rules, they will not challenge for the Stanley Cup for at least 10 years.

The owners and some general managers have been complaining about the cost of doing business — and rightly so. However, who is responsible for the high salaries paid to NHL stars?

Certainly not the player. If an 18-year-old player drafted number one is given the top capped contract of $1,025,000 for first year and if I'm drafted number two, right away my reaction is that I'm worth two-thirds or three-quarters of that total. And it snowballs right down the line. Now, when I'm a restricted free agent making $1 million a year, three teams run an offer up to $2.5 million per year by me and guess what? I'm gone, unless my team matches it.

So at age 31 I'm an unrestricted free agent making $3.5 million per year, and now I have four teams seeking my services. A top offer can hit $5 million, or much more. Free agency, restricted or otherwise, has in most cases eliminated the reason for a player to hold out for more money. If I'm worth my salt, I'll get two chances to double or triple my wages without a fight.

Who was responsible for signing an agreement with the players' union that more than doubled almost every player's salary in two or three years? The owners, of course. Now most are crying "Poor me."

I watched the recent strike in basketball with interest. When it became apparent to the union heads that the owners meant business, that they would close shop for a year if they had to, the players gave in. Every report I read said the owners got 99 percent of their major demands and gave only token ground in areas where huge sums of money were not involved. The owners had balls. Good on 'em. Sooner or later the NHL owners will get another chance to stop the spiralling costs they helped create, and I hope I'm around to see the results. Things need to get a little bit real again.

Don't get me wrong — as much as players like me were underpaid in the 1940s and '50s, I am delighted to see the present-day NHL player finally get his loaf and a half of bread. But I think the game is in trouble.

Recently Leah and I had a Saturday evening bar meal in a room where there had to be 50 people of all ages, and two big TV sets showing a Toronto game. Halfway through the second period I suddenly said, "Leah, am I the only one in the room following the action?" So we watched for 10 minutes; even though a goal was scored, no one broke the conversation or interrupted their meal to look at the screens.

The next night at home we watched Vancouver play Calgary on the tube for about five minutes, then I read the sports page of the *Globe and Mail*, occasionally glancing at the game. Leah said, "Howie, no one is trying." She was right. "Let's try the dish," I suggested, but even that provided only a dull Phoenix vs. Dallas match. I expected a great game from those two clubs, but it was a real yawner. We shut off the TV and I played computer bridge.

After a Buffalo-Dallas game a few days ago, I talked to a good friend who knows hockey and he was raving mad at the Sabres' tactics. "One man in deep, four back all night long, no forecheck at all. There weren't four scoring chances in the game. I was bored to tears," he fumed.

What is it that is making hockey boring?

Most of the owners, general managers, and coaches are under tremendous pressure to win, and less than half of the 28-going-on-30 teams have the talent to play the game as it was meant to be played. So 90 percent of the time in most games most of the effort put forth by most players is on defence. Coaches who convince their players, "Defence at the expense of offence" have jobs, keep jobs, or will find jobs.

It's a tough business on coaches; even the very best sooner or later run afoul of the players, general manager, owner, press, fans, family, and close friends. When I played, of the six teams there were only three good coaches for years — Toronto, Montreal, and Detroit. The other three teams searched and searched but couldn't find anyone who could demand and design a system to keep the puck out of the net. Today there are at least 15 to 20 coaches who do it. Almost every team is under 3 GAA per game, half of them under 2.5. Some of them are under 2.25. Amazing.

It's mainly the coach's job, with assistants, to supply the defence. It's up to the owners and general managers to supply the offence. As coach, if you can keep the peace, get maximum effort, and keep the goals against average close to 2 1/2 per game, you're more than doing your job. When you look at the superstars, stars, and two-way stars, they are spread out over about 11 teams: Anaheim, Colorado, Detroit, Carolina, Dallas, New Jersey, Ottawa, Philadelphia, Phoenix, Pittsburgh, and Toronto. So basically 11 of 16 playoff positions are gone. The rest of the clubs, mostly made up of motley crews, are going to get there on hard work, system, very good goaltending, and a group of 20 goal scorers. Boston, Buffalo, Calgary, Edmonton, St. Louis, and San Jose scrap for the final five spots and that leaves about 12 clubs in dire straits.

A league in trouble? You bet!

Is there hope? Oh yes. If there are a couple things I've learned it's to never quit, and to continue to try to change things for the better whenever you can. There are a lot of good, smart, caring people in the game, though I agree with the old chestnut that "hockey has to be the greatest game in the world to survive under the people who run it." And doubly so for community minor hockey in Canada.

But folks, don't fret. Get a cold beer, or a Coca-Cola, or a jigger of screech, a jar full of peanuts, a comfortable chair, sit back, put your feet up, and relax. Turn on an Ottawa-Leaf game on TV and enjoy, enjoy, enjoy.

We can all bitch and complain about the game (because the true fan always wants the game to get better), but when it boils right down to it, we are watching some of the best hockey ever played, anytime anywhere.

How lucky we are!

2

■ ■ ■

FROM THE
PLAYERS' BENCH
1950–1967

LEADERS, BLEEDERS, AND FEEDERS

■ ■ ■

Whenen I agreed to outline the highlights of NHL hockey during the past 50 years, beginning with the 1949–50 season, it didn't dawn on me that such a starting point would practically eliminate one of the greatest team dynasties. Naturally I refer to the Toronto Maple Leaf club that between 1946–47 and 1950–51 won four Stanley Cups. I was fortunate enough to be a member of those teams.

To this day I believe we could have won a couple more championships had owner Conn Smythe not intentionally dismantled the club. Either way, that Maple Leaf team certainly closed out the first half of the 20th century atop the hockey pinnacle — and it was an honour to be part of it.

Another observation, revealed soon after the start on this book, was that while Parts Two and Three generally attempt to divide discussion of the game into decades, there's a historical repetition of certain clubs and players dominating the league for five or seven year blocks. That trend has existed almost continuously since the

1940s and is verified by checking not only the Stanley Cup winners' list, but also the league's regular season first-place champions and overall league standings.

Only during the past 10 years of parity has that trend slipped. The Detroit Red Wings managed to win two cups and be in the running for a couple of others. Only in the first half of the 1990s was there no club really dominant for more than two or three seasons in a row — a trend particularly interesting considering the number of teams now in the league.

While few teams within the past 50 years actually qualify for "dynasty" status (according to the "experts" who decide such stuff), keen hockey buffs will note that a number of powerful clubs have pushed the puck up and down the ice. For example, the Detroit Red Wings between 1947–48 and 1956–57 finished in first spot eight times and second twice, including seven straight first-place overall finishes. However, they captured just four Cups and only two of them back to back.

Way back in "the good old days" when I played, and for a while after that, the NHL All-Star game usually featured a select All-Star team against the Stanley Cup champions. The Wings were so dominant that the league changed the All-Star game format, though they later returned to the old format.

The real test of a team's strength, depth, and talent is measured through a 70- or 80-game season, *not* the Stanley Cup. During those years, the Wings may not have won the Cup every year but they were at the top of the pinnacle. During the season, those below first or second place play a third or fourth line or four or five D-men to develop their talent. In the playoffs, with just two series with eight games to win, you shorten up, play two or three lines and four D-men and probably win.

A dynasty? Not according to the so-called hockey experts, but in my mind they sure as hell were. My goodness, they were a powerful club, and that's difficult to admit since the Wings were our hated arch-rivals in those days.

For many years I joined the thousands of other coaches, managers, players, analysts, media, and fans in passionately seeking the elusive elixir of hockey. I desired the answer to that key question, "What's the secret potion to create a winning team?"

All my adult hockey life, I've been somewhat obsessed with discovering the magic formula for a championship, and I've asked many astute teachers of the game for their answer. Most often I received similar comments suggesting a "proper blend" or certain "chemistry" of players from stars to tough guys. Yet no one I asked could adequately define the mixture for me.

Ironically, it was an Irish sports scribe who indirectly gave me the formula for dominating the Canadian game.

In May 1998 I trucked off to Ireland on a golf trip with a motley crew of friends, including broadcaster Jim Robson and former NHL player and coach Phil Maloney. While there, I grabbed a copy of the *Sunday Independent* newspaper and naturally sought out the sports section. In it I found an absolutely marvellous full-page feature by writer Tom Williams commenting on the various key "All-Ireland" hurling teams. Williams analyzed the great teams and their roster of players, and then slotted the hurlers into three basic categories: Leaders, Bleeders, and Feeders.

Leaders are the obvious stars and true leaders, feared by opponents, and as game-breakers are capable of killing other clubs in the blink of an eye. All true championship clubs need at least three Leaders in their line-up.

Bleeders are the real heart of the team, the always dependable guys who are not superstars but talented, and regularly give their all to win. They play with tremendous passion and because of that occasionally fill the role of hero or game star. Bleeders are essential to any winning club.

Feeders are the fringe players with reasonable skill who play temporary roles or contribute to the team game, but form the bottom of the depth chart. Feeders work hard, but also feed off the skills of the other two types of players. They play an important role and may even briefly bask in glory but are not guaranteed a regular pro job for long unless they eventually advance up to at least Bleeder status. Feeders often come and go, with youth, energy, and entertainment as their hook. There is no shame in or diminished respect for the role of a Feeder, for even to play at the professional level is a tremendous accomplishment. Still, Feeders seldom last more than a half-dozen years.

Players can move up and down within the categories, but rarely does a player go from Feeder to Leader. A championship team usually has an even blend of all three players with at least three Leaders on the roster. Rarely does a team with no Leaders take home all the marbles.

The Irishman's article was perfect! No one had put it quite that simply before. Williams's hurling rating system seemed a perfect thermometer to help me gauge the dynasty hockey clubs of the past 50 years.

I've picked who I think are the best players and best lines (centre, right wing, then left wing) at the end of each season. As well, and when warranted, I've analyzed dynasty or powerhouse clubs and given their players Leader, Bleeder, or Feeder ratings.

Chew on those for a while.

THE FEISTY
FIFTIES

■ ■ ■

1949–50

Overconfidence snuck and kneecapped a number of players and teams in pro sports over the years, and the Leafs of the 1949–50 era were no different. After three Stanley Cups in a row, my Maple Leafs were denied a fourth by the powerful and despised (by us) Red Wings.

I don't recall if we recognized it, but Detroit was definitely in the midst of building a dynasty team themselves and about to take over the torch from us in another year or so.

Just like 1948-49, the regular season of 1949–50 was marred with lots of fights and stickwork. The long-standing feud between Toronto and Montreal continued, but now a vicious relationship had also developed between Detroit and the Leafs. Mayhem is an appropriate word to describe a few nights I recall. The fierce competition we had with the Habs was largely a hockey grudge — but with the Wings and us it had become a true, bitter rivalry. Plain and simple, we just didn't like each other.

It seemed routine that somewhere within the evening's match

with the winged wheelers, Billy Barilko, Jimmy Thomson, Bill Juzda, Bill Ezinicki, I, or somebody would rekindle a recent or long-standing feud with the likes of Pete Babando, Ted Lindsay, Marty Pavelich, Leo Reise, or Gordie Howe.

Oddly enough, the two Wings I tangled with on an almost dating basis were Howe and Lindsay. Despite their being tough, mean players, I had no personal grudge with them, or at least not until after several battles. There were other Wings I wanted to have a go at but somehow wound up with the big two — lucky me. It seemed I would always start swinging with Lindsay and then part-way through Howe would step in and take over.

Terrible Ted played left wing and I played right so we were nose to nose most of the night. He was not big but he was mean, tough, and strong and sooner or later one of us bad-tempered little battlers would start something with the other. Ted more often than not pummelled me on an equal basis and hardly needed any help from Gordie. But all of a sudden I'd look up and there was the big fella. With Gordie I'd swing but he *connected*. Like I've said before, Gordie and I seldom actually fought. Gordie fought — I just took the shit-kickings. As insane as it may sound, I was relieved whenever I started a scrap with Ted and Gordie *didn't* step in and pound me into submission. Better Ted than dead.

It didn't help matters that the league also expanded from 60 games a season to 70 that year, which provided us the luxury of now seeing the Wings and the other four clubs at least 14 times each per season. Oh joy.

When we heard about the increase in game numbers, a few of the guys got together to discuss what we should do since our contracts (for what they were worth) included 10 more games. Vic Lynn, Joe Klukay, Sid Smith, and a couple more of us finally concluded that we should send in our big defenceman Garth Boesch to do our negotiating. In reality we all knew that Smythe would take no time in telling the rest of us that we should be glad we had jobs in the NHL. But "Bushy" was good at that sort of negotiating stuff and we encouraged him to fly at it, even though we felt like we'd sent our brave but unmatched knight into the dragon's lair. He was a bit of a hero when he returned, having wrangled $100 per game for each of us.

That was the same year Chicago coach Charlie Conacher yelled at and then grabbed referee Bill Chadwick by the shirt. After the game Charlie apparently knocked Detroit sports writer Lew Walter to the ground as well, which wasn't that common.

It was also the season of the infamous Battle of the Bulge. On December 1 Smythe embarrassed Turk Broda by suspending him until he dropped some pounds. Smythe went after a few other guys as well (including my linemate Vic Lynn), saying, "I'm not running a fat man's club." We disliked the guy — but he got our attention and certainly the media's.

Broda went along with the crap as best he could and in the end won the day by starring between the pipes. Lynn never did take the routine with much humour and I don't blame him. Within a year Vic was traded.

Detroit started strong and finished first overall with 88 points. They were led by the Production Line of Sid Abel at centre between Howe and Lindsay. The trio actually swept the top three positions in the individual scoring race with Lindsay first at 78 points, Abel second with 69, and Howe third at 68. Rocket Richard was fourth with 65, including a league-leading 43 goals.

Montreal surged past my falling Leafs into second spot in the final couple of games. The Rangers finished fourth.

Not many of us gave the Rangers much chance of surviving the Habs in their opening playoff session, however sniper Edgar Laprade (who returned from injury late in the season) led the Blueshirts to an upset over the favoured Habs.

A few years before, Laprade was the victim of one of the hardest bodychecks I ever recall, compliments of my teammate Wild Bill Ezinicki. Ezzy was like a vulture and would circle around the neutral zone from his right-wing position hunting for victims. Laprade, a centre, was dipsy-doodling with the puck up through centre ice that night when Ezzy saw him coming. The hunter took two strides, cut into the centre ice, and just as Laprade looked up and saw Ezzy coming, *blam!* the lights went out for Edgar. Ezzy hit him with his shoulder and hip and you could feel the impact from the cheap seats. Ezzy was not big but he could really hurt you and Laprade folded up like a two-dollar suitcase in a rainstorm. Maple Leaf Gardens went quiet for a few seconds after the impact because suddenly we all wondered if Laprade was even alive. When he finally twitched a bit and then moved his leg slightly, a sigh of relief was heard throughout the rink. Man, what a hit.

For my Leafs that year, it was a heartbreaking seventh-game overtime loss to Detroit that packed our bags in the opening round of the playoffs.

I maintain that the injury to Gordie Howe in the first game eventually cost us the series. Some writers, especially hacks from Detroit, suggested that Teeder Kennedy butt-ended Howe — but that was not the case. League president Clarence Campbell was at the game and later filed a judgement based on the officials' comments. His conclusion was that Kennedy was not to blame for Howe's injury.

The supposed intentional injury by Ted Kennedy was bogus. Gordie actually fell into the boards attempting to hit Kennedy, but the backlash against Teeder and the team for trying to injure the Detroit star really affected us. It also fed the Red Wings with motivation. Even with the Howe factor, however, we had our chances to wrap it up and didn't. I still remember as clear as day that in game six our sniper Max Bentley was home free from our own blueline and missed the net with his shot. He *never* did that, so what were the odds?

Either way it was Leo Reise who scored the winner for Detroit the next game and we were done like dinner.

It felt very odd for us to actually watch the final series being held in Toronto and yet not to be a part of it. The Rangers had to use Maple Leaf Gardens because the circus was booked in Madison Square Garden. I remember a couple of times looking down at the game under way and thinking that things were all wrong, and that my Leaf buddies and I were supposed to be down there playing.

The scrappy Rangers took Detroit to the seventh game and then double overtime before losing their chance to sip from the cup. Pete Babando scored the winner for Detroit.

BEST PLAYERS: Gordie Howe, Ted Lindsay — Detroit

BEST LINE: Sid Abel, Gordie Howe, and Ted Lindsay — Detroit.

1950–51

This was a year of trades with players such as Harry Lumley, Black Jack Stewart, Bob Goldham, Bert Olmstead, Pete Babando, Gaye Stewart, and Metro Prystai, among others, finding new uniforms. In November the Leafs also traded away my friends and talented teammates Vic Lynn and Bill Ezinicki. It was the beginning of the end of our dynasty club and a sign of things to come.

I was also greatly saddened by the resignation of Hap Day as Leaf coach prior to the season. During all my years in the game, I'd never known a finer hockey man. He stayed on as assistant GM but he was heading out the door.

I still maintain he was probably shoved out that door by Conn Smythe and years later I finally understood that Hap was not at all happy with Conn. And Conn had his own plan that no longer included winning or winners. What it did include was finally edging Day out of the Maple Leaf door (and also out of Smythe's personal sand and gravel business), and making room for son Stafford to take charge of the Leafs. After three Cups and plenty of glory and money gained, Conn planned on temporarily dismantling his winning team, putting the focus on Day and others in the process. Hap was a winner and so he became part of the problem for Conn and Stafford.

But we weren't done at that point — in fact we were on a roll. The Rangers went in the tank early in the year and had so many problems they hired not only a psychologist but also a hypnotist. It didn't make a pinch of difference.

It was yet another wild and woolly season that saw unlikely Ted Kennedy brawl with Montreal rookie Tom Johnson — Johnson was a hacker and the two just didn't like each other — while Ted Lindsay and now Bruin Bill Ezinicki set-to in another classic tilt. That one was simply a spillover from Billy's days as a Leaf. Old habits are hard to break and fighting the Red Wings was just so goldarn easy.

The Kennedy brawl began when Johnson gave Teeder about 10 inches of stick in the gut. Kennedy, no patsy with a stick himself, just pummelled Johnson like there was no tomorrow, and Johnson was a big boy.

The Rocket went off his rocker again, this time in a New York hotel lobby when he grabbed another referee by the neck. It was a year fraught with numerous injuries to many players, including me.

The 1950–51 also marked the first experiment in broadcasting hockey on television. There was no bigger rivalry anywhere or at any time, except perhaps Boston and Montreal, so it was a classic clash, with the Habs visiting us at Maple Leaf Gardens on March 21. I played in the game. Two seasons later regular TV broadcasts started.

Detroit took the league as regular-season champions (again) with outstanding rookie Terry Sawchuk in net. Sawchuk won Rookie of the Year and First All-Star Team honours while Detroit set a record for most points by a team at 101.

Gordie Howe likewise had a tremendous year scoring 43 goals and adding 43 assists for first place in league scoring.

Toronto started the year strong with an 11-game unbeaten streak, but injuries hurt us and we stumbled late in the regular season, finishing second. In the big picture, the bad year meant zilch because more importantly we won back the Cup.

In the opening round, we dumped Boston but not before an odd start to a series. In game one Boston surprised us 2–0, but in game two on Saturday night in Toronto we woke up and put on a show. By the end of the first period, we were tied 1–1 and the score was unchanged after the first overtime period, but the referee ended the game. Back in those days, sporting matches were not allowed to go past midnight into Sunday in Toronto — and a second full overtime would have taken us past midnight. The game simply ended in a draw. A few years later, that regulation was eliminated.

We went on to beat Boston in four straight games and then met the Canadiens in one of the greatest final-round series. Though it lasted only five games, Montreal took us into overtime every single game. It was five straight games of intense hockey, war on ice with a puck, but it was just as thrilling as it was chaotic. I remember even while on the ice that it was a tremendous series to be involved in. The energy level on the ice was unbelievable. No other series to this day has ever had every game go into overtime.

It was yours truly who cost the Leafs their only loss in the series. We fell behind 2–0 in game two but rallied to tie the game and force the overtime. At the end of my second shift, I was tired and should have gone to the bench. Instead I jumped on a pass in my own end from Cal Gardner and took off down the ice. At the Hab's blueline I tried to go wide around bruising defenceman Doug Harvey but he dove out and took the puck off my stick. When I looked back, the Rocket already had the puck and was headed back into my end. He danced around Jimmy Thomson like a hoop around a barrel, cut inside behind our other defenceman, Gus Mortson, gave goalie Turk Broda the deke, and shovelled the puck behind him. Game over.

Thankfully, the Leaf fans did not kill me but coach Joe Primeau gave me the evil eye as I slunk to the bench. I managed to vindicate myself somewhat in game four, scoring once in our win.

The Rocket had a tremendous series, scoring once in every game, including their only winner. We clashed a few times and even exchanged some jabs in a couple of games, but I don't recall any scraps with him during that series. Sid Smith, Harry Watson, Teeder Kennedy, and Billy Barilko scored our overtime winners. Billy's, of course, was the last of the series and it proved to be the last of his life. It was just about three minutes into overtime in the fifth match when Billy buried the puck on a shot from just inside the face-off circle. He did it all that series and that night. Billy hit like a football player, got into a heck of a scrap with Johnson, and then scored the winner. A great night for a goodbye. There's a well-known picture of that event with Bill flying through the air and me getting pasted into the boards behind the net by Johnson, after skating behind the Montreal net and making the pass out to Billy.

A couple of months after we won the Cup, Billy headed out on a fishing trip but his buddy's plane crashed en route home. No trace was found until 11 years later, so it was a long summer waiting to hear anything. I can't begin to express how much that accident affected our team, especially at the start of the next year. Billy was a great guy, a good friend, and tremendously talented young player. He'd have been an All-Star, for sure.

Best Players: Terry Sawchuk — Detroit; Milt Schmidt — Boston

Best Lines: Ted Kennedy, Tod Sloan, and Sid Smith — Toronto; Elmer Lach, Maurice Richard, and Bert Olmstead — Montreal

1951–52

The 1951–52 NHL Press and Radio Guide listed the six teams' rosters for the beginning of the season and the Toronto Maple Leaf line-up had Bill Barilko's name on it. But Billy never came back and training camp had an emptiness to it.

After our fourth Cup win in five years, Smythe intentionally increased his dismantling of the Leaf club, eventually spreading the players like true leaves in the wind. The team dropped to third place and a long 10-year trip into hockey darkness began. In the following years only the genius of Hap Day and King Clancy kept the Toronto Maple Leafs in the playoffs. Some outstanding goal keeping from Harry Lumley and goal scoring by Tod Sloan helped as well.

I spent a lot of the season migrating back and forth between Toronto and Ottawa as I'd won the federal Conservative MP seat for my riding of Galt, Preston, Hespeler (now Cambridge), and Waterloo South. Still, between the House of Commons, injuries, and travel, I managed to play 54 games that year. It was a brutal haul, though.

Young Bernie Geoffrion, who played just 18 NHL games the season before, continued to sparkle for Montreal, finishing sixth in league scoring and winning Rookie of the Year honours. You could tell he was going to be a dandy; he was a good skater and had a terrific shot.

Powerful Detroit finished on top of the league for the fourth straight year and eventually won the Stanley Cup. Clearly, it marked the end of the Leaf era and a dominant takeover by the Red Wings. Gordie and the boys were ready for their rule.

Howe once again captured the scoring title, this time racking up 47 goals and 39 assists while playing another full season. "Terrible" Ted Lindsay finished in second place.

Despite my tight schedule and Ted's pursuit of the scoring title, we had enough time to squeeze in a couple of good scraps during the year. One of my more memorable moments as a hockey player/politician was a tiff between Ted and me soon after I was elected to the House of Commons. At a face-off, Lindsay gave me a stick on the ankle so I whacked him back. He gave me a little jab with his stick in the gut and naturally I replied. We both did the little strut, at which point Ted looked at me and said, "Well, let's go, your 'Honourable' asshole!" We wailed on each other pretty good but in the box we laughed like hell.

Terry Sawchuk scooped the Vezina and made it look so easy.

Led by the Rocket, Montreal defeated Boston in the opening round while Detroit sank us four straight with Sawchuk shutting us out twice. The Wings received no greater competition from Montreal in the finals, shutting down the Rocket and dumping the Habs in four games — Sawchuk blanking them twice as well.

Four shutouts in eight games for Terry? Absolutely amazing.

BEST PLAYER: Terry Sawchuk — Detroit
BEST LINE: Sid Abel, Gordie Howe, and Ted Lindsay — Detroit

1952–53

I contemplated retirement prior to this year, but figured we might have a good shot at a fifth Cup. I wasn't quite satisfied, and certainly not pleased with how the year had ended. Even though I was still a Member of Parliament and the travel schedule combining politics and pro hockey was insane, I decided to play one more year.

Early in the season, however, it became apparent that things were not going to be wonderful in Toronto. Smythe traded away our talented centre Cal Gardner, champion goalie Al Rollins, Gus Mortson, and Ray Hannigan to Chicago for goalie Harry Lumley. As good as Lumley could be and did later prove to be, it was still one of the dumbest trades in hockey. But Smythe didn't give a damn. It was all part of his bigger plan to trash the team.

One week later Smythe sold my buddy and Leaf star Joe Klukay to Boston. As it turned out, Boston and Chicago ended the regular season tied for third with 69 points while Toronto managed the unthinkable and missed the playoffs with just 67. Klukay had to be worth two points to us over the schedule!

The Red Wings rolled through the regular season steaming to first spot yet again. Rookie netminder Glenn Hall provided brief but strong support when veteran Sawchuk broke his foot during a Christmas Eve practice. Hall returned to his Edmonton Flyers after his successful six-game stint; however, management made note. Gordie Howe was a powerhouse all year, and the big fella wound up winning the scoring race again, with 49 goals and 46 points for a whopping 95 points in 70 games. I remember that we marvelled at his point total. Lindsay finished in second. Former Production Line pivot-man Sid Abel surprisingly asked for a trade to Chicago, where he became player/coach. Abel was replaced at centre, first by Metro Prystai and later by sophomore Alex Delvecchio.

The rising-force team from Montreal grabbed second place and eventually grabbed the Cup over Boston in five games helped by their young backup netminder, Jacques Plante.

At the end of the year and playoffs, I could sense that a shift of power was taking place, with Detroit waning and Montreal on the rise.

Late in the season, I took a hard check into the boards in Boston and hurt my back pretty bad. As it turned out, it was the end of my career, though I came back on a recall basis the following year for five games. When I took off my skates at the end of that season, though, I had a feeling I was pretty well done playing the game for a living.

BEST PLAYER: Gordie Howe — Detroit

BEST LINE: Elmer Lach, Maurice Richard, and Bert Olmstead — Montreal

1953–54

The perennial loser New York Rangers made a pile of changes to their line-up at the start of the year, but it made little difference. Even with Johnny Bower and eventual Rookie of the Year Camille Henry, the Blueshirts still missed the playoffs. Chicago made few changes and tumbled to the bottom of the heap. It mattered not because the power in the league was now owned by Detroit and Montreal, and the rest of the clubs were really just dance partners.

Highly touted junior and senior hockey star Jean Beliveau finally signed with the Habs but broke his leg in early October. Howe plummeted to just 33 goals that year but still beat out the Rocket, Lindsay, and the hot Bernie Geoffrion for the scoring title.

Montreal would have had a better season if they had not lost control a number of times throughout the year. Penalties, misconducts, and suspensions hurt the team all season. Geoffrion went a little bonkers and broke the jaw of Ranger Ron Murphy with a vicious stick chop and was suspended from the remaining eight games against New York. The Rocket then threatened to not play if Geoffrion's suspension was not lifted, but he was soon put in place by the league president.

In the rugged playoffs that year, Detroit beat out Toronto in five games and Montreal eliminated Boston in four, setting up a classic final-round tilt.

The close competitiveness between the Wings and Canadiens was aptly displayed when the series went seven games and then into overtime in the final game. Detroit's Tony Leswick finally notched the winner on a fluky deflection.

BEST PLAYER: Gordie Howe, Detroit
BEST LINE: Alex Delvecchio, Gordie Howe, and Ted Lindsay — Detroit

1954–55

A ho-hum season was highlighted by the ongoing anger antics of the Rocket and even the loss of control one night by Terrible Ted. Lindsay was suspended 10 days for thumping a fan with his stick after the fan interfered with Howe. (Good for Ted, I figured.)

Meanwhile the Rocket had a temper tantrum on the ice on March 13, clouting Bruin Hal Laycoe on a couple of occasions with his stick, and then punching linesman Cliff Thompson twice. At one point during the fracas, Richard had his stick taken away by an official, but he picked up another lying on the ice and attacked Laycoe again.

President Campbell had seen enough of the Rocket's lack of control and respect. It was the second time Richard had attacked an official and the second time he'd picked up a discarded stick on the ice to attack a player. Maurice was suspended the final three games of the year and the playoffs, which in turn sparked the infamous Richard Riot in Montreal on March 17.

Missing the final three games of the season also cost Rocket the scoring title as teammate Boom Boom Geoffrion slipped past him to win by one point, with 75. Big Jean Beliveau finished third overall with 73 points, giving the top three scoring spots to Habs. Poor Boomer couldn't win for losing. When he surpassed Richard for the scoring title (while Richard sat idle), the Montreal fans booed him. Ironically the Rocket never won a scoring championship, twice causing his own title demise.

Once again the Wings and Canadiens battled through seven games in the final round with the home team winning every one. Smooth skating Alex Delvecchio scored twice in the 3–1 final game in Detroit.

That win marked the last time the Wings would touch the Cup for 42 years. Some suggested the famine was a karma thing or a curse maintained when the club's players later withdrew from the formation of a players' union.

Best Player: Bernie Geoffrion — Montreal

Best Lines: Alex Delvecchio, Gordie Howe, and Ted Lindsay —
Detroit
Jean Beliveau, Bernie Geoffrion, and Bert Olmstead
— Montreal

1955–56

I was coaching my second year in Pittsburgh at the time and was not as tuned in to the NHL as before, but the 1955–56 season was still a very odd year — even from a distance. Coaching changes and trades had a major impact.

Toe Blake took over from Dick Irvin as coach of the Canadiens. The former great Montreal winger would become one of the greatest coaches ever. Irvin went back to Chicago to coach, where his productive NHL career began as a player.

The biggest shock to me that year was the summertime trade by Detroit that sent Sawchuk to Boston. Weird as he was, Terry was in a league of his own as a goalie. Of course, Glenn Hall as a backup goalie wasn't exactly chopped liver. Terry later balked at the Bruins as well. Two years later, Detroit would trade Johnny Bucyk to the Bruins to get Sawchuk back. Dumb or what?

Sending Sawchuk to Boston was just one of several really questionable moves by Wings' GM Jack Adams. Soon after the Cup win in '55, he traded away several players, including Tony Leswick, Glen Skov, Vic Stasiuk, Johnny Wilson, and Sawchuk. By the time Adams was done tinkering, too many Red Wing bodies had left the team. In the past, Adams had generally tinkered with the feeders on his club. But once he started moving the leaders and bleeders, he got in hot water. The Bucyk-Sawchuk deal killed him, in my mind. Bucyk developed into a leader for many years. Adams was gone a few years later.

Jean Beliveau reached all the expectations and won the overall scoring championship with 88 points, nine more than second-place Howe. Normally a gentlemanly player, Le Gros Bill was forced to establish his turf and racked up 143 minutes in penalties doing so. He was a mountain of a man on skates during this time and dominated the ice when he was on it.

Montreal finished first in the league with 100 points, and come playoff time the final round featured familiar opponents, Detroit and Montreal. The appearance marked the sixth straight final-round showing by the Habs. When the battle was over, Montreal had won the Cup four games to one, led by Beliveau, who pumped in seven goals in the final series. The victory marked the first of five straight Stanley Cup championships for Blake and the Canadiens. The torch had been passed, or rather snatched, once again.

BEST PLAYER: Jean Beliveau — Montreal
BEST LINE: Jean Beliveau, Bernie Geoffrion, and Bert Olmstead — Montreal

1956–57

The 1956–57 season was a great learning experience both in hockey and the hockey business for me. I was named coach of the Leafs by Conn Smythe, and though I may have been simply a small part of Smythe's bigger plan, I was thrilled at the time to have the task. I knew I'd been appointed coach of a team that had been torn asunder and had as much hope of making the playoffs as someone farting against thunder, but still I jumped at the chance.

If I had been thinking clearly I would have gone to Hershey to coach (Pittsburgh was folding), but like any hockey man the chance to coach in the NHL (and my Maple Leafs, to boot) was too tempting to turn away from.

How dumb can a guy be?

We finished fifth.

The 1955–56 Habs had the most potent power plays one could imagine and they were so effective they actually led to a change in rules in the 1956–57 season regarding playing a man short. Because of their ability to score two, three, or four times when the other team was short-handed, the league decided that if a team scored while on the man advantage (for minor penalties) that the penalty would then be considered over.

No matter how good or astute hockey scouts are, or how open to advice club management might be, there are always those players who get missed in the hunt for talent — colts who never quite get the attention in junior or the minors but turn out to be thoroughbreds in the NHL.

Camille Henry was one of those guys. It was my misfortune to first meet Camille in the American Hockey League when I was coaching Pittsburgh and he was playing with Providence. Camille had won the NHL Calder Memorial Trophy as Rookie of the Year, but two seasons later, for weight and other reasons I don't know, he wound up back in the minors. The little guy constantly killed us game after game. Camille was about 5'9", but seemed taller, skinny as could be, maybe 135 pounds.

Remember Ali's saying, "Float like a butterfly, sting like a bee"? That was Henry. His skates hardly touched the ice. It was all timing, manoeuvrability, finesse, great hands, and great scoring ability. My, oh my, was he good with a puck, could he make plays and score goals. "Camille the Eel" they called him. He didn't do anything else very well, but give him the puck and Jiminy Cricket, could he move. Back then in the AHL, most coaches in the league had five checkers to every talented offensive player on the team, but having a Camille on your team made those odds more tolerable.

As a minor league coach, I was expected to also be somewhat of a scout for the Leafs. Well, I missed noticing many others I'm sure, but I didn't miss Camille. I kept telling Hap Day, "Get Henry, get him — if for no other reason than to get him out of my hair. The kid can play for you, Detroit, or the Canadiens. He can get you 35 goals, 20 of them on the power play."

I had Pittsburgh GM Baz Bastien do some homework, and we knew the Rangers would let Henry go for three of our prospects: Ab McDonald, Gerry Foley, and Larry Cahan, and although they were good players it would have been a steal.

Anyhow, the next season, 1956–57, when I coached Toronto, Camille was with the Rangers, and he killed us a few times and basically put us out of the playoffs.

When talking about memorable goals, I remember one of his like it happened yesterday. In Toronto late in that season, we were in fifth place, a couple of points behind New York in fourth, and it was life and death to get in the playoffs. Saturday night, late in the third period, Camille gets the puck at centre ice and beats two checkers, Rudy Migay on the inside and Jim Thomson on the outside, gets to the top of the circle, and Marc Reaume starts to run at him. I know right then and there that we're in trouble. You run at Camille and you're dead. So Henry just stops on a dime and Marc slides by him. Now he's 10 feet out with Migay, Thomson, and Reaume in hot pursuit and Dick Duff coming in from his left-wing position. Henry puts the puck between Dick's feet, picks it up, and goes in on goalie Ed Chadwick. ("I know where he's going — he's going upstairs under the cross bar.") Right on — Camille fakes the shot, Eddie challenges, Camille stutter-steps a little bit, goes to his right, goalie goes down, game and season — over!

When I look back he must have had the puck for at least 20 seconds and beat five guys. What a feel for the game he had, what a feel for the puck. My oh my, what a goal.

Playing for the Rangers hurt Camille Henry because that club could not create an atmosphere in which he could fully display his wares. Henry could have played for Toronto, Detroit, or Montreal and played big because those clubs had the ability to create an atmosphere in which Camille could use his talents to the full. The other clubs, including New York, didn't, and that's why Camille failed to make it big. But he did score some very great goals while in the NHL, a lot of them against me, the bugger!

Detroit had a tremendous regular season, as did Montreal, while the rest of us chased our tails. Sawchuk walked out on the Bruins and I prayed for a deal that would bring him to the Leafs. I knew what a head-case he could be but I also had watched him stop more rubber than anyone I'd known. (The Leafs eventually got Sawchuk, but that happened years later and not in time for my salvation.)

At the end of the year, the Wings won top spot again with their eighth title in nine seasons, but their celebration was very short-lived. In the opening round of the playoffs, Montreal stopped New York while Boston shocked Detroit, winning four games to one with Don Simmons in goal.

In the finals, the Rocket, Geoffrion, Beliveau, and crew were far too much for the Bruins, who fell in five games.

This was also the season when serious battles began with players over forming a players' association, while management tried to squash it. In mid-February, Ted Lindsay, Doug Harvey, Jimmy Thomson, Gus Mortson, Bill Gadsby, and some others held a press conference and announced the formation of the National Hockey League Players' Association.

In training camp I had heard whispers and rumours of a players' association starting up. I knew something was going on but I wasn't going to say anything, and intentionally wanted to know as little as possible. The players, in the main, understood that.

BEST PLAYER: Jean Beliveau — Montreal
BEST LINE: Alex Delvecchio, Gordie Howe, and Ted Lindsay — Detroit

1957–58

Hap Day decided he'd had enough of Smythe and the continuous head games, and left Toronto at the end of the season. I took over as GM early in the spring of 1958 (after getting the boot as coach). I lasted a couple of months before popping Stafford Smythe, Conn's son left to run the club, right in the mouth. If coaching had not been a set-up for disaster, my appointment as GM certainly was. I had to work with Stafford, someone I had absolutely no use for. He was arrogant and knew absolutely zero about the game, but boy, did he love to strut it.

I'd been working hard to work some deals for the Leafs, and to sign Frank Mahovlich (as well as others), but Stafford would stall or not return my calls. Then one day the little weasel called me into his office and began to dress me down for having "done nothing to improve the club." I went and retrieved my briefcase with copies of all the telegrams, letters, and calls I'd made to him and Conn. I read every one to him, then told him he knew damn well why "I" hadn't done anything.

We were nose to nose.

Stafford started in about whether I had signed Hugh Bolton, and as I was responding he interrupted, "I want his name on a contract. Go do it," and then he put both hands on my chest and pushed me. Well, that was dumb. I hauled back and popped him good right between the eyes.

As I left the room I said, "Go sign the big lug yourself."

So much for my career as a GM. Oh well.

Shortly after I had been named GM, a note had appeared on my desk from Conn Smythe advising that the Junior A Guelph Biltmores, who were in the playoffs, had a kid by the name of Edward Shack on their team who was supposed to be a sure-fire pro. Smythe suggested I should take a look at him.

My reaction was "Geeze, Stafford Smythe and Harold Ballard own the Toronto Marlboro Junior A team who played Guelph all season, so they should have a good read on Shack." This mistaken assumption was due to my short association with Staff and Harold because it became clear they thought they had all the future NHLers already playing on their team. No one else was ever going to make it but a Toronto Marlboro. With such tunnel vision, obviously they would have no real line on Shack and if they did it would have likely been "Caution — won't make it to the NHL."

Anyhow, I drove to Guelph next night, grabbed an old army buddy, Dennis Wallace, bought two tickets, two hot dogs and Cokes, and a program, and sat munching away waiting for the warm-up.

Guelph came on the ice, we grabbed the program line-up, scanned it, and saw Shack, Eddie — No. 19. Dennis and I searched the ice . . . no 19. Even when the game started, there was still no Shack to be seen.

Ten minutes into the first period, the Biltmores were down 2–0 — still no Shack. With about five minutes remaining in the first period and the Guelph club now down 3–1, just as the ref was about to drop the puck for a face-off, Eddie shows up. He one-hands himself over the boards, skates up to the face-off circle, obviously tells a teammate to take a rest, and gets ready to play.

Meanwhile, the packed house of Guelph fans are going bonkers, chanting, "Shack! Shack! Shack!" all the while, Eddie is skating in tight little circles at the wing position waiting for the puck to drop. He reminded me of a high-bred, highly strung, thoroughbred race-horse in the starting gate. Everything was there but the frothing.

The ref dropped the puck, it went to Eddie, and he took off into his own end like that racehorse coming out of the starting gate. Getting to watch and know Eddie in his good years later in the NHL I now realize that he wanted to beat all five of the other team's checkers on the way to scoring a goal. He did go end to end but when forced to shoot he was at a bad angle and the puck went off the far post. In the next one-and-a-half minutes Shack owned the puck but scored no goals.

Next shift, the tide slowly changed in Guelph's favour, and they got their second goal just before the period ended. First shift in the second period, another Shack turning, sniffing, snorting, head-shaking performance took place at the face-off circle. The puck was dropped, and Eddie swooped onto the puck and went the right way for a change, turned the D man inside out, let loose a slap shot from 20 feet out and picked the top corner — game's tied 3–3. The resounding calls for Shack filled the building once again.

At the end of the night, Guelph won handily and Eddie had four or five points. My report was something like "Eddie Shack — Good size, very good speed, good shot, very good prospect — has show-manship and will definitely sell tickets. But is totally undisciplined, can't play in a system, will break many a coach's heart before he can help a team win — and will be a fan favourite. If you want to wait five years for him to mature, get him."

As it was, the Leafs waited three years to get him and then had to suffer another two before he became a somewhat reliable and disciplined player good enough to help win a Stanley Cup or two.

Oh, there have been constant rumours (and Eddie does nothing to kill the rumour) that Mr. Edward Shack can't figure out figures. But don't believe it. "The Entertainer," also known as the "Clown Prince of Hockey," who hails from Sudbury, Ontario, could buy 10,000 shares of the local nickel mine from loose change.

For a number of years Eddie Shack was a very good NHL hockey player and a great entertainer. He had plenty of pizzazz and, in fact, still does.

I did manage to snag and sign Frank Mahovlich before I left the Leafs; however, I was never given the full chance to complete some other deals I'd been working on. As coach in Pittsburgh I was very aware of Providence goalie sensation Johnny Bower, and as Maple Leaf coach had been impressed with Bruin defenceman Allan Stanley and winger Johnny Bucyk in Detroit. That summer I talked to Detroit and Boston and confirmed that the two players were available but neither Conn nor Stafford Smythe would confirm which of the Leafs I could swap. During the process, when I popped Stafford with probably my best hockey punch, I wound up jobless. Before leaving, I highly recommended that my replacements snag the three players. Bucyk wound up in Boston in June 1957 and Punch Imlach eventually got the other two.

In the summer, star player and creator and first president of the NHL Players' Association "Terrible" Ted Lindsay was shipped to Chicago. Most of the players and folks around the league saw the move as obvious punishment for Lindsay's advocacy of players' rights. Ted later filed a suit with the league for not recognizing the association.

As a further slap to Ted and the rest of the association early in the season, the Red Wing players announced they were pulling out of the group. That temporarily crushed the association and many players never forgot nor forgave the Wings for the incident. As stated in *Golly Gee — It's Me*, I'm convinced that the gutless move by those Detroit players put a curse on them preventing them from winning the Stanley Cup for more than 40 years. Certainly they lost a lot of respect from other players who were likewise being intimidated by their owners.

I remember being disappointed with Howe, Kelly, Delvecchio, and others, and wondered how they could seemingly have left Lindsay hanging out to dry. As much as I admired the big guy's playing skills, I lost some respect for Gordie at the time.

There's all kinds of examples of winning clubs and players in my memory bank, but there were no more deserving title winners than the Maple Leaf club of that year. They earned the title with teamwork and off-ice victories, however.

The emergence of the players' association, thanks to Ted Lindsay and his gallant group, cost many a severe price. As a former player and teammate turned "management" I was segregated from the inner workings of the event by the Leaf players, and was thankful for it. They knew I was in a no-win situation, and with the Smythes involved, I was between a rock and a hard place. But the members of that club stood up and backed the players' union and Lindsay. Despite huge pressure by Conn Smythe, league president Clarence Campbell, and a high-priced lawyer, the Leaf players supported the new association. They took the flak from a very powerful and controlling group of club owners and mangers at the time. And that made them winners.

If any group of men ever deserved special mention, it is those Maple Leafs from 1957–58. They included: Gary Aldcorn, George Armstrong, Bob Baum, Ed Chadwick, Barry Cullen, Brian Cullen, Dick Duff, Billy Harris, Tim Horton, Frank Malovlich, Rudy Migay, Jim Morrison, Bob Pulford, Marc Reaume, Tod Sloan, and Ron Stewart.

Strapping, strong-skating youngster Bobby Hull started playing at centre with the Blackhawks and you could tell he was going to be something very special. Dickie Moore was unbelievable for Montreal that year and for more than a month played with a cast on his broken wrist. The gutsy little guy still won the scoring title.

Montreal finished first overall, and the surging Rangers were second. The Leafs plummeted to last place for the first time ever. I suffered mixed emotions over their dismal season, feeling somewhat redeemed by the club's bad showing, yet sorry for the players I knew and respected.

To the delight of most players, Montreal eliminated Detroit in four straight while Boston edged the Rangers to gain a berth in the final. The Bruins gave a good showing but in the end the Habs prevailed again. A battered and bruised Richard scored an overtime winner in game five.

BEST PLAYERS: Andy Bathgate — Rangers; Jacques Plante,
Dickie Moore — Montreal

BEST LINES: Bronco Horvath, Vic Stasiuk, Johnny Bucyk —
Boston;
Camille Henry, Andy Hebenton, Dave Creighton —
New York

1958-59

The Leafs picked up Johnny Bower, traded for Allan Stanley, and scooped Carl Brewer as their climb out of the league cellar was kick-started. Montreal again remained a force while both Chicago and Boston improved their line-ups immensely.

Chicago with Hull and Kenny Wharram shining as youngsters also brought in one of my favourites, little Danny Lewicki, who had great skills. As well, they had Pierre Pilote, who developed into an All-Star, and Ted Lindsay.

Montreal finished first and Toronto fourth that season. The healing seemed under way. The Leafs surprised Boston four games to three in the opening round of the playoffs but lost to the very powerful and balanced Habs in five games. The Habs were hurting without Beliveau, who had badly injured his back in the earlier round, but their depth allowed them to prevail. The Stanley Cup win marked a record fourth in a row for the Habs.

BEST PLAYERS: Dickie Moore, Jean Beliveau — Montreal

BEST LINE: Bronco Horvath, Vic Stasiuk, and Johnny Bucyk —
Boston

BY THE DECADE 1950–1959:

BEST PLAYERS: 1. Gordie Howe 2. Maurice Richard
3. Terry Sawchuk 4. Jacques Plante

BEST LINES: Alex Delvecchio/Sid Abel, Gordie Howe, and
Ted Lindsay — Detroit
Jean Beliveau, Bernie Geoffrion, and Bert Olmstead
— Montreal

Bronco Horvath, Vic Stasiuk, and Johnny Bucyk —
Boston

BEST TEAMS: Montreal, Detroit, Toronto

DYNASTIES: **Montreal Canadiens 1956–1960**

LEADERS: Rocket Richard, Jean Beliveau, Doug Harvey,
Bernie Geoffrion, Jacques Plante, Dickie Moore,
Henri Richard

BLEEDERS: Charlie Hodge, Tom Johnson, Bert Olmstead,
Ralph Backstrom, Butch Bouchard, Claude Provost,
Don Marshall, Jean-Guy Talbot, Phil Goyette

FEEDERS: Bob Turner, Dollard St. Laurent, Ken Mosdell,
Floyd Curry, Jack Leclair, Marcel Bonin,
Ab McDonald, Al Langlois, Andre Pronovost,
Bill Hicke

THE ROCKIN'
SIXTIES

■ ■ ■

(1960–1967)

During what was referred to by some as the "Dollar's Decade," the league went through a number of changes, including curved sticks, expansion to 12 teams, and player salaries taking a significant jump during the 1960s. Even my good ol' Canadian game of hockey, it seems, was affected by the decade of decadence and changing times.

When compared with the salary jumps of the 1970s due to the WHA, the 1980s because of revenue growth, and the 1990s because of expansion and TV rights, the 1960s pay-scale increase seems minor, but such was not the opinion of most team owners at the time. Many biting comments were exchanged between management, agents, players, and even fans over escalating contracts. Plenty of tension also still existed between management and players over the creation of (and long overdue, might I add) the players' association.

Realistically, the 1960s cannot be analyzed over a 10-year span because the NHL was truly two different leagues in that decade:

pre-expansion and post-expansion. When the league doubled in size from six to 12 teams for the 1967–68 season, no original team went unscathed in the player chase. Montreal, Toronto, and Chicago dominated the league in the first seven years of the decade. In the final three seasons (and early into the 1970s) the top original six clubs were Boston and Montreal while St. Louis led the expansion teams. Dominant players were Bobby Hull, Gordie Howe, Pierre Pilote, Stan Mikita, Jean Beliveau, Terry Sawchuk, Jacques Plante, Phil Esposito, Doug Harvey, Tim Horton, Jacques Laperriere, and a youngster named Bobby Orr.

Also notable was a powerful shooting style made popular by Chicago scoring star Bobby Hull and copied by teammate Stan Mikita and New York's Andy Bathgate. It was an unorthodox and erratic shot with the stick coming high above the shoulder in a windup motion before swiftly swinging back toward the ice, hitting just behind the puck and striking it forward in a powerful sweeping motion. Much like Mikita, Andy Bathgate, and a couple of others, Hull's powerful type of slap shot was causing goalies nightmares. Some players, like Hull, were quite accurate with it.

1959–60

The 1959–60 season started with tiffs everywhere. Leaf coach Punch Imlach was feuding with Mahovlich who, despite playing inconsistently, wanted a big pay raise, while goaltender Jacques Plante was scrapping with Montreal coach Toe Blake over wearing his mask in games and not just practices. When I think about it now, those goalies were crazy, absolutely nuts, not to wear masks before then. Plante went on to win his fifth straight Vezina Trophy at the end of the year, which largely shut up any critics of the new mask.

Beliveau and Geoffrion could not get flying as a line largely due to injuries to both players; however Beliveau did recover from his back injury to play 60 of the 70 games. Bronco Horvath and the Uke line played tremendously well on an otherwise faltering Bruin club.

A young centre showed promise in Chicago; his name was Stanley Mikita. He scored a goal and an assist in each of his first two games, and fans immediately took to the little whirling dervish. He slowed his pace considerably before the year ended, but due notice had been given.

When the season ended, a familiar team was in first spot. The Habs first eliminated Chicago in four straight in the opening-round playoffs and then dumped Punch and the boys four straight in the finals without breaking into a sweat. It was Montreal's fifth straight Cup and the 10th consecutive year they had appeared in the final series. The red, blue, and white machine was on a roll and nobody seemed in line to stop it.

Many folks still maintain that the 1959–60 Canadiens club was the best or one of the best teams ever assembled and I won't dispute that.

BEST PLAYERS: Bronco Horvath — Boston; Bobby Hull — Chicago
BEST LINE: Bronco Horvath, Vic Stasiuk, Johnny Bucyk — Boston

1960–61

During the league's inter-team and inter-league drafts, a few names popped up, including Ted Green, picked by Boston from Montreal (who'd just drafted him); Larry Hillman, who went to Toronto from Boston; and winger Parker MacDonald, who wound up in Detroit from New York.

Ted Lindsay and Rocket Richard had hung up their famous skates before this season started. Ironically, after dominating as one of the greatest players ever in the league, the Rocket retired having never captured the individual scoring title, while Lindsay, a major enemy who was primarily known by most as a ruffian with very good skills, held the crown.

My old Leafs, meanwhile, swapped a couple of players to New York for wild and reckless Eddie Shack. Things would never be quite the same again in Hogtown as Punch met the "Clown Prince of Hockey."

The season of 1960–61 was probably the worst in NHL history

for injuries throughout the league with only 20 or so players managing to skate all year. Among the stars injured were Dickie Moore, Doug Harvey, Ken Wharram, Bronco Horvath, Carl Brewer, Leo Boivin, Red Kelly, Johnny Bower, Dean Prentice, Gump Worsley, George Armstrong, Bob Pulford, Bernie Geoffrion, and Gordie Howe.

Toronto and Montreal battled all season both physically and statistically for top spot during a year particularly wild for fights and bench-emptying brawls. Toronto was also in a couple of major brouhahas with the Rangers and Hawks. The brawl with the Hawks, at Maple Leaf Gardens, led to police running onto the ice to break up fights.

A solid Chicago club upset Montreal in a hard-hitting opening round of the playoffs, winning the series in six games, including a triple overtime victory in game three. Superb net minding, including back-to-back shutouts by Glenn Hall, and physical prowess put the Hawks into the finals against Detroit.

Defenceman Pierre Pilote was brilliant with eight points in the series, and superstars Bobby Hull and Stan Mikita were hot as the Hawks struck gold in six games. Hull banged home two of his patented slap shots in game one while Mikita dazzled throughout and scored the winner in game five. Chicago went nuts after a long 22-year Cup drought. It's a good thing the fans enjoyed it because the Hawks haven't won the Stanley Cup since and hardly look poised to do so soon. Ironically, Mikita and Hull dominated the league scoring title in the decade but won only the single Cup.

BEST PLAYERS: Bernie Geoffrion — Montreal; Stan Mikita — Chicago; Frank Mahovlich — Toronto

BEST LINES: Bill Hay, Murray Balfour, Bobby Hull — Chicago
Stan Mikita, Ken Wharram, Ab McDonald — Chicago

1961–62

Punch and the boys restored more pride and glory to the ol' Maple Leaf uniform at the end of this season by grabbing their first

Stanley Cup in 11 years — and a sigh of relief was heard from B.C. to Newfoundland. Ironically it was the same season that we finally found out what happened to Billy Barilko. They found the wreckage of Billy's plane deep in the northern Ontario bush. It seemed only right that the Cup should come back to Toronto just like Billy. Some closure was needed.

Although I was isolated from the big league game on "The Rock," the NHL had become hugely popular, as had the Leafs and Habs. The new television market and large increase in fans had also increased the game's popularity. Watching hockey on "the telly" became a habit in many Canadian homes, as well as in the U.S. franchise cities. Television even increased the radio audience for games.

In a crowning touch to a successful season, the league also celebrated the opening of the Hockey Hall of Fame in Toronto. Hockey was booming.

Although Montreal topped the league with 98 points, including 42 wins, Toronto snagged the Stanley Cup. Toronto was very strong in second place during the regular season at 85 points. Chicago again ended the year with 74, while the Rangers, led by sniper Andy Bathgate, barely earned fourth.

Bobby Hull continued to bring fans off their feet as he scooped up the puck, rushed the length of the ice in powerful, swooshing strides, and then let go one of his surprisingly fast slap shots. Hull netted 50 goals that year en route to winning the scoring title. Bobby tied in total points with Bathgate, but Hull won the honour by virtue of more goals. Nasty little Stan Mikita also had a tremendous season in Chicago.

Gordie Howe surpassed the 500-goal mark at the end of the year and everyone figured he was going to be the sure-fire, all-time scoring champ.

All the hockey writers, and plenty of hockey folks, were predicting Chicago to take a second straight Stanley Cup. In the main the opinion was that Chicago simply had better depth. But someone forgot to tell Frank Mahovlich, Tim Horton, Bob Pulford, Johnny Bower, and crew.

BEST PLAYER: Bobby Hull — Chicago
BEST LINE: Bill Hay, Murray Balfour, Bobby Hull — Chicago

1962–63

Toronto, Chicago, and Montreal battled all year long in a tremendous race for top spot. At the end of the season-long shuffle, it was the Leafs in first. Much of the credit must go to Punch Imlach, big Frank Mahovlich, Carl Brewer, and rookie defenceman Kent Douglas, who won the Calder. I believe he was the first blueliner to win the rookie award.

Toronto finished with 82 points, just one more than Chicago. Montreal snagged third with 79 points, while Detroit was fourth with 77. Jiminy Cricket, it doesn't get much closer than that, folks!

The old master Gordie Howe showed that time could be stretched by superb conditioning, skill, and smarts as he won another scoring title. When it came to hockey, Gordie had them all mastered. In his 17th season he led the league in goals with 38 and 86 points.

Toronto had the edge in depth and it showed once again. The Leafs defeated a wounded Montreal club in five games in the opening round, and then out-hit and outplayed wild Howie Young and the Red Wings in five games in the finals. It was two in a row for Toronto and Leaf fans were delirious.

Leaf Red Kelly began wearing a makeshift helmet that year after a major head injury. Despite the wound, I remember him taking a fair bit of criticism for it from the fans and some media. The AHL made helmets mandatory the same year, I believe, and a couple of other NHL players wore them the next season.

BEST PLAYER: Gordie Howe — Detroit
BEST LINE: Alex Delvecchio, Gordie Howe, Parker MacDonald
                    — Detroit

1963-64

On November 10, Gordie Howe set a new goal-scoring record at 545, breaking the Rocket's previous total. The new marker was a short-hand affair against Montreal. The talk of the league, however, was the blistering speed of Bobby Hull's slap shots. Goalies admitted both fearing and respecting his cannonading drives. Jacques Plante told *Hockey Illustrated* in 1965 that Hull's shot "is like a piece of lead and sometimes it sinks three or four inches. You have to see it coming towards you to believe it. If he shoots it toward either corner [of the net] from 40 feet out, it's in the goal eight times out of ten. He has the hardest shot I ever saw."

Hab star netminder Charlie Hodge told the same publication, "A goalie can't possibly move as fast as Hull's shot is coming." I marvelled at the news they had clocked his shot at 108 miles an hour. Holy Jumpin' Jehoshaphat, boys, that's smoking.

Mikita and Hull put on a great two-man race for the scoring title with my favourite little spark-plug winning. Mikita racked up an impressive 50 assists and 89 points.

Despite dominating the All-Star team with five of six spots (Hull, Mikita, Ken Wharram, Pierre Pilote, and goalie Glenn Hall), the Hawks again finished a single point short of first place. Likewise, they once again missed out on the Stanley Cup. For the third straight year, the critics picked the Hawks to win the coveted hardware and for the third straight year Toronto won all the marbles. It was a script that Chicago was tired of and Toronto loved.

Young, popular pivot man Davey Keon, recently acquired Andy Bathgate, along with Don McKenney, Tim Horton, and Red Kelly led the formidable Leafs first past Montreal in seven, and then the Wings in seven more for hockey's Holy Grail. Awards were split up all over the league that year, with Hodge earning the Vezina for Montreal, Pilote the top defenceman award, and Beliveau the Hart.

BEST PLAYER: Stan Mikita — Chicago
BEST LINE: Stan Mikita, Ken Wharram, Ab McDonald — Chicago

1964–65

Punch Imlach picked up Terry Sawchuk when Detroit protected rookie Roger Crozier and Sawchuk was left available in the draft. Crozier won the Calder Trophy and selection on the first All-Star team, but Sawchuk shared the Vezina with Bower.

This was a great year for new faces in the league. The *Official 1965 Hockey League Annual* attests to the many new players on the clubs' player rosters. Toronto youth included Ronny Ellis, while Montreal had speedy little Yvan Cournoyer, Jim Roberts (back for a regular visit), Ted Harris, and Claude Larose. Chicago was keen on a lanky centre named Phil Esposito and thunder-shooting Dennis Hull, along with Alain Caron, Fred Stanfield, and puck-stopper Dave Dryden. Detroit had youngsters Gary Bergman, Lowell MacDonald, and Paul Henderson in their line-up. Rookie Bruins included Ron Schock, while the Rangers had Lou Angotti, Arnie Brown, Rod Seiling, and Jim Mikol.

When all was said and done, however, it was talent-loaded Montreal that defeated Chicago in seven games to earn the Cup. Led by Charlie Hodge and Gump Worsley in net and All-Stars Jacques Laperriere and Claude Provost, along with veteran Habs Beliveau, Henri Richard, and Ralph Backstrom, Montreal first edged the Leafs in a bruiser of a series and then sneaked by Chicago.

The Leafs' short but sweet reign was over and with it talk of another Leaf dynasty. Though Toronto would win again two years later, their dominance was done. In fact the 1965 Cup champion Canadiens were actually the beginning of a true Hab dynasty that won the Cup four times in five years (and five in seven). In retrospect, it's not unfair to think of it as an invisible dynasty, lost between the Leafs and Bruins when people think of the '60s.

BEST PLAYERS: Norm Ullman — Detroit; Pierre Pilote — Chicago
BEST LINE: Alex Delvecchio, Gordie Howe, Parker MacDonald — Detroit

1965–66

It was only a matter of time before Bobby Hull finally broke his 50-goal mark in a season and 1965–66 was the time. Only the Rocket and Boom Boom had previously shared the magic number so it seemed appropriate that someone nicknamed the Golden Jet should shatter the barrier. Indeed, the powerful centre turned left winger set a new record of 54 goals that year and set another record of 97 points for the overall scoring championship.

Montreal won the regular-season race with Chicago second, Toronto third, and Detroit fourth. Montreal and Toronto continued their decade-long rivalry in the opening round while Detroit defeated Chicago. The bruised but determined Habs then won their second Cup in a row, taking Detroit in six games. There was no denying that the Habs were a deep, talented club and had a tight hold on the cherished mug.

The league announced early in the season that it would expand to 12 teams in 1967–68, a move criticized by many who were concerned there wasn't enough talent to expand so dramatically.

BEST PLAYER: Bobby Hull — Chicago
BEST LINE: Stan Mikita, Ken Wharram, Doug Mohns — Chicago

1966–67

The most significant aspect of the season, even more than the jostling about of people for key jobs with the six planned new teams, was the arrival of sensational 18-year-old rookie defenceman Bobby Orr. No one had caused such uproar as a junior before, with perhaps the exception of the big gentleman Jean Beliveau.

Could the kid from Parry Sound actually be that good?

Bloody right, he could. Orr was gold, pure and simple. He snagged the Calder without a blink and even I was amazed at what I saw.

I'd seen Orr the year before in the Ontario Hockey Association's playoffs and he'd owned the ice. He led Oshawa all season and into the playoffs with tremendous showings night after night. But someone hit him low and he tore ligaments in his knee. After his operation, the club rushed him back too soon and the leg legacy began. I believe his knee problems started right then. I could tell the blond kid was playing on one leg because whenever he went to the bench he would turn and go into the box only one way with his knee. But in no time he'd be out on the ice again, double- and triple-shifting all night.

I expected his domination of the game to lessen when he reached the NHL, but it didn't. Hell, he changed the game, not the other way.

It took 40 years for Chicago to break their hex of never finishing first, but finally they succeeded in 1967 and the Muldoon Curse was put to rest. Once again Mikita and Hull were fabulous, with Mikita winning the scoring title on a record 62 assists, and Hull grabbing 52 goals for his third 50-plus season. The bull-like, powerhouse Blackhawk winger was truly amazing.

If ever a city deserved more Stanley Cups and never received them, it was Chicago in the early and mid-'60s. Despite owning the statistics and All-Star team selections, the club could not capture the Stanley Cup again, and once more Toronto had upset Montreal for a final Cup sip.

Montreal finished second on the regular season with the Leafs third and a surging Ranger team fourth.

The Leafs met their long adversary in the final round this time and, led by Keon, Sawchuk, Jimmy Pappin and Bob Pulford, they eliminated the Habs in six games. It was their 11th Stanley Cup.

BEST PLAYERS: Stan Mikita — Chicago; Bobby Orr — Boston
BEST LINE: Phil Esposito, Chico Maki, Bobby Hull — Chicago

3

■ ■ ■

FROM THE
BROADCAST BOOTH
1968–1999

A ROOKIE
ONCE AGAIN

■ ■ ■

For the most part I managed to slough it off, stuff it into the back of my brain, and pretend it didn't matter. But it never went away.

Ever since unlacing my skates after my final Leafs' game in the 1952–53 season, I'd felt a sense of emptiness deep in my gut. At first I thought it was because of my love for the game alone, that I simply missed playing hockey. I figured that by coaching in the American Hockey League, and later the Leafs, I would feel good again, but that was not how it worked out. The emptiness in the pit of my stomach only felt heavier, like too much lard in a pie crust.

When the chance to teach hockey in Newfoundland came along, I felt it would be the right antidote. Although it proved a tremendous move, and I made some wonderful friends, the lost feeling in my gut still remained.

When I took time to think about my feelings, I realized that I felt severed from the camaraderie of playing in the National Hockey League. Sure, I'd coached and been a general manager, but that really didn't count because as coach and GM I'd been an outsider . . . to everybody.

Without realizing it, that empty feeling began to fade a year or two after a fateful meeting in 1968 on a cold, snowy winter afternoon in downtown Montreal. My main source of income at the time (along with running the Avalon Minor Hockey system and coaching in Newfoundland) was work as an agent for companies such as Tonka, Mattel, Brunswick, Penman's, Winchester, Samsonite, and Shakespeare. In those days in order for those companies to be successful they had to match their products with the right public person, and I was lucky enough to pick up sales and distribution work for them all. As well, I'd started radio work at CJON in St. John's. On that fateful Friday afternoon in February, I was attending a toy fair in Montreal for Mattel, and the trip changed my life. On that day I ran into Ted Darling, host of *Hockey Night in Canada*, and we chatted for a bit. During the conversation Ted explained he needed someone to do guest colour work during Saturday night's game between Montreal and Chicago, and asked if I would be interested.

I was delighted and blurted out, "Yes!" before he had a chance to recant the request. The rest, as they say, is history. I had no idea at the time what an amazing series of events was about to unfold when I first stuck on the headset. My, oh my, how the world can spin.

I remember only a little from that first evening's broadcast, but obviously I did okay and created some interest because they asked me back a couple of more times that year, mainly I think because Punch Imlach called Ralph Mellanby and said, "Hey, you can send that kid into my building anytime. He did good." During the next season, 1968–69, I made six or seven TV appearances with *Hockey Night in Canada*. My visits became more numerous each year and eventually turned into a regular job, if one can call it that. To me it was always just a lot of fun, while it seemed everybody else worked their ass off. I had it easy compared to most of the fine folks who made up the broadcast crews. The technicians, producers, directors, cameramen, and people who create and produce the game that comes into your home are a tremendous group of talented, dedicated, and wonderful people.

I was mainly an analyst in the first years. I would watch the game on my own video screen and, with the engineer, select the 30- or 40-second clips that I wanted. They would quickly package one or two, add replay, and then between periods I described what was happening, or wasn't happening, to the TV audience. It worked like a charm.

In 1969–70 and again in 1970–71 I did a dozen games each season, wrapping it around my work in Newfoundland. During those years I worked mainly in Montreal with Danny Gallivan and Dick Irvin on the Canadiens' broadcasts, while on Leaf games at Maple Leaf Gardens I was usually working with Brian McFarlane, Dave Hodge, and Bill Hewitt. By 1971–72 I'd jumped to at least 15 matches for *Hockey Night in Canada* while still keeping my job at CJON. It was a rugged pace and my family paid the price, but I was getting well known by TV hockey fans and I was certainly having the time of my life.

What's more, that gnawing, heaviness in my gut was gone. That hockey camaraderie was back in my life, and even better, no bullheaded team owner was running my world.

When I look back on it now, my years at CJON radio and television with Don and Colin Jamieson in St. John's opened the door for me, and the two years I spent coaching in Pittsburgh, and finally working TV with Ralph Mellanby and others in later years, gave me the knowledge to make it big on *Hockey Night in Canada*, CBC, BCTV, NBC, and TSN.

THE

EXPANSION YEARS

■ ■ ■

1967–68

My increase in hockey broadcast work was certainly not the only expansion going on in the 1967–68 season. In fact, it was a phenomenal year for first experiences, rookies, and records. Of greatest significance, however, was the doubling of the league's size from six teams to 12.

I greeted the historical hockey event with mixed emotions and reservations. For one who grew up watching and then playing in the six-team league, it seemed very strange to suddenly have twice as many clubs. There was no doubt that the quality of the game at the NHL level would slip somewhat; the questions were how much, and for how long? Nevertheless, I was thrilled to see the game grow and to see more of my former teammates, or players I'd coached or knew, getting jobs in the National Hockey League. Yippeee!

Minnesota, Philadelphia, California, Pittsburgh, Los Angeles, and St. Louis were awarded teams for the paltry sum of $2 million each, and a massive draft of young and old hockey bodies was held that summer. Some major players were moved due to the fact that in the opening round the original six clubs were allowed to protect only 11 skaters and one goalie. Several trades and sales of players also took place, and many a backroom or telephone deal was cooked up prior to or after the draft.

Watching from a distance, I was fascinated at some of the deals, rumours, and discussions that swirled about the league. Netminders and defencemen proved to be the main hockey commodities sought. St. Louis picked up goalie Glenn Hall, defencemen Al Arbour and Doug Harvey, and forwards Red Berenson, Dickie Moore, and Jim Roberts. I was surprised that St. Louis managed to snag Hall to begin with, but it certainly paid off. Los Angeles grabbed another net veteran in Terry Sawchuk; Philadelphia snagged goalies Doug Favell and Bernie Parent (both of Boston), defencemen Ed Van Impe and Joe Watson and young forward Brit Selby; Pittsburgh drafted right winger Andy Bathgate; California (later to become Oakland) took Charlie Hodge, star blueliner Bobby Baun, tough rearguard Larry Cahan, and forward Ted Hampson while Minnesota grabbed Dave Balon number one overall. It was obvious to me that there had been some deal cooked with the Canadiens not to take Claude Larose because Claude was the very best player available. When Minnesota took Balon, Montreal protected Larose. Minnesota also picked up forwards Wayne Connelly and Ray Cullen and goalie Cesare Maniago.

The teams were split into two divisions with expansion teams in the West Division and the six original clubs in the East.

Prior to the start of the season, Boston and Chicago made a major trade that included Phil Esposito, Ken Hodge, and Fred Stanfield moving to Boston for Gilles Marotte, Jack Norris, and Pit Martin. It proved to be a disaster for Chicago and a positive move for Boston. Golly gee, when you look back at a deal like that you shake your head and wonder why? Who made that deal, and is he still in hockey?

I don't want to find out who swung that deal on Chicago's behalf because I had (and still have) friends high up in that organization. All I know is that Harry Sinden, who arrived in Boston as coach in 1966–67, had a say in the deal along with Bruin GM Hap Emms and

Milt Schmidt, and Chicago got soaked. Over the years as the coach and eventual GM (starting in October 1972), Sinden made some of the best deals in NHL history and certainly that was one of them.

In a year with so many highlights, it was that much more shocking when Minnesota North Star rookie centre Bill Masterton fell during a game against Oakland and smashed his helmet-less head on the ice. Bill died less than 36 hours later from brain injuries. His death shocked not only the players and fans at the Minnesota game, but people clean across the continent. It was the first time a player ever died playing in the NHL from an injury directly related to a game. That tragic event was still foremost in many minds the night I first sat down to work in a broadcast booth, less than a month later.

Masterton's death prompted a lot of discussion about helmet use and, absurd as it now seems, very few players adopted a helmet right away. Scoring leader Stan Mikita, however, was an exception and wore his helmet from that season onward. It would take 30 more years before every player in the league was finally wearing a helmet, and even then only due to league regulations. How dumb can you get?

Before the season was done, another major trade would rock the league with Toronto and Detroit swapping seven players. The deal saw Toronto send my friend Frank Mahovlich, along with Peter Stemkowski, Garry Unger, and the rights to Carl Brewer to Detroit for Normy Ullman, Paul Henderson, and Floyd Smith. While there was no doubt a desire to improve both clubs, there was also much inside opinion that Ullman was a bigger part of the trade than most fans realized, because of his work with the NHL Players' Association. It seemed the Red Wing management's war with the players' union was still up front and dominating some of their decisions. However, others viewed it as a "pain-relief trade" for Toronto. It was no secret that the Big M and Imlach did not get along and there'd been plenty of talk about Mahovlich being in another funk and ready to quit the game. Imlach implied more than once that Frank was a pain in his butt. To me Frank was always a fine fellow, a very gifted player, and a gentleman.

Regardless of the trades, drafts, unions, and other incidents, the real talk of the season were sophomore Bruin defenceman Bobby Orr and the scoring skills of Mikita. Stan won the scoring title again and grabbed three individual player trophies at the end of the season for the second year in a row.

Once again I marvelled at the transformation of Mikita. Not only did he rack up 87 points on the year but he also continued to stay out of trouble. In 72 games played, he collected just 14 minutes in the box. Seven minor penalties? Amazing. I'd always liked Mikita and his talents, but to accomplish that change in play two years in a row (after seasons of 154, 146, 97, and 69 minutes) gave me a whole new respect for him as a player. He adapted and improved.

Big Phil Esposito, like a sloth on skates, proved Bruins' Schmidt, Emms, and Sinden geniuses by finishing second in league scoring with 84 points, four places ahead of former linemate Bobby Hull. An aging Gordie Howe finished third in scoring.

The brash, talented Derek Sanderson was named Rookie of the Year and showed tremendous face-off and forechecking skills.

Even with all the league changes, when the rubber hit the ice for the last time that season and the red lights had all stopped blinking behind the goalies, it was the powerful Montreal Canadiens who owned Sir Stanley's coveted mug. The Habs defeated Boston, Chicago, and finally St. Louis to win the Cup. Gump Worsley was strong in Montreal's nets and Glenn Hall simply unbelievable in goal for the Blues.

Even though the Canadiens won the finals in four straight games, two went into overtime and the other two were won by single markers. I'd seen Glenn Hall play some brilliant games between the pipes for Detroit and then several years in Chicago, but during the Blues' run through the playoffs and especially during the final series I'd never seen any goalie play better.

BEST PLAYER: Stan Mikita — Chicago
BEST LINE: Stan Mikita, Ken Wharram, Doug Mohns — Chicago

1968–69

The second year of expansion was when scoring records fell like leaves in autumn. For the first time in league history, a player broke the 100-point barrier — in fact, three players did. Hard-working Phil Esposito popped in 49 goals and added an amazing 77 assists for the unbelievable figure of 126 points that year. Hull smashed all former goal-scoring records by notching 58 that season and totalled 107 points, while Howe (at age 40) finished third overall again, with a remarkable 44 goals, 59 assists, and 103 points. In the first year of expansion, teams had concentrated on defence. In year two, they let up and it cost them.

I found myself pointing out to audiences on a regular basis the "smarts" Howe had in his approach to playing the game. Again, even though his club was mediocre (just two points over .500 on the season), Gordie remained among the elite in the league. He did it largely by using his brain instead of his legs. He made perfect passes, read the plays, and created his own space. It was a regular display of wisdom on ice and I'd telestrate him to bits during broadcasts. Geez, I had fun sometimes!

Adding salt to the previous year's Bruin-Blackhawk trade, right winger Ken Hodge finished fifth overall in scoring with 45 goals and 90 points. Orr, meanwhile, shattered the scoring record for defencemen with 21 goals.

It sure didn't take Scotty Bowman long to put his stamp on the St. Louis Blues as coach and GM. With expansion, everyone said games would be more freewheeling and wide open, with goals and points by the bushel. They expected the expansion teams would really get blown out of the water. Well, in many cases they were right, but not with St. Louis.

During the summer, Bowman grabbed Jacques Plante to work with Hall in goal and also added Ranger centre Camille Henry. The Blues ended the year with just 157 goals against, 39 fewer than second-best New York. Everyone else finished with more than 200 goals against. And guess what? Glenn Hall had the best goals against average in the league at 2.17. Naturally, the Blues won the

West Division by 19 points and Bowman was on his way to fame and fortune and hockey mythology.

Montreal edged out Boston by three points in the East Division pennant race, which was a real humdinger. Anyone paying attention could see that Boston was improving day by day and becoming a real threat for the Cup, but Montreal was still the master of the league and once again took home all the marbles, earning its fourth Cup in five years and dynasty status.

Montreal beat the Bruins in six games in a classic battle in the semi-final, which saw three matches go into overtime. The clash is still remembered by many fans as one of the best ever and solidified the rivalry into a full-fledged hockey war.

After surviving the "Big, Bad Bruins," Montreal once again met the determined Blues in the finals but defeated them in four straight games. All but game three were close contests. Young Rogatien Vachon was brilliant in Montreal's goal while Serge Savard became the first defenceman to win the Conn Smythe Trophy. Savard was spectacular throughout the playoffs and I marvelled at his dexterity and his speed.

Best Player: Phil Esposito — Boston
Best Lines: Alex Delvecchio, Gordie Howe, Frank Mahovlich — Detroit
Phil Esposito, Ken Hodge, Ron Murphy/Wayne Cashman — Boston

1969–70

I've been a very lucky man and enjoyed a number of thrills and memorable experiences in my lifetime, many of them attributable to the great game of hockey. Among the highlights of my broadcasting career was the joy of watching a couple of absolutely outstanding hockey players display their skills of the game. At the top of my list of players to watch was the amazing and marvellous Bobby Orr.

It matters not how many books have been written, awards or

plaudits given — Orr has earned each and every one of them over the years. Bobby Orr changed the game of hockey — forever.

If some fans had not recognized the tremendous superstar talent Bobby Orr possessed in previous seasons, they had it aptly displayed during the 1969–70 season. Orr cleaned up on everything and everybody around the league, winning the overall scoring title; setting records for goals, assists, and total points by a defenceman and total assists by any player; winning a wheelbarrow of hardware including a record four individual league player awards; and scoring a dramatic overtime winning goal on May 10 to give Boston its first Stanley Cup in 29 years.

Beantown went bonkers.

Orr's incredible scoring performance marked the first time a defenceman won the scoring title. He was only the fourth player to exceed the 100-point barrier. Teammate Phil Esposito was second in league scoring with 99 points, while Mikita was third. The Bruins did not enjoy first-place honours in the East Division. Boston had tied with Chicago with 99 points each, but Chicago took the title based on more wins.

Another Esposito led the Hawks — Phil's little brother Tony, who won the Vezina and Calder trophies and joined his brother on the first All-Star team. Tony "O" earned his nickname by setting a record 15 shutouts that year. Montreal did the unthinkable and missed the playoffs. On the way to the Cup, the Bruins beat New York, Chicago, and then St. Louis without breaking into much of a sweat.

BEST PLAYER: Bobby Orr — Boston
BEST LINE: Phil Esposito, Ken Hodge, Wayne Cashman — Boston

1970–71

Expansion hit the league once again as Vancouver and Buffalo were allowed into the loop, though neither team iced a very competitive club. The two new teams entered the East division while Chicago was moved to the West. Figure that out — what's west of Vancouver?

I remember secretly cheering for Vancouver to win first pick and snag young Gilbert Perreault in the entry draft, but Buffalo was the lucky winner on the spin of a numbered wheel. It makes you wonder what that reversal of draft picks might have meant to Vancouver. To this day, neither club has won the Stanley Cup so I guess the question is really academic.

Hockey fans thought they'd seen impressive goal scoring and point production in seasons past, so no one was prepared, writers and broadcasters included, for the amazing goal-scoring show that Phil Esposito and the rest of the Big Bad Bruins put on in 1970–71. The crafty centreman boggled everyone by scoring 76 goals and adding the same number of assists for an unbelievable total of 152 points. Even Espo was stunned by his productivity.

Equally amazing was young Orr, who finished second overall in scoring, breaking his previous defenceman's record with 37 goals and an incredible 102 assists for 139 points. It marked the first time anyone had recorded 100 or more assists in a season.

The Bruins totally dominated the top 10 individual scoring positions with Johnny Bucyk third on the list with a career high 51 goals and 116 points. Every time I see John Bucyk's name, my mind wanders back to my frustration with not getting him when I was coach in Toronto. Just before my season as Leaf coach ended, Hap Day gave me a list of players. He'd eliminated the top 20 players in the league, then selected the top four or five players on other clubs and said, "Here. If you are coach next year, which of these players interests you? Who would you want and who would you give up for them?"

Allan Stanley was head and shoulders the best D man available that we played against. I said I'd give up any two players for him except for Dick Duff, Bob Baun, Bob Pulford, Tod Sloan, George Armstrong, or Tim Horton. Next on my wish list was Johnny Bucyk. Whenever we played Detroit, it reminded me of 1946–47 when I was a rookie with the Leafs and every time I looked up Gordie Howe was headed for our net with the puck. Same thing 10 years later, only now it was Bucyk. Gosh, what a steady talented workhorse.

Bucyk's teammate Ken Hodge was fourth with 105 points, and then the big numbers plummeted, but not the Bruins. Wayne

Cashman scored 79 points, Johnny McKenzie was eighth, and Fred Stanfield was 11th. No team ever dominated the top 10 scoring to the same level (seven of 11 spots, including the top four) either before or since that year.

Boston averaged more than five goals per game and finished first in the East. They were absolutely unbelievable to watch and, oh my, could they move the puck out of their end. A key secret to their scoring success was that six of the seven were members of two regular forward lines. Esposito centred Hodge and Cashman, while Stanfield was the pivot for Bucyk and McKenzie most of the year. The seventh player, of course, was Orr, who was virtually a fourth forward whenever he was on the ice. And a scary one at that.

However, as if in some fairy tale or storybook about grown men's hockey, the Big Bad Bruins, complete with their awesome arsenal, were brought to their knees by an young, upstart, gargantuan-sized goalie named Ken Dryden. One of the great marvels of NHL hockey history has been the uncanny ability over the years of the Habs to pull a virtual rookie goaltender out of thin air and have him shine for the club at just the right moment. Bill Durnan, George Hainsworth, Jacques Plante, Charlie Hodge, Rogie Vachon — and in 1970–71 it was Kenny Dryden, a university law student, who did the trick. I will never forget Dryden's brilliant play that playoff season as he robbed the Bruins in seven games in the opening round series.

The elimination of the Bruins that year ranks as one of the big playoff upsets, despite the tremendous hockey club that Montreal was — and given the fact Montreal was still in its final years of dynasty status. Appropriately enough, after the Bruins, the Canadiens let no one else stand in the way of their winning the Cup. En route they crushed Minnesota and then defeated Chicago in seven. The Hawks were already beaten and bruised after a long seven-game saw-off against the Rangers.

At the end of the year, Perreault won the Calder, Orr the Hart and Norris. Ed Giacomin was named the first All-Star team goalie and as good as he was that year I figured that veteran Jacques Plante had been marvellous with a much weaker Leaf team. The wonderful and popular Beliveau retired a champ.

BEST PLAYER: Bobby Orr — Boston
BEST LINE: Ken Hodge, Phil Esposito, Wayne Cashman/John Bucyk — Boston

1971–72

The Bruins learned from their previous year's experience, and while they blew through the regular season again in 1971–72 they saved some firepower and gas for the playoffs. In this season the Bruins had their cake and ate it too, winning the regular season title and the Stanley Cup.

Esposito, with 66 goals, and Orr finished atop the individual scoring race again, but this time the dynamic duo were followed by a hot-shooting Ranger forward unit of Jean Ratelle, Vic Hadfield, and Rod Gilbert, who filled the next three scoring spots. Gilbert and Ratelle had been linemates for many years in junior.

Chicago took the West title in a cakewalk over Minnesota.

Orr took his fifth Norris Trophy, and Dryden, ironically having already won the Conn Smythe Trophy, scooped the Calder.

In the playoffs, it was indeed a clash of the titans with the Rangers beating the Habs and the Bruins taking Toronto in five games in the opening rounds. Chicago and St. Louis again represented and won the West. The Rangers then swept Chicago, and Boston swept the Blues, setting up another clash of long-time rivals in the finals. In the main, though, Bobby Orr beat up the Rangers himself and the Bruins won the Cup in six games.

BEST PLAYER: Bobby Orr — Boston
BEST LINES: Phil Esposito, Ken Hodge, Wayne Cashman — Boston
Jean Ratelle, Rod Gilbert, Vic Hadfield — New York Rangers

It seemed to me that the Bruins were poised to become the next dynasty team. Their first-round banishment the year before had been attributed to two main factors: a powerful Montreal club still in its fading years as a dynasty, and overconfidence and burnout by the Bruins. While other teams were still very strong — including the Rangers, Chicago, and Montreal — the future looked bright and the Cup was favoured to go to Boston for a couple more seasons.

Several factors would change that legacy for Boston, however: further NHL expansion, the arrival of the upstart World Hockey Association, and career-ending knee problems for Orr.

Oh yeah, and in between there was a huge hockey war with the Russians.

DYNASTIES:	**Montreal 1965–1971 (five in seven):**
LEADERS:	Jean Beliveau, Henri Richard, John Ferguson, Jacques Laperriere, Gump Worsley, Yvan Cournoyer, Serge Savard, Jacques Lemaire, Ken Dryden
BLEEDERS:	Ralph Backstrom, Bobby Rousseau, Frank Mahovlich, Claude Larose, J.C. Tremblay, Dick Duff, Ted Harris, J.C. Talbot, Charlie Hodge, Gilles Tremblay, Rogatien Vachon, Pete Mahovlich, Guy Lapointe, Claude Provost
FEEDERS:	Red Berenson, Dave Balon, Jim Roberts, Jean Gauthier, Terry Harper, Noel Picard, Leon Rochefort, Noel Price, Carol Vadnais, Danny Grant, Mickey Redmond, Christian Bordeleau, Bob Murdoch, Pierre Bouchard, Phil Roberto, Marc Tardif, Larry Hillman, Bobby Sheehan, Rejean Houle

THE ULTIMATE SERIES
1972

■ ■ ■

A Nation Holds Its Breath

The 1972 Canada-Soviet hockey series ranks as one of the all-time greatest sports competitions and will long be noted as a significant bookmark in Canada's growth as a nation. The eight-game epic battle was a classic clash of hockey and ideals — on ice.

With each game, Canada's interest and emotion swelled. By the final four matches of the series in Moscow, Canada was ecstatic. A normally placid people had come alive, creating an overwhelming, unifying pride — never seen before in the country during peacetime. It was as if the nation's future depended on the "Canuck" hockey players stuffing more pucks into the "Ruskies'" net than vice-versa.

Perhaps it did.

Now dubbed the "Summit Series" the glorious shinny tournament remains one of those rare events when most Canadians can recall their location and reactions at the time. Paul Henderson's winning goal in the final game of the series sits on that same nostalgic shelf as the Kennedy assassination and the landing on the moon. Certainly I remember that moment well.

The 1972 series also held personal significance for me as part of the superstar broadcast team capturing the exhilarating moments for Canadian viewers. In turn the Canada-Soviet series became the true launching pad for my TV broadcasting career. It kick-started my career, one that would keep me busy hopping about the continent from coast to coast for more than 30 years. However, neither I nor the rest of the broadcast crew realized how big the series had become back home.

Part of the significance that makes the '72 series so special is that it was more than a mere hockey competition between two nations. These were two countries diametrically opposed in almost all ways. The build-up to and spin-off factors of the ground-breaking hockey tournament (not to mention the politics, economics, and military sensitivity) all added to the series' significance.

Most North Americans were also aware of the long-standing controversy regarding professional players from Canada not being allowed to play against the full-time "amateur" players from the Soviet Union. However, few were aware of the intense political debates over the years between the hockey bodies at various levels, as well as politicians of varying degrees. Long before the 1972 tournament ever came to fruition, intense discussions and verbal battles transpired between representatives of recently formed Hockey Canada (comprising government members, the NHL, the NHL Players' Association, and the Canadian Amateur Hockey Association) and the Soviet Union, the Russian Ice Hockey Federation, and the International Olympic Committee. The series was not dreamed up in a day.

A number of other contributing factors also intensified the 1972 series hype. Superstar Chicago winger Bobby Hull had jumped to the new league known as the World Hockey Association, signing for big bucks (back then). To all intents and purposes, Hull had become the proverbial Pied Piper of pro hockey and the NHL salary boom was born. However, the NHL and others would punish the powerful man with the blistering slap shot and banana-blade hockey stick for his insolence. Hull was not allowed to play for Team Canada.

The decision to ban Hull earned the wrath of many Canadians, including Prime Minister Pierre Elliott Trudeau, who even wrote a letter supporting Hull and others, but to no avail.

Yet above all else, what made the 1972 hockey showdown so memorable for players, fans, and broadcasters alike was that many of the best Canadian players in the National Hockey League had finally been placed on one team to meet the best of the Soviet Union. At long last it would be "our professionals" against "their professionals," a match-up Canadian hockey fans had been wishing for and speculating about for many years.

For far too long Canada had been allowed to send only its amateur, Olympic, national, or senior teams to meet the best players in the Soviet Union. Glory had been Canada's via numerous victories from Allan Cup champions or other senior hockey teams such as the Penticton Vees, Trail Smoke Eaters, and Whitby Dunlops. While those amateur clubs were steeped in talent and proudly represented the nation, they were still not the "very best" players in Canada.

With the advent of the 1972 contest, a level playing field had finally been found, and it was immediately flooded into a rink. Armchair hockey coaches from coast to coast in Canada were echoing the same thoughts: "Now that all that malarkey is changed — we'll show them what-for when it comes to hockey! Drop the puck!"

Canadian hockey fans could hardly wait to give the new kids on the hockey block a good lesson. In the minds of most Canadians, a solid thrashing was in order.

No one in the nation was fully prepared for what lay in store.

Not even me or the rest of the guys in the broadcast booth.

■ ■ ■

Team Canada's line-up was certainly filled with NHL stars and superstars, and when I looked at the broadcast line-up I realized the same was true for the TV team. The very best members of the hockey broadcast industry were behind the technical controls, cameras, and microphones. I remember feeling in awe and honoured to be working alongside folks such as Foster Hewitt, Bill Good Jr., Johnny Esaw, Renée Lecavalier, Gordon Craig, and others . . . all working together as one team on the broadcasts. The reason for such a line-up was that the two major TV networks of CTV and CBC decided to work in partnership on the eight-game series both in Canada and Russia. That pooling produced an enormous amount of broadcast knowledge in one crew. The man who put it all together for me, a man with incredible talent and an amazing sense of humour, was John Spalding, the producer and director of *Hockey Night in Canada*. Spalding worked as co-executive producer of the *Super Series* with Ralph Mellanby of *Hockey Night in Canada*. It was a star-studded broadcast line-up to complement two star-studded hockey teams. The cream of the crop — and I was honoured to be among them.

Clean across the country, from coast to coast, players and fans alike believed our guys were unquestionably far too good for the Soviets. All the scouting reports said their goaltending was "iffy" and that we would easily handle them — no question about it.

I think that was the same feeling in the minds of the players in August of 1972: they'd have a fun training camp, get in to two-thirds condition, and rub out the Ruskies. All the people in the hockey business, the media, and the fans were thinking that way. Very few were ready for what the Soviet Union had in store.

I'd never watched the Soviet Union team play, not "live," anyway. In fact, due to the pressures of work in Newfoundland, travel, and various tasks in preparation for the first broadcast, I never even saw the Soviet team practise. If I had, I would have been prepared for the shock and thrill of my life, during the next eight games.

Game One – Montreal Forum – September 2

More than 100 million TV viewers tuned in for game one of what was to be a tremendous tournament and remarkable experience.

I remember getting to the first game very early and watching the Soviets warm up. The thought went through my mind, "Hey, these people can skate, and they can handle the puck!" The velocity of their passes and the silent, controlled way they gave and received passes off the stick blade made me acknowledge that the Russians had great hand and stick control. Next to skating, puck passing is by far the most important part of the game and they were zipping the puck about with terrific accuracy. I knew right then that we had erred in our arrogance. Something was up.

So I was sitting high up in the Montreal Forum, right at the top of the arena, with a telephone line to the playback machine. The crowd was going wild with anticipation. Phil Esposito's line started and right from the face-off the puck went to Gary Bergman back at the blueline, who passed it up to Frank Mahovlich, who took a shot. The eventual star of the game, Soviet goalie Vladislav Tretiak, stopped the puck but it rebounded back out to Esposito standing in front of the net. He slashed at it once and Tretiak stopped that as well, and then Esposito reached out a country mile for the puck with his long reach and tucked in the rebound.

Thirty seconds had gone by and everybody was laughing, "Ha, ha — 1–0. This is going to be a cakewalk."

For the next five minutes, before Paul Henderson got number two for Canada, I noticed the Soviets came out of their own zone passing the puck "tic-tack-toe," and were skating full out. Soon, Team Canada could hardly touch the puck, forcing goalie Ken Dryden to make three excellent saves on Soviet scoring chances. I sat there thinking, "Holy cow — they make it look so easy," as they'd go from end to end and get a shot from a good scoring position.

Then from the face-off in the Soviet end, Bobby Clarke got it to Henderson on the inside edge of the face-off circle. He made it 2–0 with about seven minutes (6:32) gone in the game. Some of the people I was sitting near were smugly digging each other in the ribs and saying stuff like "Game over." I knew we were in deep shit.

During the next five minutes of play, the Soviets relentlessly continued to come out of their end with no problems at all. They made bullet passes from tape to tape, took our defence wide, dropped the puck back to the open man coming late into the play for a good shot on Dryden. I saw caution lights.

At 11:40 when Evgeni Zimin finally beat Team Canada's towering netminder with his first of two goals that night, my suspicions were confirmed. We were definitely in trouble. Zimin, at 5'8"and 165 pounds, had obvious dexterity on skates. I wasn't alone in quickly drawing comparisons between him and the Montreal Canadiens and Team Canada sniper Yvan "The Roadrunner" Cournoyer.

Right from the face-off, the Soviets again dominated the puck, skating freely on the Forum ice. Just before the end of the first period, Vladimir Petrov tied the game at 2–2. The noise of the boisterous Canadian crowd suddenly dropped in volume.

Between periods I told television fans that Team Canada was in "deep deep trouble." I said the Soviets stickhandled better than the Canadians did, skated as well, and never gave the puck away. I noted that Tretiak looked sensational. "The Canadian players have their hands more than full," I added.

On a recent Vancouver radio talk show, my old friend Bill Good Jr. reminded me that after the first period, I also apparently said, "Folks, we're going to lose this game."

I guess that cheesed off a lot of people. A number of Canadians were upset with the way I admired the Soviets' skill and play. I heard about that for quite a while.

Valery Kharlamov, their little right winger, simply danced around our defence twice on great passes from Alexander Maltsev to make it 4–2 at the end of the second period.

Between the second and third periods, the 19,000 fans crammed into the now extremely hot and muggy confines of the famous old Forum were a much humbler lot.

The third period was more of the same, with the Soviets dominating us in every phase of the game, including goaltending. Tretiak was superb and Dryden very iffy. He was taken aback because the Soviets wouldn't shoot at the net unless they had beaten every player on the ice. This gave Dryden time to think and, despite being relatively intelligent, he thought wrong many more times than right.

Clarke tipped a shot from Ron Ellis past Tretiak about eight minutes into the third period and briefly there was hope. However, the skilled Soviet puck control, precision passing, pattern plays, and strong skating could be denied only so long, and eventually the flashy Boris Mikhailov beat Dryden on a weak long shot to regain a two-goal Soviet lead.

For some reason, probably frustration, Canada again decided to try to physically stop the visitors for the remainder of the game. Once again the Soviets simply danced around their hosts and deposited two more goals, including a second by the "Russian Roadrunner" Zimin. When it was time to assess the damage done, the Soviets had thumped Team Canada 7-3.

At the end of the game, we wrapped up fairly quickly and once again I praised the Soviet skills, suggesting Canada had its work cut out for the rest of the series. Even as we ended the show, it was obvious to most of us in the broadcast booth that Canadian hockey fans were not alone in their shock. So were we.

Not only did the Soviets match us in skill; they were superior in physical conditioning and mentally far more focused. Even Sinden admitted to being impressed by the Soviet system and skill. "We got beaten by one fine hockey team. . . . I didn't expect the Russian team to skate as well as they did for 60 minutes. They beat us to most of the pucks, particularly in our own end," he told Canadian Press writers. "I was stunned by how well they played."

Team captain and leader Phil Esposito, was shaken by the defeat and told reporters the loss was a matter of conditioning and timing. He shrugged off his several missed opportunities as if they were to be expected and told us, "If it's around Christmas time, I don't miss those babies."

When he was reminded later by the media that the score was a 7–3 pasting, Phil boiled back, "You'll never see that happen again!"

Probably most profound of all, however, were the words of the guy facing the pucks: Ken Dryden. "When I played for the [Canadian] Nationals, I thought they [Soviets] were better. But I thought this team could beat them. They're probably better than this one, too," Dryden told us.

Game Two — Maple Leaf Gardens, Toronto — September 4

It was a sombre, serious practice held the following day at Maple Leaf Gardens, site of the second game. The players' giggles and over-confident bravado had disappeared, replaced by a quiet, simmering determination. I knew game two would be different in one aspect for sure; the Canadian players were at least now tuned in to the reality of the situation. They had received the wake-up call.

Sinden and Ferguson saw the flaws in their opening line-up and injected some rugged but talented players into their roster. On defence they added Pat Stapleton, Bill White, and Serge Savard, while up-front they inserted Wayne Cashman, Jean-Paul Parise, and Bill Goldsworthy. Slick centre Stan Mikita was also added. The team was much tougher both up-front and on defence. The minute the guys in the broadcast booth saw the line-up, they knew it was not going to be a game of simply speed, skill, and finesse. That would come *after* they decided who was the toughest.

In the second game the toughies did their job and did it exceptionally well. Team Canada came out flying and hitting, and took the body at most opportunities. The two teams battled back and forth through a scoreless first period, with Team Canada managing to slow the overall game pace and control the Soviet movement.

The restless Toronto crowd was finally satisfied when Phil Esposito put Canada in the driver's seat seven minutes into the second period, set up perfectly by Park and Cashman.

Sinden was obviously on to something as the solid Canadian bodychecking continued; tempers started to flare, and the aggressive play by the Canadians appeared to be clogging up that synchronised Soviet machine. Both teams were now carrying their sticks pretty high, and the cheap shots and chippy play increased.

Early in the third period (1:19), little Yvan Cournoyer made it 2–0 with a beautiful power-play goal. Park roared up the right side of the ice with the puck and fed it nicely to the Roadrunner, who snapped a great wrist shot past a surprised Tretiak. The Russians caught the Canadian lads flat-footed a few minutes later, scoring a power-play goal to get close 2–1, but then Pete Mahovlich went to work and scored as nice a goal as has ever been scored anywhere. The hulking 6'5", 205-pound forward faked out a Soviet defenceman and then buried a pretty forehand deke behind a sprawled Tretiak. Older brother Frank then popped in the final marker, and it was all over for the night — 4–1 Team Canada. While the Mahovlich brothers notched the game-clinching markers, it was the other brother combination that earned game star status, Tony and Phil Esposito.

Game Three — Winnipeg Arena — September 6

Fully aware of the huge task ahead of them now, the Canadian fellas worked full out at practices in a rigorous attempt to get in better condition.

Despite the significance of the early pivotal match held in Winnipeg, I hardly recall a thing about it. The stunning news of the massacre of 11 Israeli athletes by Arab terrorists the morning before at the Munich Olympics overwhelmed all of us. It numbed me completely; it hit a nerve.

Prior to the opening face-off, one minute of silence was observed in memory of the Israeli athletes and that passive tone seemed to remain throughout the night. It was a fast-paced and entertaining match, yet seemingly both sides were less impassioned. Even the fans seemed subdued. Nevertheless the game went on and the coaches planned accordingly.

Canada replaced Minnesota North Star grinding forward Bill Goldsworthy with slick New York Ranger centre Jean Ratelle in the line-up and the move paid off as Ratelle gave Canada a 2–1 lead near the end of the first period. The USSR battled back twice from two-goal deficits to eventually tie the game 4–4 by the end of the second period. A scoreless third period resulted in the match remaining a draw. Perhaps that score was fitting considering the Israeli tragedy.

For the third straight game, Canada had out-shot the USSR, this time 38–25, but again had a difficult time beating the impressive Tretiak. Tony Esposito was great in the first half of the game and not so hot in the second half. At the end of the night, I remember thinking that a tie was a hell of a lot better than a loss, and we could have quite easily lost the game. But the talk of the series to that point was Tretiak, who was just truly outstanding.

Game Four — Pacific Coliseum, Vancouver — September 8

The fourth match in Vancouver saw the numbers game finally catch up to Sinden and Ferguson. It had only been a matter of time.

In game four the coaches dressed some very good players but I'm not sure they were the players who deserved to be playing against the competition the Soviets were giving us. In order to keep the large number of players happy, and prevent some of them from jumping ship, management figured they would go with eight or nine regular guys and jump four or five around in the line-up. It was an effort to keep everyone content, but it was an impossible situation. Management had not made up their mind about who the best 15 or 16 guys were to go with and it blew up in their face.

Canada was without the injured Savard and Lapointe, and that hurt them terribly. Sinden started Ken Dryden in goal, and I thought he was very average. When Goldsworthy took two very foolish penalties, not team penalties, or good penalties (if there is such a thing), Mikhailov scored two great goals in a row and we were down 2–0. Dryden was hot and cold in that period.

In the second period, Canada played terribly, running around like a bunch of chickens with their heads cut off. Gilbert Perreault put Canada close at 2–1 but the Soviets scored two more markers and jumped ahead 4–1. The game was basically over at the end of the second period. The Soviet line of Vikulov, Kharlamov, and Maltsev dominated the ice that night. Dryden played very questionably while Tretiak was good — not great, but good enough to win.

Team Canada lost the game even though the trend continued of out-shooting the Russians, this time 41–31, including a whopping 23–6 attempts in the final period. That great number of shots was an indication we were starting to get into shape.

While there may have been signs of hope for the upcoming four games in Russia, the impatient Vancouver hockey fans displayed their frustration with Team Canada's performance and heartily booed the players at the end of the game.

A lot of Team Canada players and members were hurt by the response. They recognized that the game had not been a classic, however not through a lack of caring or heart. Captain Esposito, in true "Espo" style, let his feelings be known loud and clear to viewers after the game. He told the TV and press that his Team Canada mates deserved better treatment and respect from Canadian hockey fans and chastised the booing crowd for their attitude.

He was right. It had been a great humiliation to many Canadian hockey fans to have a Soviet team come over here and beat us in our own backyard with two wins, one tie, and one loss in four games. The Soviets seemingly outplayed Canada by a wide margin. Actually they probably hadn't, but the score indicated so and probably the television and press reported it that way. Canada, when playing five men aside, had as many chances as the Soviets. If the goalies had been swapped, we would have won or at least tied.

I did not get to hear Esposito's "live" reaction to the booing because I was running from one location to another at the time, but I saw it on tape later and it was definitely vintage Esposito — straight from the heart. He was right on the money.

I maintain that his TV performance that night had as much to do with the club eventually winning the series as his tremendous on-ice performance. His team leadership directly created the coming together of Team Canada when they hit Europe.

Still, the fans booed the team and I think that particular incident also had a lot to do with the reaction of management, Esposito, and members of Team Canada in putting their nose to the grindstone between the last game in Canada and the first one in the Soviet Union. With two weeks between the last game in Canada and the first in Moscow on September 22, Team Canada had valuable time to regroup, get in better shape, and prepare for the biggest four games in Canadian hockey history.

Now that Team Canada trailed the eight-game series with only four matches left, every shift of every game was important. Few thought the Canuck boys had a chance of winning the series. "Unless our goaltending is as good as or better than theirs, our goose is cooked," I told listeners at the end of game four.

There was no shortage of those wishing to advise Team Canada on how to plan their game in Russia. Suddenly all of Canada was a collection of armchair coaches. Most agreed, however, that Canada needed to use not only brawn but also brains if they were to have a hope of winning. They had to play smart hockey. In an "official" TV home program printed by Ford Motors and CTV for the four games in Russia, I wrote that mental discipline would count most.

"If we use the same tactics (foolish, emotional penalties) in Moscow as we did in Canada there'll be enough players in the penalty box for a good game of Growl (a Newfoundland card game for up to eight players). Team Canada's problem will be compounded by the larger ice surface. I just hope we are approaching these Moscow games with the same attitude the Soviets brought to Canada — they came to learn something. If we do, we'll come home a whole lot wiser," I cautioned.

Organizers of the event may not have done a whole bunch right in that series but one decision that proved a bigger plus than we knew at the time was to play a couple of exhibition games in Sweden before hitting the Soviet Union. The club management wisely elected to fly the players to Europe early rather than remain in Canada and leave just before the series resumed. That smart schedule allowed for four days of travel and ten days' practice or exhibition games. Not only did the stop in Sweden reduce travel fatigue but it greatly improved the overall player conditioning. In a feisty, nasty pair of games in Sweden, we won 4–1 and tied 4–4, with scraps on the ice and even in the corridors.

Our eventual arrival in Russia was a real shock to many members of the Team Canada contingent, and had it not been for the break first in Sweden I'd hate to imagine how horrendous our initial Soviet Union experience would have been. But nothing could have prepared Team Canada, the broadcast crew, or the rest of the Canadian entourage (who met us in the Soviet Union) for what awaited us there. The Iron Curtain had been raised only two years before and Air Canada had only just begun routes in to Moscow. Despite the recent impact of western culture on their lifestyle, the Soviet Union was still another world and the bulk of Team Canada members felt like total strangers in a strange land.

The contrasts were stark and were immediately reflected in the quality of life and the state of the people and homes. Women were out in the cold streets with brooms, people dressed very drably but in the best they had, few vehicles were about except those of the government or rich, and everywhere the military was on the watch. Nowhere would you find three or more people gathered to talk, and if such was the case a soldier soon came and moved the people along.

It didn't help that immediately after landing in Moscow, we learned that our imported milk, steaks, and beer had all mysteriously disappeared. From the very first, a sense of uneasiness and mistrust towards our hosts permeated the Canadian contingent.

The broadcast crew arrived in Moscow a couple of days ahead in order to figure out how we were going to get our work done. We needed to learn what we could and could not do from a technical broadcast perspective. We soon found out there were a whole lot of things that we couldn't do, and a lot of other things that were going to make our job much more difficult. From day one it was like working in a maze intentionally designed to slow and aggravate us.

The problem was not in the technology aspect, in fact in many ways they were light years ahead of us. Their broadcast centre was huge, at least a block long and broadcasting to over five time zones in numerous languages. They had technology and equipment in their facility that we had never seen the likes of. The control rooms they gave us to use were the best they had; they had full-length wall schematic panels tracking each and every camera and line.

"It was a dicey situation because we had to be diplomatic, but we weren't about to take their nonsense either. They were wanting to see just where the lines were with us," Spalding reminded me later. He was right; we had to set a tempo right off the bat indicating just how much bullshit we would put up with.

Compared to the tasks of other broadcast folks like Craig,

Mellanby, Spalding, Hewitt, and others, my stress and workload was nothing. My role was simply to observe the game from a broadcast booth (stuffed high up in the heavens) and pick out a highlight or two for between periods. Hopefully our people would then be able to get it transferred from the video machine to the projectionist's machine and get it on tape.

Bill Good Jr., as host, would lead me into the show. Then they'd play the highlight footage for me on my monitor, and I would talk my way through it to the TV listeners. That process is a piece of cake, a very simple task to do, and one person can do it here in Canada with no problem.

But not so in Russia back in 1972.

Just getting the broadcasts to run smoothly was one huge chore. The next one, of course, was for the technical crew to feed the game and highlight packages back to Canada.

As the series progressed, the absurdity of the Russian system continued. In order for me to get a 45-second clip (which meant maybe two areas of play of about a minute each) and to get it transferred to another tape would take them three to four hours.

After each game in Russia, the Canadian broadcast team would prepare an exciting highlight package to be aired in Canada for the televised opening of the next game. The three-minute openings sometimes took them four hours to complete, and I have no idea how the other fellas had the patience to put together the openings.

Obviously the Russian technicians were not prepared or were not allowed to do what we would ask them to. It often took 10 minutes for them to find the opening John Spalding or someone else wanted for the show. It was a case of total inefficiency and ineptness.

To further aggravate the situation, none of the Canadian broadcast crew was permitted to operate or even touch a machine. Finally, after about the third go-round of the absurdity, producer Harrison decided enough was enough and started to use the oldest bargaining process in the world — the buy-off.

Since the majority of the technicians were women, Ron would con them with perfume, sweets, and that sort of stuff, and in return they would allow him to run the tape machines.

1. *Slender Stanley* — The Stanley Cup was not as big when I first laid my mitts on it as it is today. Winning the Cup was the ultimate reward in my first season. I'm lucky to have held the Cup four times. Some very deserving players never got the chance. – HOCKEY HALL OF FAME

2. *Bill Barilko* — Billy was a dazzler on and off the ice, and was particularly popular with his Leaf teammates. When Billy died in a plane crash on August 26, 1951, while on a fishing trip, some of the Leaf spark flickered and died. It wasn't the same without him.

3. *Kroehler Kids* — Golly gee, that's me in the middle. As a kid I had it made. I played hockey all winter long on rivers, damns, backyard rinks, and in Junior A and B. My days with the Stratford Kroehlers were wonderful.

1. *Johnny Bower* – The crafty netminder spent a number of years in the American Hockey League, where I found him when I was with the Leafs. I tried to get Leaf management to snag him during my brief stint as coach–general manager, but he didn't arrive in time to help me out. – CLEVELAND BARONS

2. *Rocket Richard* – The Rocket was without a doubt one of the fiercest competitors in the game, and was extremely talented to boot. He was as quick and mean as a rattlesnake.

3. *Fred Shero* – Freddy the Fog was a solid pro in the American Hockey League, and had great success as an NHL coach in the 1970s. He had some odd ways of doing things in leading the Philadelphia Flyers to two Cups. – CLEVELAND BARONS

1. *Bill Ezinicki* – Wild Bill, though not a big guy, was one of the hardest hitters in the NHL. Ezzy made and received two of the biggest hits I ever saw.

2. *Tragedy on Ice* – Minnesota North Star forward Bill Masterton hit his head on the ice in a game against Oakland on January 13, 1968, and died two days later in hospital. The tragedy, which occurred just weeks before my first TV broadcast, rocked the hockey world. – Minnesota North Stars

3. *Baz Doran* – Also known as Bomber Doran, Baz was a talented American League star in Syracuse in the late 1930s. I was thrilled to play Old-timers hockey with him in Parksville, BC, forty years later. What fun!

1

2

3

1. *Jean Beliveau* – On the ice Big Jean could leave you in a crumpled heap, but he was truly a gentleman's gentleman. He was a fabulous centre and a tremendous leader, both on and off the ice. – Montreal Canadiens

2. *Stan Mikita* – Without a doubt, Mikita was one of the craftiest centres ever to play the game. – Chicago Blackhawks

3. *Pure Gold* – Bobby Orr was a star at both ends of the rink. Here he snags a rebound off the pad of goalie Gerry Cheevers. – Associated Press

1. *Bobby Baun* – Bruising Bobby played for many years, a miracle considering the kind of hard-hitting, no-nonsense rearguard he was. I rank him as one of the toughest players ever. When the Oakland Seals joined the league, they did well in grabbing Baun early.
– Oakland Seals

2. *Jacques Lemaire* – A slick centre, Lemaire was one of the few players who understood the unpredictable yet talented Guy Lafleur. Ironically, Lemaire pushed Guy out of the game too early, in my opinion.
– Montreal Canadiens

3. *The Golden Jet* – Power, speed, and skill – that about summed up Bobby Hull. He was tremendously strong, and his slapshot was legendary. What a sniper! – Associated Press

HOWIE MEEKER ON: WHAT'S WRONG WITH OUR GAME.

1

2

1. *Ulf Nilsson* — As talented as Anders Hedberg was, to me Ulf Nilsson was the true superstar of the two Swedish NHL pioneers. My, oh my, what Nilsson could do with the puck. He dominated the WHA before starring in the NHL. — NEW YORK RANGERS

2. *Big Bad Bruins* — The Bruins took exception to a 1971 loss in Los Angeles, and the fur began to fly. King Matt Ravlich has Derek Sanderson of the Bruins in a chokehold, and big Ken Hodge is jumping in to help out his Bruin teammate. The brawling Bruins and the wild Flyers kept the league hopping in the 1970s. The number of brawls and fights in the NHL has fallen off dramatically in recent years, but players now carry their sticks like war clubs more than ever. — ASSOCIATED PRESS

1. *Final Visit* – Gordie Howe (left) always took the time to talk with people. Here, after his final NHL game in Vancouver as a member of the Hartford Whalers, he signs pictures for fans visiting from Kamloops. – CHARLIE HODGE

2. *Welcome to North America* – Igor Larionov (third from the left) is flanked by Canucks brass at his first-ever press conference in North America. Larionov's arrival in Vancouver created great excitement. He was one of the first Russians to play in the NHL. – CHARLIE HODGE

3. *Parade of Champions* – The New York Islanders easily defeated the Vancouver Canucks to win the 1981–82 Stanley Cup in what was known as the "White Towel" series. – CHARLIE HODGE

1. *The KLM Line* — Vic Lynn (left) and Teeder Kennedy were both superb players, but, sadly for them, they were put on a line with me. Here I'm reunited with my Maple Leaf linemates at the Overwaitea Old-timers Tournament in Nanaimo in 1998. – CHARLIE HODGE

2. *Emphasizing a Point* — I had an awful lot of fun between periods pointing out my thoughts on games for TSN. On most nights, it wasn't hard to find something of interest for the viewers. On this TSN broadcast, I was upset with the defensive play of (more than likely) the Vancouver Canucks. – CHARLIE HODGE

3. *A Rose Between Two . . .* — My lovely wife Leah and I pose with Frank Mahovlich during the Boys' Club of New York Hall of Fame dinner. The Big M is a marvellous man, and we enjoyed seeing him again.

The whole situation from a broadcasting perspective, however, was very frustrating. We had our own little war as well. For our technical people to do what they did, despite the odds, was heroic. They did a hell of a job, equal to that of what the hockey team did.

In addition to the sensation and reality of being in a strange land, Team Canada was still having some problems coming together as one big happy family of hockey players. In a strange way, the horrible booing by fans in Vancouver acted as a bonding agent for the tossed-together team of stars and regular season enemies. Still, the numbers game of an extra 15 players continued to plague development of team morale.

Game Five — Palace of Sports, Moscow — September 22

I saw both teams practise one day and — bang! — we were into the fifth game. At the time, many fans considered that match-up as the single most important game in hockey history (until game eight).

It would be a night of learning, not just for the players but Canadian viewers as well. Suddenly we were in the world of the Soviets. We were in their homes and their arenas and we started to see hockey in another way. Canadian players and fans had to adapt to Soviet fans whistling instead of booing, and their constant chant of "Shaibu, shaibu!" (The puck, the puck!)

Team Canada suddenly seemed united and inspired. I have no doubt that Captain Phil Esposito had something to do with that. The Canadian lads came out flying in the game, despite the larger ice surface and dingy, somewhat menacing confines of the Luzhniki Arena at the Lenin Central Stadium. Parise put Canada up 1–0. Clarke and Henderson added singles in the second for a comfortable 3–0 lead as the Canadian fans rocked with joy at the arena's north end.

When five minutes into the third period Henderson added his second goal of the night for a 4–1 lead, the Canadian fans went bonkers. Victory seemed assured.

Someone, however, forgot to tell the Ruskies.

The Soviets scored twice within eight seconds, and four times within five minutes and forty-six seconds to win the game 5–4. Vikulov stuffed home the winner.

I understand that most of Canada sat stunned in silence at the turnaround. If so, they were not alone. Even the guys in the broadcast booth were stupefied by the turn of events.

Tony O use to break every rule in the book and make it work, making saves he had no right to make. He was a guesser, a dipper, a diver, a swimmer, went down early . . . but most nights he made it work. Most nights he was brilliant. But not that night.

Despite the club's excellent practices, improved conditioning, and a solid game, Team Canada had lost again. It was a good game, but more significant to me than the players' effort was the crazy, enthusiastic pack of about 2,750 Canadian fans stuffed together at the north end of the dull, cold, miserable Moscow Arena. During the opening ceremonies, they all stood proudly and belted out the Canadian national anthem with such pride and passion that I cried. I knew I wasn't alone in my feelings, because when I looked over at Foster Hewitt, he had big tears in his eyes as well.

Right from the start of game five, those fans were there screaming and cheering Team Canada, and that passionate support never died.

That memorable moment at the beginning of the game was surpassed, however, by the fans' reaction at the conclusion of the game. The Canadian club had blown a late third-period, three-goal lead, and yet the fans stood and cheered madly when the game was over. As the players skated off the ice, every single Canadian fan remained on their feet, clapping, shouting, and waving flags. You'd have thought the guys had won the game, not blown it. As much as the Vancouver fans' booing had hurt the Canadian players after game four, the Canadian fans in Russia did just the opposite. The Canadian team was pumped, despite the loss.

The day before game five, Vic Hadfield, Richard Martin, Gilbert Perreault, and Jocelyn Guevremont packed up their bags and headed back to Canada. The departure brought criticism from many fans and media, even though the majority of players and those in the know understood the exodus.

Game Six — Sports Palace, Moscow — September 24

Canada dug down and found what they needed for game six and won. I'm still amazed that Canada won the game because they collected seven penalties at key times. One of those eight penalties was a five-minute major picked up by a feisty Esposito. Phil earned an additional two minutes for being dumb and bumping the referee.

The Soviets received only two minor penalties the whole game. Throughout the series, penalties were a handicap that Canada had to battle. There is no denying Canada deserved most of their penalties in game six but the Russians deserved at least as many penalties and were never nailed. An overall 10-to-two penalty ratio was not a fair representation of that hockey game. My memory keeps going back to when Canada was holding on to a one-goal lead very, very late in the game (17:39) and the referee called Ron Ellis for a penalty. I just shook my head and said, "That's impossible."

I maintain the sixth game's victorious outcome was largely due to the return of defenceman Serge Savard and the fine play of the Canadian defence. Every game of the series the D improved but there was no denying that the return of Savard that night was the biggest factor in the win. He was a leader all night: Brad Park, Pat Stapleton, Gary Bergman, and Guy Lapointe played excellent games, and very physical. Big Bill White clobbered everybody within his huge reach, but Savard was brilliant in all aspects, especially carrying the puck out of Canada's end.

Canada also prospered from a few changes in the forward ranks. Hot-shooting Dennis Hull (replacing the departed Vic Hadfield) scored a goal from Rod Gilbert, while line-up insert Red Berenson made a great play on a marker by Cournoyer. Ken Dryden was very good in net, especially in the third period. It was a key game and something was in the making, you could sense it. The fella who scored the winning goal was, of course, Paul Henderson unassisted, and he was certainly on a roll. Henderson won the game by snapping in a shot from just inside the blueline. All of the scoring in the 3–2 Canuck victory was done in a furious second period of play.

Game Seven — Sports Palace, Moscow — September 26

Canadians from coast to coast could no longer contain themselves from being swept up in the hockey frenzy. Millions of Canadians flocked to the television sets in what had become an instant piece of Canadian folklore. At the time, none of us, except maybe for the few in contact with Canada (Craig, Mellanby, and Johnny Esaw) had any idea of what was going on in Canada. The players, however, were swamped with volumes of letters and telegrams of support. More than 50,000 Canadian names were pinned up around the dressing room as team members prepared for one of the biggest games of their lives. The game six victory had set the stage for a sports miracle.

While millions of Canadians remained frozen in front of the television at home, the Esposito brothers put on an impressive performance on the Moscow ice. What a show it was.

Coach Sinden went back with Tony O between the pipes, a hunch that proved correct, and Phil Esposito, who got the ball rolling again for Canada as he banged in two goals, keeping the score tied 2–2 after the first period. Gritty little Ron Ellis, who didn't score much in the series but did a great job checking up and down his wing, made a great play to Esposito for the opening marker. On the second Esposito goal with 2:26 left in the period, Savard made an amazing play to set up the marker. Stopping the puck at the blueline, he performed his patented "Savardian spin-o-rama" manoeuvre (spinning in a complete circle with his stick on the puck, avoiding an attacking player) and then passed the puck to Esposito in the slot. A scoreless but eventful second period led to the tense third-period climax.

Rod Gilbert scored from Jean Ratelle as that great New York Ranger combination also played well. I don't remember the line of Gilbert, Ratelle, and Hull doing much in the whole series, but I'll never forget the goal by Gilbert that put Team Canada ahead.

Just a few minutes later, Yakushev, an outstanding hockey player, scored on a pretty tip-in play from Lutchenko, and their best centre Maltsev, to tie the game, setting the stage for Henderson's goal at 17:54. Serge Savard once again made a tremendous pass, this time to set up Henderson's winner. Henderson beat four Russians at the Soviet blueline and then beat Tretiak.

Canada had won 4–3 and the fans went nuts.

It was only the second game in which the Soviets out-shot Team Canada, 31–25, but a chink was showing in the Soviet armour — Tretiak appeared human after all.

With the game seven victory, the teams were deadlocked at three wins apiece and a tie. The eighth game would indeed decide the world champions of elite hockey. The stage was set for a super sports spectacle. Two nations held their breath.

Game Eight – Sports Palace, Moscow – September 28

Soviet players skate extremely well with the puck, handle the puck very well, give and take a pass as good as anybody, and play a disciplined system better than anyone else in the world. In hockey you have to be disciplined in many ways, particularly in your own end. But to be disciplined on offence can be a great handicap. That is part of the reason why Canadians play the game of hockey better than anyone else — their defence is not always disciplined.

Canadians look, analyze, and react. The reactions of the great hockey players are right a very high percentage of the time. They look, analyze, and are not afraid to react. In that way there is no pressure to play the game. In Canada, at the end of the game the coach can say, "You're not going to play the next game, I don't like what you did." You can say, "Okay, release me and I'll go play somewhere else. I've got talent and there will be teams that want me. I'll make a living somewhere else." In the Soviet Union, they couldn't go and make a living somewhere else. They made a living in hockey or they were in deep trouble.

It was that unbridled Canadian free spirit, and Canadian players' ability to take risks, that won the day in all-important game eight. Canada needed to win the final game in order to win the series.

That incredible effort, however, almost never made it back to Canadian viewers. The entire broadcast almost never happened.

We had planned to use a fight scene from game seven between Gary Bergman and Boris Mikhailov, where Mikhailov kicked Bergman with his skate, as part of our highlight package opening the final show. However, Soviet broadcast and security officials intervened when they heard about it, saying they weren't going to let us use it. When we went ahead and picked the footage out from the game reel at the broadcast studio, their technicians immediately went to the big boss. He came down and said we couldn't use it, the film would not leave there. They were going to confiscate the tape.

Well, you don't confiscate anything on John Spalding so John snuck it out and we put it in the opening anyway. Shit hit the fan, big time! Just before we went on air, the Russians found out we had the kicking scene planned for the opening, and up to about 15 seconds before we started, they were still threatening to take us off the air. It was absolutely bizarre.

Back on the ice, the game was starting, and I'm glad to say our viewers didn't miss a single moment of the highly anticipated match. Sinden returned to Ken Dryden in goal for the final game and for the first 40 minutes he played absolutely terribly, with occasional brief glimpses of brilliance. After the first two periods, Canada was down 5–3. In the third period, though, Dryden sure redeemed himself. He was downright amazing.

Canada looked in deep trouble going into the final 20 minutes of play. Then right on cue, big Phil Esposito kick-started Canada. His early marker (2:27) narrowed the gap to just 5–4. Peter Mahovlich made a superb play and pass to Phil, who buried the biscuit.

Ten minutes later Esposito struck again, snatching the puck from a Soviet player behind the net. He then threw the puck in front to Cournoyer and the Roadrunner took three or four whacks at it and finally put it in the net. Yippee — halfway through the period and we had a tie!

After Canada tied the game 5–5, the Russians hardly touched the puck. In retrospect it seemed they were scared to touch the puck, scared to analyze and react. Canada absolutely dominated the game from that point on. You could feel the whole game shift.

Dryden was sensational early in the third and saved Canada's bacon long enough for Cournoyer to tie the game (12:56). Then, very late in the game (19:26), Esposito stole the puck yet again and gave it to Henderson, seemingly a man with the Midas touch. Paul shot the puck, Tretiak made the save, and Henderson got his own rebound and put it in the net — Canada 6–5.

Canada had won an unbelievable series and Canadian fans went nuts. Players swarmed off the bench to pile on Henderson. Pat Stapleton scooped up the historical puck and joined the throng. While Canadians everywhere went delirious with delight, television sets across the Soviet Union went black. The head Ruskie honchoes had made a decision at the control station.

The entire hockey world seemed to go berserk on that goal and pandemonium broke out everywhere — except in the broadcast booth and control centre.

"When Paul scored his goal, I understood what that meant to my Russian broadcast brothers and there was no way I could cheer. As broadcasters, cheering at that moment would not have been appropriate anyway, but still it was absolutely dead quiet in the control truck when the puck went in. Everywhere else people were going bonkers, but not in there," Spalding recalls.

For some, Serge Savard among them, Henderson's winner marked the greatest all-time goal in sports history. The Team Canada defenceman later ranked that goal as his highlight memory of his 17-year career, including winning eight Stanley Cups.

Phil Esposito had had an amazing night with two goals and two assists, while Henderson had another pinch of magic in his miraculous bag of hockey tricks. Despite the heroics up-front, the real star of the final game was Kenny Dryden. He made at least three tremendous stops in the third period.

It was a hell of a hockey series. There will never be another like it and I am still delighted I had the opportunity to be there. There were some outstanding performances by the Canadians — some of them not directly related to hockey. The character of Phil Esposito and the Canadian players will always stand out in my mind when I think back to 1972. Prior to the fifth game (the first match in the Soviet Union), the biggest name in Canada was Phil Esposito, especially after his scathing TV speech to the fans who had booed team Canada following the loss in Vancouver. Before the game started, the whole world was watching the player introductions, and when Esposito's name was called, he left the blueline and skated a few strides, but when he went to stop, his left skate hit something on the ice and Esposito fell on the seat of his hockey pants. The Soviet crowd howled in delight. It was the best pratfall I'd ever seen in my life. But instead of being embarrassed, Esposito just got up, bowed to the crowd, bowed to the cameras, and with a big grin on his face joined his teammates, who were all doubled over laughing. He followed that up with a helluva hockey game and a great series.

But that's Canada, that's the Canadian spirit, that's what our hockey players are about. They can turn adversity into an advantage. That is why we can play the game better than anyone else can.

There were other major contributing factors to why Canada won the series, but none more significant than the hockey fans themselves, especially those dedicated Canadian fans in Russia. The wonderful reaction of the fans after Canada losing the fifth game was a very positive experience. I believe that incident was the key factor in turning the series around. The Canadian player is a good guy but Canadian fans are great people.

Of all players involved it was Phil Esposito who made the largest single contribution to Canada's slim victory. No one touched the marvellous performance by the towering centre.

Team Canada picked a great leader in Esposito. I still maintain that no player in my lifetime has been so significant in a team winning not only a game but also a series, as Phil Esposito was in 1972. I've never seen anyone else display leadership on and off the ice like he did. He was amazing. I didn't think any one person could influence the outcome of a team sport, game after game, through a whole eight-game series. But Esposito was just not going to allow his team to lose, and he was not going to allow anybody on the ice to have a sub-par performance. He led by performance, playing both ways in the game, working, hitting, skating, checking. His intensity level was always at a maximum. The timing of his goals and assists in key games was amazing. Especially in game eight. He was the guy who won the series. It was the most out-standing performance I've seen in anything, be it business or in sport, certainly in hockey. A lot of guys made great, great contributions but Phil was the guy that won it.

The Soviet team all played impressively, but several Soviet players had particularly superb performances — Alexander Yakushev, Vladislav Tretiak, Vladimir Shadrin, Alexander Maltsev, Boris Petrov, Valery Kharlamov, and Boris Mikhailov.

I particularly liked Maltsev. He never scored any goals but was a great playmaker, a tough little nut. Valery Vasiliev was a standout on a defence unit that was very big, very mobile, and excellent with the puck. They were not used to the really rough forechecking by the Canadians at first, but it didn't take them too long to adjust.

Team Canada's line-up was filled with stars and superstars and while the majority of players performed admirably, it was the club's blueline brigade that most impressed me. Led by Savard, Lapointe, Stapleton, Bergman, Park, and White, the defence turned in eight consistent performances.

I thought in all, Stapleton was as good as anyone else on the ice. That surprised me because I didn't think the little guy had all the tools. I knew he had the heart, but I didn't think he had the mental and physical toughness, or the skill to do the job. He was not a big man or a strong man. But he was a smart little son of a gun.

The defencemen all played superbly, game in and game out. No forward, with the exception of Esposito, turned in as solid a performance, every shift.

I enjoyed Moscow very much. I found it a historical marvel and a very interesting experience despite its many negatives. The food was lousy, but, hell, I spent four years in the army so I'll eat just about any food.

Our room was very small and I shared mine with Bill Good Jr. He is a huge man but our beds were only about 5'10". I fit into them pretty good but Bill had a couple of feet hanging out the end of them and I often think back to that picture and chuckle. Bill Jr. was a great guy to spend time with on the road.

"To this day I swear that our rooms were bugged," Spalding

attests. "We'd say things like 'I wish we could get some soap' or 'Did you know the light bulb was out?' and the next thing you knew they would be replaced or fixed. All during that series we felt we were being scrutinized. Our rooms were searched without a doubt."

The beer and wine was all right and the food was edible. I kind of enjoyed the place. I never realized, I guess, how poor Russia was until we were on the way home. We stopped in Prague, Czechoslovakia, for an exhibition game, and the people there threw a wonderful party for us. I'll never forget how good the wine tasted and the food was — and the desserts were unbelievable. It was an amazing shift in hospitality with the finest of food and alcohol served to us in quality crystal and silverware.

At one point in the evening I was admiring a beautiful bottle opener-jigger with a Czech crest on it. I sensed someone watching and when I glanced up the bartender was looking at me. With a grin he nodded at my hand and the opener, then gestured that I should keep it, put it in my pocket. I looked at him with a quizzical look and he repeated the gesture. So I smiled and did as he suggested. I still have the jigger somewhere. It is a moment frozen in my mind because it was such a shock and change in attitude from the Soviet Union.

I guess victory has a way of making the trip home seem a lot shorter than it is so the return trip to Canada was a blur. One thing that wasn't a blur was seeing all the fans at the airport — it was pretty amazing to all of us. We knew that Canadians had been wired to the series but none of us over there could understand just what sort of frenzy was going on at home. We understood when we arrived.

That 1972 series was of great significance to every one involved in the trip and for some it truly changed their lives. Fellas like Paul Henderson wound up a few years later affirming their faith largely because of the series and the stress it brought him, while for others it had different impacts. Certainly the 1972 series affected Howie Meeker. It changed my life for sure — the series greatly enhanced my career as a broadcaster and put me in the homes of millions of

Canadians. It was my launching pad, so to speak. It was a marvellous experience and one I will always treasure.

It is only in looking back now at that series and time period that I realize we actually learned more about the world and life than we did hockey. John Spalding points out that we were fighting an ideology as much as facing any hockey test. We believed that we had to win because our social system, belief structure, and values were the right and only way. We had to win because we had invented the game.

"Now when we look at the Olympics and at all the national teams we can enjoy them and see the talent of the players. The '72 series had little to do with that, so much of the focus (consciously or otherwise) was on the other stuff, the better system, the better league . . . superiority. None or little of that thinking exists anymore," Spalding muses.

From a hockey perspective I don't think many of us learned as much from the Soviets and the series at that time as we should have. We are learning more from the European players now than we did back in the 1970s and '80s, and early '90s.

I think we've learned some lessons, but even today we are still doing many, many things wrong.

Perhaps one of the best summations of that incredible series was a comment by the likeable and articulate Ken Dryden. In an article titled "Summit Series: 25 Years Later" in the September 12, 1997, Toronto *Globe and Mail*, Dryden said, "It's like that old Winston Churchill phrase, 'The greatest feeling anybody can have is being shot at and missed.' And that's what it felt like. We were shot at and it whizzed right by our ears."

Indeed.

TEAM CANADA

GOAL: Ken Dryden, Tony Esposito, Ed Johnston

DEFENCE: Don Awrey, Gary Bergman, Jocelyn Guevremont, Bobby Orr, Brad Park, Serge Savard, Rod Seiling,

Pat Stapleton, Bill White, Brian Glennie,
Guy Lapointe

RIGHT WING: Wayne Cashman, Yvan Cournoyer, Ron Ellis,
Rod Gilbert, Bill Goldsworthy, Mickey Redmond,
Dale Tallon

CENTRE: Red Berenson, Bobby Clarke, Marcel Dionne,
Phil Esposito, Gilbert Perreault, Jean Ratelle,
Stan Mikita

LEFT WING: Vic Hadfield, Paul Henderson, Dennis Hull,
Frank Mahovlich, Pete Mahovlich, Richard Martin,
Jean-Paul Parise

COACH: Harry Sinden, John Ferguson

USSR NATIONAL TEAM

GOAL: Vladislav Tretiak, Victor Zinger,
Alexander Sidelnikov

DEFENCE: Alexander Ragulin, Vladimir Lutchenko,
Victor Kuzkin, Alexander Gusev,
Gennadiy Tsigankov, Valery Vasiliev,
Evgeni Paladiev, Yuri Liapkin, Yuri Shatalov

FORWARDS: Vladimir Vikulov, Alexander Maltsev,
Valery Kharlamov, Boris Mikhailov,
Anatoli Firsov, Viacheslav Starshinov,
Vladimir Shadrin, Alexander Yakushev,
Evgeni Mishakov, Viacheslav Solodukhin,
Viacheslav Anisin, Alexander Bodunov,
Yuri Lebedev, Vladimir Petrov, Yuri Blinov,
Yevgeni Zimin, Martyniuk

COACH: Vsevolod Bobrov, Boris Kulagin

C A N Y O U S A Y T H A T
O N T V?

■ ■ ■

Like a number of others involved in the incredible 1972 Soviet Series, I landed on my feet running after the September clash, and also like many others the series greatly affected my life. Certainly it raised my profile on TV and made me a more interesting commodity in the eyes of CBC.

In 1973 the number of broadcasts I did for *Hockey Night in Canada* increased and I became a familiar fixture in many Canadian homes. *Hockey Night in Canada* now appeared entrenched as part of the Canadian culture and I was lucky enough to be a small part of it.

I worked around 35 games that year and the playoffs. As well, I worked in extra productions and projects such as *Showdown* with Brian McFarlane, a series that ran for three or four years. I also later produced another show with Ralph Mellanby and Jerry Petrie called *Pro Tips*, used between periods. Guy Lafleur, Larry Robinson, Bob Smith, and Mark Messier were some of the players who helped out and it worked great.

I've been asked numerous times over the years how I adopted

my "style" and where I got my colourful, unique terms and phraseology I used during broadcasts. There isn't one clear answer. As far as style, I never really thought about whether I had one. I simply saw my job as two-fold: to entertain and educate the viewer — and in that order.

As a Member of Parliament, coach, and broadcaster in Newfoundland radio and TV I'd found that it was not only what you said, but how you said it, that folks tuned in to. If you weren't interesting, they'd soon stop listening. If you weren't a bit dynamic or at least getting their attention, the message was probably not going to get through. You had to get the player, the opposition member, media, or the viewer tuned in first before anything else was going to happen.

My "style"? Hell, it was just a case of survival, of learning how to be heard and remembered. I'd also learned (and from whom I'm not exactly sure but certainly Hap Day had an influence) that the best thing to be was yourself. Be honest in how you feel, say it, and then be prepared to stand by it. I've always been an excitable fellow, a fireball with a lot of conviction, especially where the game is concerned.

I suppose my down-home way, whiny voice, and pointed opinions appealed to many folks as very average, very guy-next-door, very Canadian.

As far as terminology, it was all of the above and more. Growing up with a military and hockey background, I'd learned to curse almost through osmosis. Given the wrong set of circumstances, I was able to peel paint with the best of them. It was not something I was proud of but it was certainly part of my environment. I was raised in small-town Ontario, and later spent many years in Newfoundland, both of which provided me with a variable potpourri of expressions, terms, and slang words. When I was on national TV and radio doing live broadcasts of a hockey game, though, there was no place for profanity, accidental or not. In the heat of excitement, slipping into locker-room lingo is not difficult and so I had to work hard not to slip up. I would make a point of seeking something colourful and creative to say to fill the void left by the saltier language I self-censored. Sometimes the terms were planned, sometimes they were simply split-second salvations such as "Jumpin' Jehoshaphat," or "Jiminy Cricket" instead of taking the Lord's name in vain. "Sssssshooot the puck" rather than "shit," "pitter-patter" with the puck rather than "piss around with . . ." and on and on. Much like Trudeau's famous "fuddle duddle."

As explained in *Golly Gee — It's Me*, I first saw the telestrator used in broadcasts of Canadian Football League games. I asked broadcast crew Ralph Mellanby, John Shannon, and Larry Brown, "Can you get me one of those things," and they did. I played around with it a bit, figured it might work just dandy, and then easily convinced the *Hockey Night in Canada* producers and production crew to give it a whirl. The telestrator was a video screen that worked like a TV, except I could write on the screen with a marker. I'd pick out plays during the period, then during my between-period show time I'd have it replayed and highlight players with circles and x's to show the viewer what was happening. For example, I would circle Orr (with the puck behind the net), then draw lines and arrows to show how he was about to create open ice, or pass the puck. When I wanted a clean screen I just pushed a button and the markings disappeared. Then I could start with another play or highlight. It was a wonderful tool to help educate the viewer about the game and help them see how plays develop or errors are made. We had no idea how well it would work or popular it would be, and it saved my ass more than once and probably extended my job a lot longer than I might have without it. It was a marvellous teaching tool to serve the hockey viewer better.

As a hockey broadcaster I was feeling pretty lucky that once again I had found a way to remain involved in the game. As well, that particular void I'd had in my gut for several years was now gone, although I was working with a new set of teammates. Broadcasting wasn't the player's bench or the battle trench, but it had the same sort of team camaraderie. For some men that sort of esprit de corps is imperative or at least very important and the need for it never leaves their lives. At that time in my life, I needed that team bond a great deal.

Of course having such a great crew of people around made the job a joy. All of them were and are very talented technical and on-air people with skill, wit, and dedication. On air I worked mainly with Dave Hodge, Dick Irvin, Brian McFarlane, Danny Gallivan, Foster and Bill Hewitt, Bill Good Jr., and Don Whitman during that period. Over my broadcast years I also worked with other wonderful folks including Steve Armitage, Harry Neale, John Garrett, Mickey Redmond, Gary Dornhoefer, Bernie Pascal, John McKeechie, John Wells, Jim Van Horne, Gary Green, Ryan Walter, Eddie Westfall, Jiggs McDonald, Jim Hughson, Paul Romanuk, and others.

The time between 1973 and the end of the decade was an absolutely wonderful period to be involved in hockey. Because I was a broadcaster, I often had the best seats in the house and my oh my, what a thrill every night was. Some of the finest players and teams ever involved in the game were playing and the changes, controversy, and excitement never ended. Boston had Orr, Phil Esposito, Ken Hodge, Wayne Cashman; Philly with Bobby Clarke, Bernie Parent, and Reg Leach; and Montreal had the cream of the crop that decade with, well, everyone . . . Kenny Dryden, Guy Lafleur, Steve Shutt, Serge Savard, Jacques Lemaire, and on and on.

It was a decade of more expansion, the rise and fall of the WHA, Soviet ice wars, player contracts . . . you name it. And I had a ringside seat. How lucky can you get?

1972-73

Still a-buzz from the incredible Soviet Series, Bobby Hull's banishment, the WHA's raiding and subsequent lawsuits and legal cases, an expansion draft involving the New York Islanders and Atlanta Flames, retirements, injuries and promising rookies, the NHL opened under keen scrutiny by all — including yours truly.

Understandably, some of the fellas who played with Team Canada had slow starts to the regular season; however, this was not the case with all of them. Good ole Phil Esposito simply never stopped after Russia and came out of the NHL regular-season gate like a gangbuster. With little opposition, he roared to the league scoring title once again. Espo racked up 55 more goals to his impressive skyrocketing career tally and set up 75 helpers for 130 points.

That brash little buzz saw with no front teeth and an attitude to explain why finished number two in league scoring. Flyer Bobby Clarke, also hot off the Team Canada experience, had tallied 104 points. Bobby had caught the attention of all Canada for his controversial "Soviet Slash." It was Clarke who viciously chopped down Russian superstar Valeri Kharlamov late in the '72 Series. I was not alone in suggesting that Clarke had played as valuable a role in that series for his infamous hack as had Henderson for his goal scoring or Espo for his leadership.

By Jiminy when Clarke was on the ice things happened. He kept the same spark-plug-like momentum going all regular season and led his Philadelphia teammates to new heights for expansion clubs.

Mr. Marvellous, Bobby Orr, continued to do the unbelievable on a pair of skates and one good knee. In better knee condition than during the Soviet Series, Bobby returned for a tremendous regular season and finished with 29 goals and 101 points for third place in league scoring, despite missing 15 games. Amazing. Twice that year I clearly remember watching Bobby skate with the puck from behind his net the entire length of the ice, past several players, and then around the other team's goal before scoring.

Now somewhere earlier in this book you've read about my feelings on the length of a hockey stick, and how important it is. It took me many years to learn all the advantages of the right length and the disadvantages of one too long. When we were covering games from Montreal, I used to beg producers John Shannon and Larry Brown to get a shot of the Montreal Canadiens' bench while the national anthem was being sung. There would be 15 players standing with their sticks in front of them, all cut well below the chin. I'd have my tape man record it and use it between periods. But even that didn't seem to convince kids, parents, or minor hockey coaches to cut their sticks.

I was pretty passionate about the stick length issue by the 1972–73 season and I vividly remember my first broadcast involving Rick MacLeish that year. I watched the Flyers warm up, and there was a young player with half his blade on the ice, the rest rockered and curved. The puck was constantly going under the toe or heel of the blade while he was carrying the puck. "Who's that dumb kid, how did he ever get to the NHL? He can't even carry the puck," I noted to myself. In the second shift after the game starts, Rick takes a pass at centre ice and heads for Jacques Laperriere. When their sticks are about two feet apart, the puck goes under the toe of Rick's stick and squirts free, Jacques reaches for it but by the time he gets there, MacLeish has recovered it, gone around the big D man, and shot the puck high over Dryden's shoulder for a goal.

I said, "Oh, folks, he's just a lucky kid," and used it as a highlight between periods, only to demonstrate the theory "Play the man, not the puck," plus Rick's fake to get Dryden down before putting the puck up in the attic. But I began to watch MacLeish and after a bit discovered he was a bit of a con man. He'd learned that, when on the attack and when he lost the puck, it was so obvious to the retreating D man that it would break his concentration on taking the body. The puck was there, so tempting, and possible . . . the defenceman's entire physical and mental reaction became "Loose puck, I can get it, why not?" But the instant the D man's concentration was broken, MacLeish would regain possession and beat him cleanly — time after time after time for years.

My bosses Ron Harrison, John Shannon, Larry Isaac, and others would routinely ask, "Well, Howie, what are we looking for tonight?" But I'd learned early in the TV sports business that if you look for it, it won't happen. My stock answer always was "Not a thing, gentlemen, just let it happen and I'll pick it out." But when we did a Philly game the answer was "Rick MacLeish carrying the puck."

Yes, there are some NHL players with longer than normal hockey sticks who make it work, but very few. Warning, kids: Don't you try it!

Mickey Redmond of Detroit, another hard-shooting winger, also broke the once elusive 50-goal barrier with 52 on the year. What a sniper he was.

Despite their good showing on the season, Boston had definitely been stung by the WHA and expansion draft, losing players such as

Derek Sanderson, Gerry Cheevers, Johnny McKenzie, and Eddie Westfall. And while Boston, the New York Rangers, Philadelphia, and Chicago were all showing plenty of power and potential that season, the Habs, it seemed, could never be counted out of it. In fact, another Montreal dynasty was in the making and the Canadiens were clearly the top team that regular season.

One of my favourite centres of that era, Jacques Lemaire, slammed home 44 goals. He finished fifth in league scoring with 95 points. My friend, big Frank Mahovlich, now relocated again, had blossomed in his new home of Montreal, snapped in 38 goals, and finished tied for seventh overall, while fans in Toronto and Detroit just shook their heads. Kenny Dryden had a tremendous regular season and playoffs, and the Habs won the Cup over Chicago.

The Blackhawks gave Montreal a battle in the final playoff round that year, but without their number one rocket man, Bobby Hull, they were simply no match for Montreal. When the season was over, Hull's glaring absence on the NHL All-Star team roster was filled by the Big M.

The upstart World Hockey Association held its major draft in February of 1972 for the new 12-team league. By the time the season was under way, a large number of NHL players, more than 60 in fact, had jumped to the new league. They joined a motley crew of American Hockey League, Western Hockey League, college, university, retired, junior, and even a few European players on the new league's dozen rosters. More than 240 new jobs had been created in the world of North American pro hockey.

Maple Leaf goalie Bernie Parent was the first "star" to sign with a WHA team, joining the Screaming Eagles of Miami. I still remember their logo and uniform: an eagle with wings back and talons out in full attack mode. Before the season began, however, Miami became the Philadelphia Blazers and Parent wound up there joining Derek Sanderson (briefly) and John McKenzie. The birth of the player bartering war had taken place.

Bobby Hull was the first "superstar" to sign and was the original rolling rock in the avalanche shift of players. Owners of the new league were smart enough to realize they had to find a marquee player if they were to have a chance of survival. Bobby inked his landmark deal in late June with Ben Hatskins and the Winnipeg Jets. At the time, Hull signed a whopping deal worth more than $2.5 million over 10 years and we all were shocked. However, as it turned out all of the WHA clubs had wisely paid a share of the deal just to get Hull into the league as a draw.

In a too-little, too-late reaction to the very real new hockey league, NHL gurus announced the expansion of the league to the New York Islanders and Atlanta Flames. It was a blatant attempt to hurt the new WHA markets in Georgia and New York. It worked, but the WHA got revenge as they snagged more than six of the Islanders 20 expansion picks, and even though Miami did not last long in fact, neither did Atlanta. There was little love lost between the two leagues but it was a war fought strictly at management and ownership level.

On the ice there was some good hockey played, and some very bad hockey. Other former NHL players to dress during the WHA inaugural season included Val Fonteyne, Reg Fleming, Brian Conacher, Wayne Carleton, Tom Webster, Jim Dorey, Rick Ley, Jim Watson, Ted Green, Tom Williams, Kent Douglas, Norm Ferguson, Les Binkley, and Ab McDonald.

André Lacroix of Philadelphia won the overall scoring title with 124 points including 50 goals, while Ron Ward of the New York Raiders was second. Hull finished tied for fourth in scoring and hit for 51 goals on the year.

Winnipeg, led by Norm Beaudin (13 playoff goals) and Bobby Hull, met New England Whalers in the finals. Tom Webster, Larry Pleau, Jim Dorey (former Leaf tough guy), and Tim Sheehy starred for New England, who won the first battle royal for the AVCO World Trophy title in five games. Dorey, surprisingly, contributed 16 assists from the blueline in the playoffs.

BEST NHL PLAYER: Bobby Orr — Boston
BEST WHA PLAYER: André Lacroix — Philadelphia
BEST NHL LINE: Jean Ratelle, Rod Gilbert, Vic Hadfield — New York Rangers

BEST WHA LINE: Christian Bordeleau, Norm Beaudin and
Bobby Hull — Winnipeg

1973–74

Bernie Parent was many things and one of them was entertaining. Not only was he among the first players to leap from the NHL to the WHA, he was also one of the first to jump back again, becoming one of the final players needed to create a winning team in Philadelphia. When his WHA team, the Blazers, moved from Philly to Vancouver at the beginning of the year, Bernie decided to stay put in the City of Brotherly Love and switch leagues rather than homes. His resistance to moving brought him the coveted Stanley Cup.

In his earlier years with Toronto and the WHA, Bernie never impressed me much. He was a guesser, dipper, diver, flopper. When you play like that, you're super — if things are going good. When they're not so good, you're terrible. When Bernie returned to the NHL with the Flyers, he'd matured somewhat as a netminder. Maybe it was the 40 or 50 shots a night he'd taken in the WHA, but he stood up and stayed square to the puck. It helped that his six big, tough, rough, mean defencemen didn't give the opposition too many second shots. It's hard to get to the puck or shoot it when you're lying on your back staring at the roof. Bernie was first-rate all his years with Philly. Geeze, I wish the present-day goaltenders would stand up like he did.

For pure mayhem, and rough and rumble hockey, I don't think I've seen anything like the Broad Street Bullies from Philadelphia. In most games, including playoffs, their role-player tough guys ran around the rink for 40 minutes bodychecking and beating on anything that moved in the other team's colours. Clarke and the other goal scorers would play hockey just long enough to get the necessary number of goals needed to win, before the mayhem would return. Said mayhem would continue until the clock ran out, and sometimes even after.

It was a time in pro hockey when brawn ruled brains, when intimidation won over skill, speed, and finesse. It was the wrong analysis or assumption of why we'd narrowly defeated the Soviets the year before, but that was how coach Fred Shero and the club appeared to view it, largely because most of his toughies *could* play hockey.

Shero was the original spin doctor. He covered the opposition's star players one on one, one on three, and one on twenty. Geeze, did the Philadelphia team ever come together for him and play consistently tough, mean, hard-hitting hockey. His toughies could play the game in the atmosphere they created. The Flyers were inspired by tough guys like Dave "The Hammer" Schultz and Bob "Battleship" Kelly.

Not too many teams or players were anxious to force the issue with the Flyers. If you went into their barn and played tough, you were asking for a physical beating, while getting thumped on the scoreboard. So Philadelphia usually set the pace of the game and the opposition really didn't attack as fast as normal. The additional half-second gained by the defenders got them to the puck quicker, with enough time left to either make a pass or (better still) chip it against the boards and out. Shero and company created an atmosphere in which the team's talent could best perform. Half his toughies, especially D-men, wouldn't have lasted in a freewheeling wide-open atmosphere, but hey, Philadelphia won two Stanley Cups.

Everyone who played regularly on those teams were good hockey players.

Eventually the spin doctor's magic became old hat, and when that happens it's moving or retirement time. For a time, though, the rough-stuff, intimidation crap worked. And it started that season.

I always believed there was definitely a place for roughness and toughness in the physical, fast, harsh game of hockey, including the occasional fight, but Philadelphia turned it into a full-scale war, and even I had to shake my head many a night in front of the TV cameras. The Flyers made the Big Bad Bruins look gentle, and the mayhem spilled over into other games and other teams for a couple of years before eventually settling down again.

"We take the most direct route to the puck and we arrive in ill humour," Clarke once explained to *Inside Sports Hockey*. They did it often, and in the process totaled 1,750 minutes in penalties on the season. Either way, Philadelphia topped the Western Division over Chicago that year in a wild, absolutely wild, season.

The powerful but WHA-scarred Bruins earned top spot overall in the East Division and the league. Boston ended the season with 113 points while Philadelphia had 112. Phil Esposito continued to shine for the Bruins along with wingers Ken Hodge and Wayne Cashman. The line finished first, third, and fourth in league scoring. Only the unbelievable Bobby Orr, in second, broke up the trio. Espo scored 68 goals and had 145 points to earn his fourth consecutive scoring title. Orr picked up 90 assists within his 122 points.

My oh my, what a series of years Esposito, Hodge, and Cashman put together as a forward line, with Phil going four straight years as scoring champ — absolutely amazing. The scary thing is that Milt Schmidt and Harry Sinden found the two players who could play with Phil mentally and physically and match his work ethic. Ironically, winger Kenny Hodge came as part of the package for Espo from Chicago, but the Hawks had seldom played the two together.

In Hodge, Esposito, and Cashman, plus Orr, there was magic. There never has been (or ever will be) a shift of four players on any team as good as or better than that quartet. They scored 200 goals and averaged 50 goals each and an amazing 461 points. That's an average of 115 each! Simply amazing. The line was big, strong, and talented, but the key player was Cashman. Oh man, was he tough, mean, and hard working. Without a doubt, he was the best in the league for work in the corners — his or his opponents', although no one was too keen to go into a Bruin corner. Besides, it would just get to Bobby O and out the puck would come. Cash had paid his dues for his rewards in injuries. In 1968–69, he played just 51 games. In the early 1970s he averaged 50 points and 100 minutes a season but in 1971–72 and especially 1972–73, he put it all together. Cashman meant as much to the Boston Bruins' success as anybody. I was delighted I didn't have to go into a corner with him.

Kenny Hodge, noted for his accurate shooting, was a classic example of timing, timing, timing. He had very good hands and was tough, but best of all he had incredible timing. That combination was murder when you had Espo, Orr, and Cashman on the ice, and then tossed in Hodge. He had everything needed to excel — size, strength, skill — but his head and timing were a perfect fit for the other skilled players. My, were they fun to watch.

When Kenny later went to New York, he quickly lost his confidence and his timing. When that happened, the cycle only got worse; then Ken seemed to simply lose heart and left the game. Too bad.

Spitfire Flyer Bobby Clarke was fifth overall in league scoring that season while classy Leaf centre Darryl Sittler made lots of noise for Toronto and finished eighth.

In the opening-round playoffs, tight defence won out with the Rangers upsetting the very strong Habs. The other three series were predictable, with Chicago dumping L.A., Boston beating Toronto, and Philadelphia eliminating Atlanta. Tough intimidation hockey ruled the rest of the playoffs as the Flyers went seven games against the Rangers while Boston scraped past Chicago in six. I remember being amazed that any two teams were still standing for the final series, and two warriors at that — Philadelphia and Boston.

In the end it was stingy defence and goaltending (along with the tough stuff) that won the day. Parent and a solid defence led by original Flyers Joe Watson and Ed Van Impe stoned Esposito, Hodge, Orr, and the Boston gang, and after six games the Flyers became the first expansion team to win the Stanley Cup.

When year two rolled around for the WHA, a few clubs were in new homes, including Philadelphia shifting to Vancouver and the Ottawa Nationals becoming the Toronto Toros. There were still 12 teams, much to the chagrin of the NHL.

Most devastating of all to the NHL, however, was the return from retirement of the grand man of hockey himself, Gordie Howe. At 45 (but still built like a brick), "Elbows" returned, but he chose the WHA instead. Once again, the new rebel league was pumped full of publicity.

I don't think it bothered Gordie a whole bunch that the NHL wasn't happy about his move. The NHL had never really treated

Gordie with the respect I believe it should have. Gordie and I did not see eye to eye on a couple of key issues, and he did one or two things I was not impressed about. Gordie allowed his team to vote against and then throw out the union back in Lindsay's day and then he played for half of what he was worth, so everyone in the league suffered. Still, Howe was a great guy and an incredible hockey player. He was already an excellent ambassador of the game. For Howe to choose the WHA and not the NHL was a slap in the face, and one the old, arrogant league totally deserved.

NHL puppet media types and spin doctors, along with various columnists and hockey people, pooh-poohed Gordie's return. Many questioned whether the comeback was just wishful thinking on the part of the old man, and they joked about him playing with his boys. Some even suggested it was just a publicity stunt. Sure he was great, but at age 45?

Not only did the old man shut up the critics by scoring 31 goals and 100 points on the season, he also helped his Houston Aeros club to the playoffs and eventually the AVCO World Trophy championship. Gordie was successfully joined by his two sons, Mark and Marty, on the team, which was a big part of the draw for Gord.

When the owner of the *Toronto Telegram* newspaper bought the Toronto Toros and brought them to Hogtown for the 1973–74 season, I was delighted. I was living in Newfoundland then and worked a lot of Saturday night Leaf games. The Toros usually played Friday night, so I'd catch the first plane out of St. John's and make the game on time. I knew most of the players on all the teams but always found time to talk to Big Frank and Paul Henderson.

WHA games were usually freewheeling, wide-open contests and fun to watch if you didn't care who won.

Mike "Shaky" Walton led Minnesota Fighting Saints to second place in the Western Division. Walton led the league in scoring with 117 points, including 57 goals. Mike was a great player when he wanted to be.

In the bizarre WHA playoffs that season (when both Chicago and New England had to play "home games" away from home), Chicago surprisingly advanced past the Whalers and then Toronto into the finals against Houston. However, Pat Stapleton, Ralph Backstrom, and Rosaire Paiement weren't enough against Murray Hall, Frank Hughes, Larry Lund, Paul Popiel, and the three Howes. Lund, a former Western Hockey League star, led the Whaler team in the playoffs with 23 points while Gordie Howe picked up 17. The fans ate it up.

BEST NHL PLAYER: Bobby Orr, Phil Esposito — Boston
BEST WHA PLAYER: Gordie Howe — Houston; André Lacroix — New York-New Jersey
BEST NHL LINE: Phil Esposito, Ken Hodge, Wayne Cashman — Boston
BEST WHA LINE: Mike Walton, Wayne Connelly, G. Morrison — Minnesota

1974–75

Attempting to keep ahead of the rival WHA bandits, the NHL grew by yet two more clubs: the Kansas City Scouts and Washington Capitals. All the expansion actually achieved was to create additional financial woes for most involved, though Washington survived. Kansas City eventually became the (Denver) Colorado Rockies and later the New Jersey Devils. The two new teams merely provided easier fodder for the Bruins, Flyers, Habs, and emerging powerful teams such as the Buffalo Sabres and New York Islanders.

With 18 teams, the league split into four divisions, and Buffalo, Montreal, and Philadelphia all topped their own division with 113 point totals each. Most critics said the division make-up made no sense geographically, nor by rivalry, and for the most part they were correct. For instance, the Norris Division had Montreal with Los Angeles and Washington, while California was in the Adams with Toronto and Boston. Just brilliant!

It was a wild year filled with fights and craziness, and I recall thinking that a couple of teams were trying to emulate the Philadelphia roughhouse tactics. The goons and all the fighting hurt the game a lot. It had gone past its limit of acceptance.

However, it also drew in plenty of fans during times when most teams needed a hook to fill the rink. The talent pool was simply too thin on superstars and stars to spread them onto all teams in the two large leagues, and so other means of drawing fans were attempted by some owners and management.

New Bruin coach Don Cherry promised he was going to beef up the Bruins, claiming that Philadelphia had merely copied the winning "play mean" formula he had used as a successful minor league coach.

Without any goonery on his part, Bobby Orr — the amazing one-knee wonder — captured the scoring championship once again. If there were still any sceptics after he'd won his first scoring title, Orr silenced them with his second showing. Bobby was brilliant that year, scoring a phenomenal record for defencemen of 46 goals and set up 89 others for 135 points.

On numerous evenings I showed Orr performing one of his spectacular dashing rushes up the ice as one of my between-period highlights. "Like a hoop around a barrel" became a term I used for him many times as he turned someone inside out. That expression became somewhat synonymous with me, however it should have been synonymous with Bobby Orr instead because it was the magical number four who inspired it to pop out of my mouth one night.

In the scoring race, not even Espo with 61 goals could catch Orr. Phil ended in second with 127 points while Detroit's sensational centre Marcel Dionne was third at 121.

Another superstar in the making (and one of my favourites of all time), young Guy Lafleur, woke everyone up in Montreal with a simply fantastic year. "The Flower" scored 53 goals and added 66 assists for 119 points and fourth spot overall. Few players ever excelled at on-ice leadership like Guy. He had an insatiable desire to win. That tremendous spirit glowed from him that season, and you could tell for sure that Lafleur was going to dominate the game, in his own way, like only a few others had. No one would ever duplicate Orr, Howe, or Richard in their unique ways, but it was reassuring for fans to know that another shining light of the calibre of Guy Lafleur was arriving on the hockey scene. The 1971 first-round top draft pick, Guy was finally meeting and exceeding the high expectations that had been heaped on him the first few seasons in hockey-mad Montreal.

Guy told me later that he'd been given a bit of advice, perhaps a touch tersely, by his idol, Jean Beliveau. It seems Le Gros Bill admonished young Guy for not giving 100 per cent every shift, every game. Well . . . the lecture certainly seemed to have worked.

Three young fleet-footed stars in Buffalo again pooled their talents on a forward line and all finished in the top 10 scoring. René Robert hit the 100-point mark for seventh place, while Gilbert Perreault with 96 was ninth, and Richard Martin, who was picked fifth in the same draft as Lafleur, with 52 goals and 95 points, was 10th. Perreault was the first-round top pick in 1970, the season before Guy.

Holy cow, that line, dubbed the "French Connection," was really something to watch. Gilbert made the line go, Richard had amazing outside speed and a fast accurate rising shot, and René had phenomenal timing and some ruggedness. Let the big guy Perreault go, and when he and Martin were in dire straits, Robert would be wide open like an airplane hangar's doors and in she goes. René and Richard were a perfect fit for the Buffalo centre superstar. My oh my, Perreault could motor. He was one of the fastest skating centres I ever saw.

The third member of the Bill Barber-Bobby Clarke combo in Philadelphia was another young sniper named Reg Leach, who came to the Flyers at the request of Clarke that season. Bobby had told Flyer management that Leach, his former Flin Flon Bomber junior linemate, was a sniper and would net them 50 goals a year. A year later Clarke was proved right.

Kenny Dryden also returned after a one-year retirement and helped the Habs in the regular season, but not enough in the playoffs.

The league's four new divisions and two conferences created the potential for a new set of clashes in the playoffs. For the first time ever, two expansion teams met in the Stanley Cup final: the impressive, fast Buffalo Sabres, and the defending champions, the rock-hard Philadelphia Flyers.

Goalie Bernie Parent won his second straight Conn Smythe Trophy as Philadelphia took the Cup in six games. Parent earned a shutout in the final game, just in case there was any doubt who should haul in the hardware as playoff MVP.

To reach the finals, Philadelphia rolled four straight over Toronto, then played seven tough games against the Islanders. Buffalo trundled by Chicago in five and then surprised Montreal in six games.

The WHA was not about to miss any opportunity to gain national or international attention, so in 1974 the new league also engaged in an eight-game battle with the U.S.S.R. Team Canada (WHA) wound up winning just one, tying three, and losing four games against the Soviet National Team, a result that did little to enhance either the WHA or the Canadian hockey image.

Bobby Hull was tremendous as he led Canada in his long-awaited meeting with the Soviets, racking up nine points in eight games. Ralph Backstrom had eight points while Gordie Howe and André Lacroix earned seven each. Alexander Yakushev and veteran Valeri Kharlamov, two familiar Russians, led the U.S.S.R with eight points apiece.

I was lucky enough to be involved in broadcasting that Soviet–Team Canada confrontation, and though it lacked the same lustre as the 1972 series, it was still good hockey and a real honour to be a part of it. Our old pros gave a good showing, but simply did not have the young legs or team skills to beat the younger, better disciplined, skilled Ruskies. In Canada we played all right, but in Moscow, for the final four games, we could not quite click. Still Hull, among others, gave a tremendous showing and I pondered on how such an impassioned Bobby Hull might have helped Team Canada in 1972. My mind could not get past visualizing Hull playing with Esposito again, especially the way in which Espo and Hull had separately led their teams against the Soviets. What if. . .?

During the WHA regular season, the big news was that Frank Mahovlich and Paul Henderson had found their way to the WHA and joined a couple of other former NHLers in building the Toronto Toros into a competitive team with the Maple Leafs. Other Toros included Les Binkley, Tony Featherstone, youngster Pat Hickey, and Czech

Vaclav Nedomansky. Former Leaf Billy Harris was coach, and was replaced by Bob LeDuc midway through the 1974–75 season.

The biggest score of the WHA in 1974–75, however, was the acquisition of four Swedish hockey stars in Winnipeg. Defencemen Lars-Erik Sjoberg, goalie Curt Larsson, and star forwards Ulf Nilsson and Anders Hedberg arrived in the cold Manitoba capital causing a bit of a hockey heat wave. The Quebec Nordiques improved their club by losing moody Jacques Plante as GM-coach and gaining junior rookie centre sensation Real Cloutier.

"In a province that deserves better, the Quebec Nordiques have failed to make the playoffs two straight years. This could make it three," the *Popular Sports Face-off* magazine of January 1997 predicted.

Like most predictions, it proved wrong.

The fast-skating, smooth-passing Nordiques finished first in the Canadian Division with 92 points, while the Whalers won the East with 91 and the Houston Aeros were first in the West with a strong 106 points.

André Lacroix of (transplanted) San Diego once again led the league in scoring with an amazing 147 points on 41 goals and 106 assists. Lacroix continued to shine despite playing with nomad clubs that seemed to never have a permanent home, and a spinning door of players. Bobby Hull went nuts in the goal-scoring category, topping Espo's pro goal season record of 76 by one marker. Bobby's 77 goals helped him to the second spot overall in league scoring with 142 points assisted by his super-talented Swedish linemates Nilsson and Hedberg.

In the playoff finals, the Howe clan and crew proved too strong defeating Quebec four straight. Mark Howe led Houston with 22 playoff points, while Dad earned 20. Marc Tardif was the top Quebec point man with 21.

Best NHL Players: Bobby Orr — Boston; Bernie Parent — Philadelphia

Best WHA Players: Bobby Hull — Winnipeg; André Lacroix — San Diego

BEST NHL LINE: Gilbert Perreault, René Robert,
Richard Martin — Buffalo

BEST WHA LINE: Ulf Nilsson, Anders Hedberg, Bobby Hull —
Winnipeg

1975-76

In my mind, 1975–76 ranks as one of the darkest years of the 50 covered in this book and for many reasons, not the least of which was injuries, both physical and financial. The season started on a down note for many fans (especially those in Boston) with the news that Bobby Orr needed more major surgery on his damaged left knee. It was the fourth time he had gone under the knife, and as it turned out it marked the beginning of the end for Bobby. He played just 10 games that year, notching 18 points, but sadly never played another game after that for his beloved Bruins.

Bruin fans were in for even a bigger shock 12 games into the season when star centre Phil Esposito was part of a deal that sent him to the New York Rangers with Carol Vadnais for stars Jean Ratelle, Brad Park, and Joe Zanussi. It was the end of Espo and Orr dominating the top of the individual scoring race. Neither former Boston player finished in the top 10 scoring list that year, while Ratelle finished sixth overall. Espo was devastated by the trade at first, and it took him several games to adjust.

The Bruins finished first in their division with 113 points; Park and Ratelle had a solid year while veteran goalie Gerry Cheevers rejoined the team late in the year from Cleveland of the WHA.

How good was the Esposito trade for Boston? Well, after the deal, the Bruins lost just 10 of their remaining 68 games. The Rangers stumbled to fourth in their division with just 67 points. Geez, you'd think people would have learned not to deal with Harry Sinden. What a wheeler dealer!

Montreal was back where it belonged at the top of the pile. The two years of goon hockey that had dominated the league were slowly starting to dissipate and the rightful heirs of hockey, those who displayed speed and skill, were about to continue their dynasty-building in a big way. Led by the flowing, flashy Guy Lafleur, who earned the individual scoring title, the Canadiens won everything that counted in 1975–76. They ended the year with a whopping 127 points, including a record 58 wins and only 11 losses.

More important to coach Scotty Bowman was that his team had adhered much better that season to a style of solid team defence. "We start out with this in mind. That if you win the Vezina Trophy, you're almost certain to win the Stanley Cup," Bowman said.

Goalie Ken Dryden responded, as did the whole team. The Habs lost just three times at home, the club's defence was the best in the league, and Dryden was on the First All-Star team and won the Vezina. The club also won the Cup.

While Montreal proved the darlings of the game, the nasty Philadelphia Flyers were certainly no slouches. That year the Flyers, led by Clarke, Barber, and Leach, went a record-tying 23 consecutive games undefeated. Clarke won his third Most Valuable Player award in four years.

In Montreal "The Flower" scored a solid 56 goals and wound up with 125 points on the regular season, beating out Bobby Clarke, at 119, for the individual scoring title. Young Gilbert Perreault of Buffalo had an outstanding year and finished third with 113. Darryl Sittler of Toronto went crazy one night in February, scoring an unbelievable 10 points against Boston.

Although all those players were magnificent during the season, it should also be noted that the 1975–76 season was an unprecedented year for goal scoring and massive total points by several players. Never before had four players broken the 50-goal mark and finished in the top 10, nor had nine players hit the 100-point barrier in a season. Only the year before had the old century mark record of four players been reset at seven.

Can you imagine three of the six divisions in 1999–2000 averaging close to 300 goals scored per team? Now don't get me wrong. I am all for scoring goals, but for 14 out of 18 teams to average 3.64 goals per game was insane.

We had pretty good broadcast crews and some of them were

hockey people and knew the game. The on-air guys usually left the hotel for the arena at 4 p.m. for an 8 p.m. game and naturally we talked hockey. Mostly about rumours, trades, teams in trouble, players, and who was hot or cold, that sort of stuff. Very seldom did we discuss the philosophy of the game, but when we did, I always went back to my roots, my real training under coach Hap Day. His philosophy was that for each game he would accept that the opposition would earn one goal, you gave them through mistakes one goal, and the officiating cost you half-a-goal a game. Therefore he'd expect his coach to keep the goals against to just under three per game, and if he didn't he'd fire the coach.

I still wholly subscribed to that belief and would argue it anytime, anywhere. When I get on the soap box, the heads bow, the eyes roll, and I can hear the young guys say, "Geeze, the old man is bonkers," but I still maintain 3.41 per season is way too many goals against. Yet today there are not near enough goals.

Anyway, a superb young New York Islander centre named Bryan Trottier earned the Calder Memorial Trophy as Rookie of the Year, and you could see right off the bat that he had the hockey savvy to do well. His brightness helped reduce the dim future of the financially troubled Islander team. (Once again, not a lot seems to have changed.) Trottier racked up a remarkable 95 points, including an amazing 63 assists.

The Habs, however, were a far more powerful hockey club than many "experts" even realized, and it was proven in the decisive way they marched to the Cup final that year, beating very solid clubs on the way. In their first match-up, the Habs breezed past Chicago 4–0 and then took on the powerful and ever improving New York Islanders (who'd edged out tough Buffalo). It took Montreal five matches before shaking New York, but in the end their speed and passing won the day.

The Flyers, meanwhile, battled their way past the Leafs and the Bruins to the finals, but the grind eventually got to them.

In the finals, Philly again tried their intimidation techniques in their quest of a third Cup but the Broad Street Bullies were left clutching at air as the Habs were simply too quick and slick for them. Montreal out-skated, out-passed, and out-scored Philadelphia in four games and won yet another Cup.

Even though his club failed to win the Cup, Flyer sniper Reg Leach was awarded the Conn Smythe Trophy as the playoff top player. Leach scored a record 19 goals during his pursuit.

I'm convinced that a big part of Reg Leach's scoring success was that he went unidentified or unnoticed most of the time. During the warm-up as you watched the Flyers skate about, you'd look for stars you normally recognized like Bobby Clarke, Bill Barber, Rick MacLeish, and the various toughies. Then you'd finally think, Leach — what's his number, where is he? You'd look for a while and then figure he was not dressed or must be hurt. When the game started and the first line came out, though, there he was.

On TV I'd save clips for the telestrator replays of some great goals by Leach. "Stop it right there — back it up — Reggie scores, but where'd he come from?" I'd squeak in disbelief.

"But where the hell was he when the puck went end to end?" My mind would search, and indeed I would stop the film and wind it back, time after time, to find where the elusive Leach had come from. He not only was "absent from the scene" with his long-range set-up passes and assists, but he also appeared at the last second on goals he scored himself.

Even with my high wide-angle camera I could never find him until the last 10 feet of the play. He'd seem to come out of nowhere and put the puck in the net. Not always, but a lot of the time. I can hardly remember seeing Leach carry the puck on his side of centre ice, but it seemed he suddenly appeared with the thing on his stick bursting in from the wing towards the net. *Bang!* In it went.

Reg was a prolific junior scorer in his home province of Manitoba. When he first came into the NHL, it was not with a big bang in either Boston or California. He finally arrived in Philly, though, and was reunited with Flin Flon teammate Bobby Clarke, and exploded. During his first Flyer season in 1974–75, he dented the twine 45 times and the next year popped home 61 goals. He hit the 50-goal plateau once again 1979–80. Not bad for a guy you couldn't find in a warm-up.

Despite the Montreal win, some fans felt Guy Lafleur had not played well, that he was not in the game. What the fans were not aware of (and the broadcast crew learned about near the end of the series and kept quiet about) was that Lafleur was under threat of a kidnapping during the playoffs and was under tight security. "I went through hell," Lafleur said later.

The WHA started to show major cracks in year four as a couple of teams switched town before the season began and a couple more folded during the year. What started as a 14-team loop ended the year in great confusion as a 12-team league with Minnesota and Denver-Ottawa in the dumpster.

Partway through the 1975–76 season, goalie John Garrett joined the Toros from Minnesota, and I found a new source of supreme pleasure in watching the occasional Toros game. I'd always respected and loved a good standup goalie, and Garrett was a classic example. Turk Broda, Gil Mayer (Pittsburgh Hornets), Bill Durham, Frank Brimsek, John Bower, and Terry Sawchuk were good at staying on their feet but Garrett was sensational. After watching Garrett closely for four or five games, I got the feeling John wouldn't leave his feet to pick up a $100 bill. Watching him reminded me of a Hap Day coaching expression, "He played the [goal] post like a door on a hinge." Garrett squarely faced the puck, never got beat short side or between the legs, and he covered the five-hole better than most. Garrett also attacked the puck carrier just as soon as the opponent indicated what he was going to do.

Golly gee, John was entertaining. Sure he'd get beat five of 50 shots, but he made goaltending look easy and was he fun to watch. Years later he performed the same magic for the Vancouver Canucks. One night in Winnipeg he stopped 45 shots, and I never saw better goaltending, or goaltending made to look easy. No guessing, flopping, swimming, no diving . . . he just got square to the shooter, stood there, and let them hit him.

In recent years John has done colour work for *Hockey Night in Canada* and today there isn't a better one in the business. John Garrett — as good a standup goalie as anyone, ever.

Off-ice financial woes and on-ice mayhem and brawls continued in the league as things got pretty ugly for a time. The absurdity of the violence and concern about it was highlighted when superstar Bobby Hull protested against it by holding a one-game refusal to play. Hull took a lot of flak and criticism about his protest, but I thought it took a hell of a lot of guts and I admired him for it.

On ice Marc Tardif won the scoring title, including 71 goals and 148 points. Bobby Hull finished second overall with 123 points, while Real Cloutier finished third at 114 points, including an impressive 60 goals. It marked the fifth straight year that Hull had scored 50 or more goals, an amazing feat.

Absurd as it was, 10 teams made the playoffs but nobody, including Howe and the Aeros, could stop Hull, Hedberg, Nilsson, and the Jets from winning the AVCO Cup. Nilsson led the playoff race with 26 points, Hull was second with 20, and Hedberg third with 19, including 13 goals. I remember watching the three of them one night and marvelling at their puck-handling skills. The two Europeans, especially, took a tremendous amount of physical abuse and cheap shots by players through the year, but they kept going and scoring. They, along with the Stastnys and Borje Salming, were the first real indication of the tremendous European influence and influx that was about to grow in the NHL. I said it then about the Europeans and people laughed, but I guess time has a way of sometimes making us fools and sometimes visionaries. Either way, Hedberg and Nilsson were certainly sweet to watch with the puck, which gave Hull plenty of opportunity to do what he did best — shoot the puck. What a tremendous line that was, one of the best I've ever seen.

Nilsson was likely the most gifted of the three for pure skill. He was a marvellous skater with tremendous stickhandling and passing skills. My oh my, how he could dipsy-doodle and make the puck pay attention. Hedberg, on the other hand, was a strong-skating, hard-shooting port-side sniper who was also nifty at passing. Hedberg had the scoring nose of a bloodhound and would either shoot the puck and then break to the net for a rebound, or feed to Hull and drive to the net for Hull's rebound or return pass. Gosh, they were something to watch play.

BEST NHL PLAYER:	Guy Lafleur — Montreal
BEST WHA PLAYER:	Marc Tardif — Quebec
BEST NHL LINE:	Bobby Clarke, Reg Leach, Bill Barber — Philadelphia
	Pete Mahovlich, Guy Lafleur, Steve Shutt — Montreal
BEST WHA LINE:	Ulf Nilsson, Anders Hedberg, Bobby Hull — Winnipeg

1976–77

A couple of key players missed much of the 1976–77 season in both leagues with Frank Mahovlich and Bobby Hull out for the WHA and Bobby Orr, Yvan Cournoyer, Keith Magnusson, and others absent for much of the NHL.

Problems began for Chicago early in the year with news that Orr, who'd signed up in the summer, would likely not see much (if any) action that year. It seemed the clock might be up on the Wonder Kid's left knee, and no bloody wonder. I was amazed he even continued to try, though I admired his tenacity.

On October 30, Magnusson had his jaw smashed in a brutal blindsided cross-check by Brian "Bugsy" Watson of Detroit, and by mid-November the Hawks were without Orr, Magnusson, Bill White, Stan Mikita, and Dennis Hull all due to injuries.

Even though the Canadiens also had a number of regulars on the wounded shelf for much of the year, no one was capable of really stopping the red, white, and blue machine from Montreal. Quite simply, the 1976–77 version of the Canadiens was probably one of the finest, if not the finest, hockey clubs ever assembled. That was aptly displayed by their amazing season, which unbelievably topped their performance in 1975–76. The squad lost just eight games all year (including only one at home), won a record 60 games, and tied 12 during their grinding 80-game schedule.

Appropriately, the gifted Guy Lafleur repeated as scoring champ, notching 56 goals again and adding 80 assists for 136 points. The diminutive and deadly L.A. King's centre, Marcel Dionne, finished second overall with 53 goals and 122 points, while Lafleur's line-mate Steve Shutt was third with 105 points, including 60 markers. Those were three real snipers.

At the beginning of the year, the Kansas City Scouts were shipped to Colorado and became the inept Rockies. The only team to play worse than the Rockies with 54 points was the pathetic Red Wings, who fell to last place with just 41. It seemed the old Detroit-player association hex was in full swing. The Cleveland Barons (formerly California Seals) mustered 63.

In the playoffs Lafleur continued to display his magic as he led his club with an incredible 26 points in just 14 playoff games and won the Conn Smythe award. Jacques Lemaire was also brilliant, scoring three game-winning goals, including an overtime thriller.

Montreal steam-rollered St. Louis four straight, then edged the tal-ented Islanders four games to two in a great skating series. Boston, meanwhile, used their intimidation game, adapted from Philadelphia, to help them move past L.A. Then they beat the Flyers at their own game in the semi-finals four in a row. In the finals, however, the bullying Bruins were left behind and went down four straight to Guy and the fleet-footed gang. A stingy Dryden and Montreal defence gave up just six goals in the four-game final. It was a tremendous display of defence, positional play, and discipline by Montreal.

The Quebec Nordiques and Houston Aeros were once again the toast of the WHA, which started with 12 teams on the season and ended with 11. Smooth-skating Real Cloutier finally found top spot in league scoring after two years of real promise. The super for-ward earned 141 points for the title, including 66 goals.

The "Swedish Express" Anders Hedberg went crazy in the goal-scoring category with 70, while Ulf Nilsson helped out with an outstanding 85 assists. Hedberg's big numbers were especially impressive early in the season when on February 6 against the Calgary Cowboys he set a new pro-hockey record, notching goals number 49, 50, and 51 in just 47 games. In the process of setting the record, Hedberg scored 11 goals in three games including two four-goal nights back to back. The NHL snobs, of course, refused to recognize the feat just like they refused to recognize the league.

American-born Robbie Ftorek was named the WHA's player of the year, another indication of how American players were also steadily improving NHL team rosters. Ftorek was a tricky, speedy little pivot man.

In the playoffs, Winnipeg and Quebec collided in an entertaining seven-game series with Quebec winning the final match. It was a strange, unpredictable series as the clubs seemed to take turns dominating each other. After a 2–1 Winnipeg opener, the goals flowed. Quebec won game two 6–1 with Winnipeg winning by the same score in game three. Quebec sneaked the only other close victory in game four and then easily won game five 8–3. Winnipeg scorers went wild in game six pounding Quebec 12–3. The Nordiques then bounced back again with a vengeance, winning the crucial final match 8–2. There was no consistency or continuity but it was exciting. The win for the Nordiques meant that the two top pro hockey leagues on the continent were dominated by teams from Quebec.

BEST NHL PLAYER: Guy Lafleur — Montreal
BEST WHA PLAYER: Real Cloutier — Quebec; Anders Hedberg — Winnipeg
BEST NHL LINE: Pete Mahovlich/Jacques Lemaire, Guy Lafleur, Steve Shutt — Montreal
BEST WHA LINE: Christian Bordeleau, Real Cloutier, Marc Tardif — Quebec
                    Ulf Nilsson, Anders Hedberg, Bobby Hull — Winnipeg

1977–78

Much of the off-season summertime chat was the fuss over Team Canada's dubious showing in the eight-team World Hockey Championships held in Vienna in late April and early May. Canada had not taken part in the tournament since 1969 when it quit in protest after the International Ice Hockey Federation refused to let Canada use professionals. This year, however, Canada was permitted to send a makeshift team of players eliminated from the playoffs. But even with the likes of Phil Esposito, Tony Esposito, Jim Rutherford, Pierre Larouche, Rod Gilbert, and Ron Ellis, Canada not only failed to win a medal, but didn't place a single player on the World All-Star team. Some members also played some very questionable hockey bordering on thuggery. Most Canadians felt upset and concerned about it.

The Czechs won it all with the two Stastny brothers strutting their stuff, Sweden second, the Soviets finished third, while Team Canada embarrassed themselves, and Alan Eagleson showed his true nature in front of the whole world. Following an 8–1 pasting by the Soviets, Eagleson berated an International Ice Hockey Federation official with insults and obscenities. He blamed the referees for Canada's deplorable on-ice conduct as well as the loss. There was no denying that the officiating had been bad, and even my 1972 hero, Esposito, said, "Canada should just stick to the Canada Cup every four years in Canada. I don't ever want to go through this kind of torment with the referees again. It just gives me ulcers and I don't need that." At the time I agreed with him.

Team Canada GM Derek Holmes had a different perspective, saying he was not proud of the intimidation trash. "The skill level is the difference. The Russians are masterful craftsmen and technicians. What else can I say? If you say anything critical [of Team Canada's rough play and behaviour] or even offer your opinions, you're branded a communist."

Before the NHL season began, a few other interesting off-ice moves took place, including the junior draft, more WHA merger talks, and the naming of former NHL chairman of the board John Ziegler as NHL president succeeding Clarence Campbell.

"Great, they just went from dumb to dumber — when it comes to hockey," I remember thinking at the time. Nothing I saw from Ziegler over the years gave me reason to think differently.

It was the year of the right-wing worries for New York Rangers. Star Rod Gilbert was one more player in a growing list to have problems with New York GM John Ferguson. Fergie was obviously cleaning out the old New York house and it seemed Rod was on the dustbin list. The veteran Ranger star finally asked to be traded and left the team for a couple of weeks. Midseason they signed retired Bruin Dallas Smith, and many suggested that Fergie wanted a Boston clone in New York as he kept grabbing former Bruins.

The Wings also grabbed goalie Ron Low from Washington and began their ascent out of the basement of the league. Bobby Kromm was the 10th coach for Detroit since the 1969–70 season. It would not be hard for Kromm to beat the team's previous season point total of 41 points. Meanwhile, Lindsay let it be known that he would gladly take over the Rod Gilbert problem in Detroit but the Big Apple did not bite. Sadly, Rod played just 19 games that year, retired, and then faded away.

The New York Islanders snagged a Laval junior sniper named Mike Bossy as their 15th overall draft choice, and if that wasn't the steal of the decade, I'm not sure what was. According to *Inside Sports Hockey*, when Bossy told Islander owner Bill Torrey he would score 50 goals for him, Torrey laughed. Bossy scored 53 and set a record for rookie goals in the process, finishing a remarkable sixth in the regular-season scoring parade. Everybody paid attention, and he was the obvious choice for the Calder Trophy at the end of the year.

For some reason I was in New York early in the 1977–78 season with Brian McFarlane (I think it was to see the Hanna-Barbera cartoon people to get the rights for *Peter Puck* in Canada), and there was a Saturday night game in New York — Islanders vs. Rangers. I said, "Brian, let's go." I thought it would be enjoyable to attend a game as just a spectator but it's a $25 cab ride from Broadway and we had to buy tickets, so I was surprised when Brian said, "Sure, should be fun."

During the warm-up I always watch goalies first. Islanders Chico Resch and Billy Smith were alternating between the pipes taking shots. I watched defenceman Denis Potvin take shots, then my gaze turned to centre Bryan Trottier, Clark Gillies, and finally a tall gangly kid on the right side doing line rushes with the puck.

"Who's the kid with 'Trotts'?" I asked Brian.

"That's their newest rookie, kid named Bossy. Good hands," McFarlane responded.

Good hands? What an understatement that was, as I was about

to see. I checked out the program stats. "Let's see . . . 'Mike Bossy, Islander's first pick in draft, fifteenth overall, a centre and right wing with Laval.' Hmmm, scored a lot of goals in junior all right. We'll see."

I remember thinking that if Bossy turned out okay, he'd be the first decent Islander draft pick since they grabbed Gillies in the first round and Trottier in the second of the 1974 draft. Potvin had been nabbed number one in the 1973 junior feast as well.

The Islanders opened the game with Trottier's line on first and Trottier snagged the face-off, plunked it perfectly onto the stick of Potvin at his own blueline; Potvin passed it over to Gillies, then back to Trottier — tic-tac-toe, from one end of the ice to the other. Trottier fed it back to Gillies, who fired a shot at the net, but young Bossy, in perfect position, missed the deflection. The puck bounced into the corner, Bossy wheeled into the deep slot while Gillies and Trottier fought a couple of Rangers for possession from the corner to behind the net. Bossy stayed deep, the puck squirted free, and it looked certain that Trottier was going to be the first to it. But Bossy burst past a deep checker, took the now obvious pass on the face off spot, made a quick fake, the goalie went down, and he tucked the shot high in the short side.

The red light flared angrily and I sat back with a grin.

"Geeze, he's going to be a great one. That kid is money in the bank," I chuckled. Brian just grinned and nodded his head.

Bossy had it all — timing, excellent hands, very good shot, competitive, and very smart. He was a brilliant performer and a natural goal scorer if ever there was one.

The kid knocked in a rookie record of goals (almost doubling my once-upon-a-time rookie record from many years before), and I was lucky enough to see a few of them. Over the next 10 seasons he played, Bossy shot 573 goals and tallied an amazing 1,126 points in just 752 regular-season games. Think about those numbers for just a couple of seconds and they become boggling.

While he'd been in junior hockey, the scouts had questioned his bravery. Some didn't think Bossy was aggressive or tough enough to perform in the NHL. An old buddy of mine, Billy Cupolo, who played for Boston, always claimed that a player "just has to be brave enough to go where he has to go to get the job done." Bossy was.

Fifteenth draft pick overall? Ha! The true test of a genuine sniper is what he does under pressure and the heat is never higher than in the playoffs. Few can match Bossy's performance in the extra season as well. In 129 playoff games, Mike notched 85 goals and 75 assists for 160 points, well over a point a game.

I don't know why he was never tagged "Machine Gun" Bossy — he was deadly enough with the puck.

Anyway, Bossy along with young centre Bryan Trottier, Denis Potvin, Clark Gillies, and goaltenders Billy Smith and Chico Resch were letting it be known that they had future plans for the Cup — when Montreal was done. However, the Habs were in no hurry. In fact it seemed their only weakness was their overall strength. The Montreal club and farm system was bursting with players who had great potential, but some were fleeing the system and signing with other teams or leagues because they had no chance to play and other teams were offering more money and glory. It was an enviable problem to have. From the goal out, Montreal was very deep in talent. Bunny (Michel) Laroque and Ken Dryden guarded the net, while the blueline talent was unbelievable as well. Larry Robinson, Serge Savard and Guy Lapointe were the superstars with defence support from Pierre Bouchard, Bill Nyrop, huge Gilles Lupien, and Brian Engblom. Yikes! Defensive forwards included Bob Gainey, Doug Jarvis, Doug Risebrough, and Mario Tremblay. No wonder nobody scored on those guys.

If that was not enough, Montreal's snipers included Yvan Cournoyer, Pierre Larouche, Rejean Houle, Pierre Mondou, and three guys named Guy Lafleur, Steve Shutt, and Jacques Lemaire.

Whenever I think about classy centremen with superb passing and play-making skills, the first name that pops into mind is Jacques Lemaire. While not a superstar, Lemaire certainly achieved star status as a famed Canadiens' pivot man. In 12 seasons (853 games) with Montreal, he scored 366 goals and 835 points and he was particularly brilliant in playoff action, earning 139 points in 145 games and winning eight Cups.

Jacques was born to do many things, but one of them, I'm sure, was to play centre and to play alongside Lafleur. High on the list of combinations of players who seemed to click over the years are Lemaire, Lafleur, and Shutt.

It was uncanny to watch Lemaire work, especially with Guy. When he gave the puck to The Flower, it was as if he could read Guy like a book — and he was the only player on the team who could. Guy played the game his way and nothing was planned. He played full-speed ahead and his basic attitude with his linemates was "Just follow me and when we get in trouble, I'll make something work. Just be there." Amazingly, Lemaire always was, and quite often so was defenceman Larry Robinson.

Lemaire instinctively filled in or went directly to the best offensive or defensive position according to Guy's movements. When I sat high in the broadcast area of the Forum, I'd marvel at Lemaire's understanding of Lafleur, as well as Shutt, the opposition, and the game as it should be played.

After his stint as Montreal Canadiens coach, he was still scouting for the club, and I often met him in a pub after a game and, my oh my, was he interesting to talk to. Jacques had the game and its complexities figured out pretty good, as his stint with New Jersey later showed. Oh, he never was too complimentary toward coach Scotty Bowman, but that was between him and Scotty. Lemaire played the game very well, but it was his mind, his insight, and his game knowledge that intrigued me.

However, I also believe that when Lemaire was a coach years later, his insistence that Lafleur play a "team" game and do more checking or play to a planned defence or offence took away Guy's creativity and caused him to retire six years too soon. Some day, somewhere, over a cold one I might learn the answer to that mystery.

During the 1977–78 season, however, Lemaire, his new linemates, and the rest of the powerful Habs were just too much for everybody else, and they won their division and league with 129 points. Detroit, while some distance behind, had climbed into second spot in the Norris Division with 78. Boston topped the Adams with 113 points, the Islanders won the Patrick race with 111 points while Chicago was the best of the worst, winning the pathetic Smythe Division.

Lafleur earned his third straight scoring title with 132 points on 60 goals. A hot Maple Leaf team, led by Sittler, upset the Islanders in the quarter finals of the playoffs but were then thumped by Montreal. Boston, meanwhile, sifted Chicago four straight and then defeated the Flyers in a robust five-game affair. Boston gave the Habs a fight but after six matches the powerful and balanced Habs had their third straight Stanley Cup rings.

During the second to last year of its existence, the WHA was showing cracks; the writing was on the wall when six teams formally applied for entry into the NHL. The two leagues even discussed a merger. NHL voters finally said no to the plan that summer but it was clearly only a matter of time.

Before the 1977–78 WHA season had begun, Phoenix, Calgary, and San Diego packed it in, the remaining eight teams forming one large division. As well, the teams played a touring Soviet Union team and a Czechoslovakian team once each, with the results counting as part of the regular season.

The Howe clan moved their skills to New England, joining Davey Keon, Johnny McKenzie, Ted Green, and some other familiar faces. In the playoffs, the big scrap came down to Howe, Keon, McKenzie, and the Whalers against the faster, regular-season champion Winnipeg Jets with the younger, swifter Canadian team winning the AVCO Cup.

BEST NHL PLAYER:	Guy Lafleur — Montreal
BEST WHA PLAYER:	Anders Hedberg — Winnipeg
BEST NHL LINES:	Jacques Lemaire, Guy Lafleur, Steve Shutt — Montreal; Bryan Trottier, Mike Bossy, Clark Gillies — New York Islanders
BEST WHA LINE:	Ulf Nilsson, Anders Hedberg, Bobby Hull — Winnipeg

1978-79

Swedish WHA stars Anders Hedberg and Ulf Nilsson signalled the start of the end of the WHA when they signed lucrative two-year deals with the New York Rangers prior to the start of the 1978–79 year. The deal was one of the first made by GM John Ferguson that made any sense and it was also one of his last. After the deal was cinched, but before Hedberg arrived, Ferguson and coach Jean-Guy Talbot were toast.

For the life of me I couldn't figure out the Rangers' firing of Ferguson. He was 15 games below .500 during the previous two years but with Hedberg, Nilsson, and top draft Ron Duguay, his seven and eight games below .500 would easily be eight to 10 games on the plus side above. The Rangers went on to have two plus years with Fred Shero as coach and general manager. As coach, Shero was fine, but not as a GM. The Flyers players had had it up to here with his witch-doctor routine and quit on him after a while; his style could work for a few years as coach, but not as a manager. The guy who had really made it all work back in Philly was Eddie Shore's top defenceman in the minors, Keith Allen. Allen was the best behind-the-scenes executive in hockey — not Shero. Freddy was a great coach, super hockey man with many great motivational tricks, but no GM. In two more seasons the Rangers tumbled again and so did Freddy the Fog.

But, in true Shero fashion, stuff happened right away that first year in New York. Ferguson had anticipated the Rangers would have an opening at the controversial right-wing position long before Don Murdoch received a 40-game suspension by Mr. Ziegler for his cocaine charge the summer before. Never a dull moment in New York. Aside from superstar Hedberg for the starboard position, the Rangers had also drafted youngster Duguay in 1977.

The Rangers made lots of noise while the rival Islanders simply grew up another year. Its metamorphosis would eventually make it a new hockey dynasty. The never-rattled, always calm Islander centre Bryan Trottier broke free of anyone else that year and in the end he rightfully earned the scoring championship with 47 goals and 134 points.

It had been many a year since New York hockey fans had much to cheer about, but in 1978–79, suddenly things changed. Not only were the Islanders and the Rangers chock-full of stars, but both teams were solid contenders for the Stanley Cup. As fate would have it, however, the two clubs met each other early in the playoffs, and when the subway series (so-called because both teams were in New York) was ended, the Rangers had upset the slightly favoured Islanders in six.

Reality hit New York hard and quick in the Cup finals, however. Montreal was caught off guard in the opening game, dropping the match 4–1, but that was all the wake-up they needed as Les Canadiens replied with four straight victories to earn their fourth mighty mug in a row.

Over in the WHA, without Gordie Howe and clan, Houston could not draw the crowds and folded in August, leaving just seven teams in the faltering league. Early in December, the Indianapolis Racers also collapsed, sending the league on the skids. Players from the club were distributed throughout the league. A coveted 17-year-old whiz-kid named Wayne Gretzky had gone to Edmonton in November.

In late December of 1978, Gretzky skated onto the ice for an Oilers-Cincinnati Stinger match and scored three times, recording his first pro hat-trick. The Stingers, led by young Mike Gartner and Robbie Ftorek, were impressed, as were the fans, and the Oilers won the game 5–2 to end a five-game losing streak. It was the start of something very, very special. With a rookie total of 110 points including 46 goals, Gretzky earned third spot overall in league scoring. Everyone said the skinny kid was pretty good, but would never last. Critics quickly suggested that sooner or later someone big would hit him and that would be the end of the lad. I had to admit that I also wondered how well he would survive in the hockey world.

In the playoffs it was the powerful Winnipeg Jets who won the AVCO Cup one more time. Without Hedberg and Nilsson, but with plenty of ex-Aeros, the Jets defeated Gretzky and his new Edmonton friends in the finals in six games. Dave Semenko scored with 12 seconds left in game six to register the WHA's final goal ever.

The season 1978–79 proved to be the WHA's final year. On March 22, 1979, the NHL agreed to take in four WHA teams for the next NHL season. Behind every cloud there is a silver lining, and such was the case with the demise of the upstart league. In its final season the WHA introduced one of the finest athletes of all time to pro hockey, Wayne Gretzky.

BEST NHL PLAYER: Marcel Dionne — Los Angeles
BEST WHA PLAYER: Real Cloutier — Quebec; Wayne Gretzky — Indianapolis/ Edmonton
BEST NHL LINE: Bryan Trottier, Mike Bossy, Clark Gillies — New York Islanders
BEST WHA LINE: Kent Nilsson, Terry Ruskowski, Morris Lukowich, — Winnipeg

THE BEST DECADE

When I reflect upon the past 50 years of hockey and look at the various decades, I suppose the 1970s would rank as the overall top 10 years. For pure joy of watching hockey played at its best, you can look to the Montreal dynasty teams of that decade. As a full-time broadcaster, I was constantly amazed and thrilled with the hockey displayed before me night after night by that team. In addition to the Habs, the '70s had the amazing talented Big Bad Boston Bruins at the beginning, then the fearsome Flyers, and later the emerging New York Islander dynasty. This decade also had the 1972 Summit Series, then other Soviet matches in 1974 and 1976 and the start of Canada Cups. For stars, superstars, and star-gazers, it was an amazing time that brought us Lafleur, Bossy, Perreault, Dionne, Potvin, Dryden, Sittler, Clarke, Trottier, and more of Orr, Esposito, Ratelle, Lemaire, Hull, Howe, Park, Parent . . .

It's one thing, and true, to say that the league and the WHA expanded too much and too fast, and that the quality of hockey was temporarily set back in the '70s. However, it is also fair to say that a tremendous number of talented players came into the league and brought amazing skills with them. The league recovered to a reasonably consistent high quality of hockey in short order. That was due to strong junior players coming into the league and the steady influx of European and American players.

Montreal's incredibly strong hold on the league as a powerhouse and dynasty should not be diminished by the realities of league expansion. Actually, in many ways that growth only adds to the amazing accomplishment of the Canadiens' ability to stay at the top. Montreal lost countless numbers of talented players, junior drafts and otherwise, who signed with other clubs, demanded trades, played in Europe, or quit the game because the Canadiens were just too solid a team to crack the line-up.

During the decade other powerful clubs would easily have reached true dynasty status if not for the mighty Habs simply never disappearing. Rarely did the league find more than two potential dynasty teams competing in the same era, but the '70s did. Boston, Philadelphia, and the Islanders were all very powerful clubs teetering on that dynasty title, while Buffalo was making lots of noise. For hockey fans it was an exciting and explosive decade of hockey. What a time to be in hockey — YAHOO!

DECADE'S BEST PLAYERS:	1. Bobby Orr 2. Guy Lafleur 3. Phil Esposito.
DECADE'S BEST LINES:	Jacques Lemaire, Guy Lafleur, Steve Shutt — Montreal Phil Esposito, Ken Hodge, Wayne Cashman — Boston Gilbert Perreault, Rene Robert, Richard Martin — Buffalo
WHA ALL TIME BEST PLAYERS:	André Lacroix, Bobby Hull
BEST LINE:	Ulf Nilsson, Anders Hedberg, Bobby Hull — Winnipeg

1970s DYNASTIES:	**Montreal Canadiens — 1971, 1973, 1976–79** (six Cups in nine seasons)
LEADERS:	Ken Dryden, Guy Lafleur, Steve Shutt, Larry Robinson, Jacques Lemaire, Jean Beliveau, Henri Richard, Serge Savard, Jacques Laperriere, Yvan Cournoyer
BLEEDERS:	Guy Lapointe, Peter Mahovlich, Frank Mahovlich, J.C. Tremblay, Rejean Houle, Claude Larose, Marc Tardif, Jim Roberts, Doug Risebrough, Bob Gainey, Mario Tremblay, Yvan Lambert, Pierre Larouche, Michael Laroque, Doug Jarvis, Pierre Bouchard, Rod Langway, John Ferguson
FEEDERS:	Terry Harper, Mark Napier, Bob Murdoch, Phil Roberto, Leon Rochefort, Chuck Lefley, Murray Wilson, Bill Nyrop, Rick Chartraw, Mike Polich, Pierre Mondou, Brian Engblom, Gilles Lupien, Bobby Sheehan, Cam Connor, Pat Hughes, Don Awrey
HONOURABLE MENTION:	**Boston Bruins, Philadelphia Flyers.**
	Boston Bruins: 1970, 1972 (two Cups); Cup finalists in '74, '77, '78
LEADERS:	Bobby Orr, Phil Esposito, Johnny Bucyk, Gerry Cheevers, Ken Hodge, Brad Park, Jean Ratelle, Wayne Cashman
BLEEDERS:	Ed Westfall, Dallas Smith, Ed Johnston, John McKenzie, Derek Sanderson, Fred Stanfield, Rick Smith, Ted Green, Gregg Sheppard, Terry O'Reilly, Don Awrey, Peter McNab, Bobby Schmautz, Rick Middleton, Gilles Gilbert, Carol Vadnais, Gary Doak, Mike Milbury
FEEDERS:	Bill Speers, Don Marcotte, Jim Lorentz, Ron Grahame, Bill Lesuk, Wayne Carleton,

Garnet Bailey, Mike Walton, André Savard,
Dave Forbes, Rich Leduc, Darryl Edestrand,
Al Sims, Matti Hagman, Earl Anderson,
John Wensink, Stan Jonathon, Bob Miller,
Dennis O'Brien

Philadelphia Flyers 1974, 1975
(finalists in '76 and '80)

LEADERS: Bobby Clarke, Reg Leach, Bernie Parent,
Rick MacLeish, Bill Barber

BLEEDERS: Joe Watson, Ed Van Impe, André Dupont,
Bill Flett, Orest Kindrachuk, Terry Crisp,
Tom Bladon, Bob Kelly, Jimmy Watson, Mel
Bridgman, Ross Lonsberry, Ken Linseman,
Paul Holmgren, Simon Nolet, Pete Peeters,
Barry Ashbee

FEEDERS: Dave Schultz, Don Saleski, Larry Goodenough,
Ted Harris, Gary Dornhoefer, Bruce Cowick,
Jack McIlhargey, Terry Murray, Wayne
Stephenson, Bill Clement, Bob Dailey, Behn
Wilson, Mike Busniuk, Tom Gorence, John
Paddock, Norm Barnes, Al Hill, Phil Myre

STOP IT THERE, BACK IT UP!

■ ■ ■

The expression "The more things change the more they stay the same" perfectly summarizes the National Hockey League, especially during the 1980s. For starters, the tradition of two or three solid hockey teams carving out dynasties continued during the new decade — but the uniforms and names changed. Instead of the Red Wings, Leafs, or Bruins, it was the Islanders, Oilers, and Flames who claimed the title "champions." Even the mighty Canadiens who'd owned the league for the better part of the previous 30 years picked up just one Stanley Cup in the decade.

Other similarities between the 1980s and earlier decades included the arrival of key dominant players, further expansion, the WHA teams, plenty of controversy, and several more European and American players joining the regular NHL ranks. Indeed, the decade held highlights and low points, joys and sorrows, heroes and villains, and once again I was lucky enough to be part of it all.

The flip of the calendar to a new decade seemed to symbolize that it was also time to pass on the dynasty torch. After years of threatening, the matured and honed New York Islanders finally stepped up and grabbed the mantle at the end of the 1979–80 season. New York was led by a core of Canadian-born stars including solid centre Bryan Trottier, pure sniper Mike Bossy, rugged Clark Gillies, superb blueliner Denis Potvin, and goalies Chico Resch and the guy I dubbed "Wild" — Billy Smith. The Islanders totally dominated the race for the Cup during the first four years of the decade.

After Trottier, Bossy, and the rest of the crew were done their run, it was time for the powerful Edmonton Oilers to place a chokehold on the Cup. The Oilers won Lord Stanley's mug five times in seven seasons (four times in five years) between 1984 and 1990. Only Montreal and Calgary interrupted their string.

The 1960s had Howe, Richard, Beliveau, Sawchuk . . . and the 1970s featured Hull, Esposito, Orr, Lafleur, Dryden . . . but the 1980s brought us "The Magicians." No other players came close to dominating the decade like Wayne Gretzky and, later, Mario Lemieux.

The deceptive, intuitive, brilliant Gretzky absolutely smashed every goal-scoring and point record he could reach during the decade. In the process, he also led his dazzling collection of teammates to four titles. Joined by the likes of Mark Messier, fast-skating Paul Coffey, Finnish superstar Jari Kurri, and goalies Andy Moog and Grant Fuhr, the Oilers were a machine unmatched, except perhaps by the Canadiens of the late 1960s and early '70s. The Oilers were the first club to crack the mark of 400 goals scored in a season and did it a number of times. Once again, the majority of the club was made up of Canadian-born players, with Kurri emerging as the NHL's first genuine consistent superstar from Europe.

Lemieux was magic from the moment he stepped into the Steel City. Mario is a big man and few hockey players of similar size have ever shown near the amount of dexterity and fluidity that he did. Lemieux was smooth, graceful, and incredibly coordinated, not to mention strong as an ox. Sadly for Mario, he had few skilled teammates during his first two or three years in the league. He was largely surrounded by plumbers and diggers.

The brilliance of Gretzky and Lemieux diminished the incredible skills and performances of other tremendous players during that decade, including the talented Marcel Dionne in L.A. After carrying the Kings for a couple of seasons by himself, Dionne was finally united on a forward line with regular wingers Dave Taylor on the right side, and recruited NHL retread and CHL and AHL star Charlie Simmer on the left. The trio clicked immediately and "The Triple Crown Line" was born, led by the bright light Dionne at pivot position.

The '80s boasted the slick skills of the amazing Slovak brothers Peter, Marion, and Anton Stastny — all with Quebec. The decade also featured a crew of high-quality, speedster, rearguard snipers in Paul Coffey, Denis Potvin, Mark Howe, and Bruin super-sensation Ray Bourque. Up front there was the gritty and talented Mark Messier, the smooth Steve Yzerman, the continued brilliance of Trottier and Bossy, and the arrival of young Brett Hull.

It was a decade of tremendous scoring output, surpassing in average goals and points any other time period. Starting in the late 1970s and running throughout the entire 1980s, the top 10 scoring race was filled with 100 plus point-getters. That trend slowed down again late in the following decade when clutch-and-grab hockey, and a level of parity, again hit the league.

The 1980s marked more growth for me in the broadcasting business as I worked a number of games as an analyst with the BCTV network in Vancouver in addition to my regular *Hockey Night in Canada* broadcasts. Most of my time in Vancouver was spent working with CTV. Bernie Pascal did play by play, the very talented and delightful Jim Robson and Jim Hughson of TSN largely covered Vancouver Canucks games. I also got to know CTV colour and CKNW radio man John McKeechie (another immensely talented and very funny man) along with the other tremendous media folks in the Vancouver area.

Later during the decade I also worked with NBC and got to know hockey and sports director Scotty Connell very well and we became good friends.

1979-80

The shift into the new decade was appropriately saluted with the merger of the World Hockey Association and the National Hockey League. Four teams — Edmonton, Hartford, Winnipeg, and Quebec — made the shift, while the remainder of the WHA clubs became mere trivia. Long negotiations took place before the merger (or expansion, takeover, absorption, buy-out, depending upon your view) was completed. The result, however, was very significant. The league exploded from 17 to 21 teams with a balanced 80-game schedule.

In my view, the four clubs were taken to the cleaners when they joined the NHL, and most folks I knew figured the same way. Many fans, broadcasters, and other media wanted to see the WHA teams integrate as they were, intact, into the league. Many of us wanted to see how well they would actually compete, but Ziegler and the greedy NHL brass were not about to let that happen.

The feeding frenzy began when the four WHA teams were allowed to keep only two goalies and two skaters in the "re-entry" draft, and the NHL clubs then pillaged and plundered to their hearts content. Some of the "parent" NHL clubs had waited a number of years to get their pound of flesh back from the bandit league, and they relished the opportunity when it finally arrived. When the dark day was finally over, some of the NHL teams (who'd mauled the WHA survivors by claiming back or drafting new players not protected by the fledgling four) still claimed to be unhappy.

Despite the pillage party, the "new" clubs all managed to protect more than four of their original club members through a series of deals including trades, understandings, retirements, and comebacks, and cash deals with individual NHL clubs.

The Edmonton Oilers came out looking fairly good considering they'd lost their five top defencemen, including Paul Shmyr, Dave Langevin, and Risto Siltanen when they entered the NHL. But GM Larry Gordon (at the start of the year) and coach Glen Sather quickly got to work. When the season began, they had a roster including Wayne Gretzky, Dave Dryden, Kevin Lowe, Mark Messier,

Lee Fogolin, Blair MacDonald, Brett Callighen, and a university kid named Glenn Anderson. As the future would show, not bad, though at the time they were a bunch of no-names to most of us in the broadcast booth.

Quebec looked like the team to beat of the four WHA new kids as they managed to secure some stars and steal a few others. The Nordiques boasted a starting roster that included sniper Real Cloutier, Serge Bernier, Marc Tardif, Michel Goulet, Robbie Ftorek, goalie Richard Brodeur, Paul Baxter, and junior drafts Dale Hunter and Lee Norwood.

The badly depleted Jets decided to load up with toughness to compete in their first NHL season.

The Whalers paraded Gordie Howe in their line-up, along with another long-tooth smoothy in Davey Keon. Hartford had further skill in the two Howe boys, Mark and Marty, on defence joining Rick Ley, John Garrett between the pipes, and André Lacroix and Mike Rogers up front. Interesting but not threatening.

It seemed that while no NHL team was about to cut any mercy or slack toward helping one of the "new" clubs, neither were they pre-pared to help, in any way, their own NHL brethren. Either way, the WHA newcomers certainly were mangled badly before their inau-gural NHL season, and it was not a particularly warm welcome to the family.

The addition of the four WHA teams, the re-entry draft, and recent previous league expansion meant a thinning of the player pool. That in turn led to further recruiting of European and American players. Canadians no longer had a monopoly on the NHL job market.

Ironically, one of the NHL's best went the other way. Jacques Lemaire shocked many when he announced he was leaving the Canadiens to take a job as player-coach in Switzerland.

More than 100 other players changed positions before the 1979–80 season began. Eight coaches were replaced for the start of the season, including Don Cherry, who headed to Colorado, Floyd Smith to Toronto, Fred Creighton to Boston, and Scotty Bowman left Montreal for Buffalo. Bernie Geoffrion started the season as coach with the Habs, but was replaced halfway through by Claude Ruel.

In that remarkable year, which was filled with many firsts, it was teenager Wayne Gretzky who truly dazzled the watching world and stole the spotlight. Few heralded stars ever manage to match the hyped expectations that await them in the pro pressure-cooker world of hockey, but Wayne did. In fact he left most fans in awe, and he left me scrambling for replay footage in every game.

Gretzky, playing with wingers Brett Callighen and B.J. MacDonald, scored 51 goals and assisted on 86 other markers for an amazing 137 points. Not bad for a kid many experts continued to predict was one hard bodycheck away from oblivion.

"I've been hearing that forever, Mr. Meeker. Every league I've played in they said the same thing and guys have tried to knock me down, take me out of the play, but I'm still here. I think and hope I can handle most of the rough stuff and hits in the NHL," Wayne told me during that first season. "I like to go into corners or go behind the net to set up goals, and to do that I must expect to get hit. Mainly, though, I just try to keep moving my feet. Let's face it, if I just stood in front of the net or the slot like Esposito or bigger players can, I'd get killed. People think I'm clever or crafty and that's why I get away from bodychecks, but in fact I just get out of the way to save my life, to stay alive," Gretzky grinned.

For years after that initial conversation with Wayne, I looked closely to try to find him in the corners, with the puck or fighting for it. He was forever behind the net, but in the corners? Never.

The Oilers, however, were paying less-talented people good money to work the corners, and Wayne had enough sense to spend as little time as possible along the fence. When he absolutely had to, and the situation (such as in the playoffs) called for corner work, he was there. It was 15 years before anyone made him pay the price.

Hitting Gretzky was easier said than done. When Winnipeg was at the top of their game with Nilsson, Hedberg, and Hull leading the way in the WHA, they had another pretty good Swedish performer in defenceman Lars Sjoberg. I watched him play quite a bit and he was big, strong, mobile, a good puck handler, and tough. Best of all he liked to hit.

In 1979–80, about halfway through Gretzky's first full year in the

NHL, I was in Winnipeg to televise an Oilers-Jet game. Wayne was tearing up the league. I cornered Lars coming out of the dressing room after the game day morning skate and naturally the conversation turned to the kid superstar who would be the Jets' problem that evening.

"Lars, no one lays a glove on this kid. You mean to tell me that you can't catch him in a corner and make him pay the price?" I confronted him.

"Honest, I try. I go in the corner behind him and yet he leaves me standing there lost when he goes out with the puck. Sometimes two of us go in, both with the idea of taking the body. Geeze, you feel sheepish when he beats us both. Howie, the kid's got eyes in the back of his head. We couldn't hit him with a handful of beans," Lars said, shaking his head.

I often recall that conversation with Lars, especially when I hear some diehard say, "They would have killed Gretzky in the old six-team league." Pure rubbish. Hell, we weren't fast enough (or even all that big and tough) back then, or smart enough to have caught Gretzky with a friggin' string of fishing nets.

Wayne's amazing first NHL season point production left him tied for first place with Marcel Dionne in the individual point-scoring championship. Dionne's 53 goals, however, gave the veteran King centre the title.

I remember, aside from Gretzky, watching another amazing young defenceman in a Bruin uniform emerge as a star that year, and his name was Raymond Bourque. From the first game I broadcast with him playing I was a fan. Ray was not Bobby Orr nor was he trying to be, yet few players have ever come close to being the same offensive threat and dominance from the blueline position. Bourque not only possessed beautiful skating, passing, and stickhandling skills, but had a hard, deadly accurate shot. His impressive skills earned him Rookie of the Year honours that year, and my respect over the next 20 years. Ray consistently remained a superstar for two decades and continued to be one of the best rearguards at safely moving the puck out of his own end. Tremendous talent and absolutely amazing timing.

One night while I was working a game in Toronto early in the season, Ralph Mellanby came to me and said, "Howie, your Saturday scheduled game in Montreal — you can't work it."

"Sure I can," I said. "I can get off from CJON-TV [St. John's] in time for the flights."

"That's not the problem. I just got word from the public relations man there that Montreal management has vetoed your presence. In other words, they won't let you work in his building."

I was shocked and a little ticked off, to say the least. Still, Mr. Grundman had the hammer and it was myself and hockey fans who were hurt by it. For five years, none of us could find out why I had been banned, and I never pushed the point, though I realize now that I should have. However, Dick Irvin thought the reason revolved around a Leaf-Canadiens game I worked the year before, when in a very excited moment, and referring to the Leafs, I said "we" instead of "Toronto, visitors, Leafs, guys in blue," anything but "we." The implication was that, as a broadcaster, I favoured that team.

I suspect Scotty Bowman was originally part of the decision to have me eventually booted from the Forum. Apparently the next morning at a Canadiens practice after the game at which I'd made the critical comment, Bowman called reporters over and complained about what I'd said.

The 1979–80 season also saw the emergence of L.A. winger Charlie Simmer as a scorer. The year before Kings' coach (and Simmer's old minor-pro coach) Bob Pulford was in need of a left winger and decided to call up Charlie from the Springfield scrap heap. Simmer instantly connected with Dionne and Dave Taylor and the Kings were suddenly a team to watch. The line started off just as hot in the 1979–80 year and lit up the league all season.

At the end of the year, Bourque joined veteran Larry Robinson on the first All-Star team defence, while Lafleur claimed his traditional right-wing honours. Dionne edged Gretzky for the slot position while Simmer was so impressive he won the left-wing nod. Gretzky did not qualify for the rookie award due to his WHA service.

Montreal owned the Norris Division with 107 points, 33 ahead of second-place Los Angeles Kings. Buffalo, Philadelphia, and

Chicago won their respective divisions but the standings meant little as an absurd 16 of the 21 teams made the playoffs.

I ranted and raved, saying the regular season was obviously a stupid waste of time and that it meant not a galdarn, cotton-picking thing — nothing, zilch! (I think those were the words I used!) Still, the opening round had some exciting hockey. Edmonton and Hartford qualified for the extra round and if not for key injuries so would have the Nordiques.

Just before the trading deadline, the New York Islanders picked up Butch Goring from the Los Angeles Kings for Dave Lewis and others, and though Lewis was a very solid defenceman, Goring would turn out to be a vital cog in the next couple years of Islander history. As a Los Angeles Kings centre for more than eight years, Butch Goring was durable, consistent on offence (he averaged close to 70 points and 30 goals a year), and while on defence checked and worked as hard as anyone. If he was not the best second line centre in the league, he was certainly not far off. During 1978–79 the little buzz saw had 87 points, including 36 goals, but they still traded him, believe it or not. It was robbery in the realm of Boston abusing the Canucks by stealing Cam Neely.

For the next five years, Goring played second and third line centre for the Stanley Cup winners. He was outstanding at killing penalties and played the second shift on the power play. He even won a Conn Smythe Trophy as the playoff MVP and deserved every inch of it.

No wonder the Kings have been sucking air ever since, knowing how good Butch Goring was. He was not by any means a graceful or skilled hockey player. In my view, Goring was a hacker, grabber, pusher, holder, tripper, elbower . . . He got a piece of everyone he ever went after, with stick, body, skate, hand, and he was a first-class lunch-pail hockey player. But Geeze, I can't ever remember him going to the penalty box.

His stats have to be wrong. In ten and a half years with the Kings, five years in New York, and half a season in Boston, Goring managed just 102 penalty minutes. In 1,107 games, the way he played and he only got 102 minutes?

For four straight seasons he received just one minor penalty each year. In 1980–81 he never received a single penalty even though he played in 78 games. Unreal. Absolutely amazing. He should go to the Hall of Fame on that alone.

Oh yeah, he picked up 888 points during all those games as well.

Revenge was almost immediate for Butch as the Islanders defeated L.A. in their opening round of the playoffs three games to one, including an 8–1 pasting in the first game. With Goring taking a leadership role, the Islanders also eliminated Boston in five games and then the talented Buffalo Sabres in six.

In the Stanley Cup final series led by Mike Bossy, Denis Potvin, Trottier, and the emotional net-minding of Billy Smith, the Islanders edged the tough and talented Flyers in six games to win the Cup. Bossy scored four goals and had 11 points in the finals, while Potvin had nine points including five goals.

BEST PLAYERS:	Marcel Dionne — Los Angeles; Wayne Gretzky — Edmonton
BEST LINES:	Marcel Dionne, Dave Taylor, Charlie Simmer — Los Angeles
	Mike Rogers, Blaine Stoughton, Pat Boutette — Hartford
	Pierre Larouche, Guy Lafleur, Steve Shutt — Montreal

1980–81

Two Czech superstar brothers, Peter and Anton Stastny, arrived in Quebec in dramatic fashion in 1980 and were the start of a wave of European players who would influence a shift in the NHL game. Their skating and wide-open passing plays helped change NHL hockey by increasing the tempo and further nullifying the recent goon tactics. In the hands of these hockey craftsmen, power plays became precision instruments of destruction.

The Stastny brothers had defected from the Czech National Team during a tournament in Austria, flew to Canada, and quickly joined the Nordiques. The defection caused considerable international discussion; however, the two would be joined by their older brother (and Czech hockey legend), Marian Stastny, the following season with Czech hockey sanctioning. In February that first season, Peter picked up four goals and four assists in an 11–7 pasting of Gary Green's Washington Capitals. His younger brother Anton, playing on the same line, had a remarkable three goals and five assists for eight points as well. The 16-point combination is the most ever scored by brothers in one game. That incredible performance made everyone sit up and take note.

A number of solid rookies came into the league, including defenceman Paul Coffey (sixth pick), Larry Murphy (fourth), and a sharp-shooting centre named Denis Savard (third). It was Savard, or rather his lack of selection by Les Canadiens as the first draft pick overall, that I believe contributed to my ban from the Forum. For a number of years starting that season, I was barred from working in the Montreal Forum, though Canadiens' management would deny it.

When Sam Pollock had been running things for Montreal, I had a good working relationship with the hockey club though the Francophone technicians were a major problem. I sat upstairs beside Dick and Danny with a telephone line hooked to the tape recorder. I had a hard time getting the technician to answer the phone and when he did, he spoke mainly in French or screwed up the in and the out of the action I wanted or would show something completely different than I had asked for. The union was so strong nothing could be done. That really made it hard for me to do the job. Still, it was an absolute pleasure working a game in the Forum, seeing the city, the people, staying at the Mount Royal Hotel — ah, now that was first-class. The city itself, well there's none more exciting, and the hockey teams were always top notch. On top of that being at the Forum meant working with the very talented Danny Gallivan and Dick Irvin. Folks, there were none better. As a bonus Red Fisher and other press were real good folk. To be paid for "working" such an exciting weekend made it even better.

Anyhow, Sam Pollock left the club. Rumour has it (and it comes from a pretty good source) that while Scotty Bowman was doing so well as coach for the Canadiens, he had offers to work elsewhere.

To keep Bowman with the Canadiens, Pollock intimated when he retired he would recommend that Scotty become general manager. So what happens? Instead of making Scotty Bowman the general manager, the Montreal owners hired Irving Grundman for the job. Grundman ran a bowling alley and was involved in the operation of the Forum. Well, the guy might have known a five-pin bowling ball from a 10-pin, but what he knew about hockey, and the people who play it, you could write on the head of a pin. So Grundman took over, Bowman hit the road, and the hockey team went into the whizzer (by Montreal standards).

Unless you were a hermit moose hunter stuck in the middle of nowhere, you knew that the best junior hockey player available in the draft was Denis Savard. The small but speedy French Canadian centre was already a legend in Quebec and had played most of his hockey in the Forum for the famous Junior Canadiens. The Quebecois fans were just itching for another young Lafleur, Beliveau, Geoffrion, or Richard. But instead of choosing Savard, the all-mighty Mr. Grundman overruled the majority of his scouts and selected Doug Wickenheiser, a tall, scoring Regina Pat centre from western Canada. With due respect to Wickenheiser, who was certainly talented, he was not the potential buzz-saw star that Savard was, nor, again unlike Savard, was he a French Canadian sensation who was (and still is) of great significance to Hab fans. Everybody went crazy saying Grundman had screwed up.

Years later, when Denis was on the downside of his career, the Habs finally brought him home to Montreal. But in the process they gave up the youthful and very talented Chris Chelios.

All of this happened at a time that I was terribly disappointed in Toronto's performance, and with the club itself, and I praised (some even suggested preached) the Canadiens' skills and work ethic. If there was a team in the league that I respected more than anyone else, it was the Canadiens.

Either way, Savard had a hell of a rookie season for Chicago and career and I felt good about that at least. Another rookie came along that year with a dashing name and equally interesting style for Minnesota — Dino Ciccarelli.

I admire the little guy as a hockey player. What a talent, along with an understanding of the game, what hand-eye coordination, what balls, and, geeze, what meanness. Funny though, I remember that was not my first impression of the kid from Sarnia, Ontario, with the Italian-sounding name that broadcasters loved to roll off their lips.

Dino was first stuck in Minnesota when he arrived in the National Hockey League, and *Hockey Night in Canada* didn't get to broadcast many of his games, especially in his first year, when he played just 32 times. However, the North Stars visited Maple Leaf Gardens one night and I scratched a few notes about Ciccarelli.

"What a competitor, no doubt. He has excellent timing, and goes to net at the exact right second. On the negative side, sure he can score goals but he's not too good with the puck, and isn't a very good passer especially out of his own zone or coming through centre ice. He will eventually get killed or seriously injured (because he's so small)," I scribbled.

Well, I was right about the "rights" and wrong about the "wrongs." That same year in the playoffs, and again the next year, we saw a lot more of Minnesota, and did Dino improve his game or what? Early the next season, the North Stars were in Toronto and by the second period I couldn't believe what the kid was doing with the puck. Tape-to-tape 10-foot, 30-foot, 50-foot passes from anywhere on the ice to open teammates. By far (and keep in mind it was the Canadiens they were playing) he was the best passer on the ice. Holy smokes, what a metamorphosis.

"How the hell did he do that in such a short time?" I asked myself.

It didn't take long to find out.

As Minnesota improved, we seemed to cover more of their games, and I along with the other on-air broadcast crew always went to the game-day morning skate for both teams. Dino would be first on the ice with a pail of pucks and shoot 25 or 30 at the posts and crossbar from the deep slot area. Nine out of 10 would hit iron. He would then go to the goal line, directly behind the face-off spot, stand so the heel of his stick was on the goal line, and shoot for the far post, then the crossbar, then the near post. Honest, folks, nine out of 10 shots would hit their target. A shooter or what? Yikes! We could have used him back in 1944.

One day years later when Dino was spinning his magic for the Red Wings, I was in their dressing room checking out sticks and skates, something I always do, and I came to Ciccarelli's and picked it up. It was perfectly balanced and felt just like my fly rod. The new-fangled sticks today with their wood, fiberglass, or aluminum shafts and replaceable blades are amazing.

I put the blade on the floor and my next thought was, "It *feels* like my fly rod — but it *looks* like my nine iron." It had an almost wedge shape at the bottom, which would certainly roof any puck. Then the light went on why he can put the puck almost straight up in the air. He laughed when I mentioned it to him after the practice; he gave me one of his sticks but advised that I take the existing blade off knowing I didn't have the skill to carry, pass or shoot the puck with that blade. He suggested I use one of the other three that he's personally designed and uses, one with less angle and loft.

Anyhow, Dino Ciccarelli had a gift but he also worked, and worked, and worked at improving his skills. Even in the early twilight of his career in 1996–97 playing with Tampa Bay for 77 games, he smoked in 35 goals and tallied 60 points. (*Nobody* gets 35 in Tampa Bay!) He'd easily have notched 50 playing for a real hockey team.

By the end of the 1996–97 season, Dino had played 1,156 regular-season games and tallied 1,160 points, including 586 goals. He recorded six years of 40 or more goals, including two seasons of netting 50 or more. As well, Ciccarelli snagged 118 points in the playoffs, including 73 goals, 14 of them in the 1980–81 run. To me, those are Hall of Fame numbers.

Even as a real long-tooth playing in just 14 games for Florida in the 1998–99 season, an injured and aged Ciccarelli showed his stuff. Dino scored six goals and an assist, including five of his six on the power play. Always a sniper.

Dino apparently got himself in a variety of snags outside of the arena during his younger days (he had a habit of taking out garbage bags naked) and yet continued through the controversies to produce well. It will be interesting to see if his on-ice skills are acknowledged in the future despite his bad-boy reputation off ice (valid or not). In my mind, there's no doubt that a spot should be getting cleared off right now at the Hall of Fame for the kid.

Meanwhile, in year two of his NHL career, Wayne Gretzky started to hit his full stride, and it was a full dozen steps ahead of all the rest. Like cream, he soon separated himself from the rest of the league. When the year was over, Wayne had amassed an unbelievable 164 points on 55 goals and 109 assists, breaking Esposito's old total point record.

Any sceptics about his talents by that point couldn't be taken seriously.

Next to the Stastny caper, the story of the year was the play of the Islanders and the surprisingly strong St. Louis Blues. Led by coach Red Berenson and GM Emile Francis, the Blues climbed into the upper echelon with strong goaltending and a couple of bright young forwards. Francis had selected goalie Mike Liut in the re-entry draft and was credited with most of the St. Louis improvement. He was brilliant all season. Centre Bernie Federko was again solid, grabbing a terrific 104 points for the Blues combined with his solid wingers Blair Chapman, a former Kelowna (B.C.) Buckaroo junior star, and Viking, Alberta, hero Brian Sutter.

However, the swift New York Islanders were like sharks on the scent of blood when it came to the Stanley Cup. After their first taste of the championship, the Islanders took a liking to the title and would not let go. They could play the game any way you wanted and win. Despite (once again) the wrong predictions of numerous "hockey experts," the Islanders showed they'd been no fluke the year before and took all the marbles. At the end of the year, they led the Patrick and the league with 110 points.

In the playoffs, the Islanders defeated Toronto, Edmonton, and the Rangers prior to meeting the Minnesota North Stars in the finals. It was a long and bumpy road to say the least. Minnesota had fought hard to get to their first final series ever and dumped Boston, Buffalo, and Calgary on the way.

In the finals, it was a battle of right wingers, with the Islanders sending out Mike Bossy against the North Stars' big dipper rookie Ciccarelli — another pure goal scorer. In the end it was Bossy who won the shoot-out as the Islanders won the Cup in five games.

Bossy set a new playoff record with 17 goals and 18 assists for 35 points in 18 games, including a record nine power-play goals. Ciccarelli set two new playoff marks for rookies with 21 points and 14 goals. Dynamo Butch Goring won the Conn Smythe Trophy, and the trade looked even better for the Isle.

BEST PLAYERS: Wayne Gretzky — Edmonton; Mike Bossy —
New York Islanders
BEST LINES: Marcel Dionne, Dave Taylor, Charlie Simmer —
Los Angeles
Bryan Trottier, Mike Bossy, Clark Gillies —
New York Islanders
Peter Stastny, Anton Stastny, Michel Goulet —
Quebec
Wayne Gretzky, Jari Kurri, and Mark Messier/Dave
Semenko/Glenn Anderson — Edmonton

1981–82

Just when I thought I'd seen it all, Gretzky went absolutely nuts in the point production parade. He was truly brilliant to watch and I spent many an hour, on camera and off, shaking my head in disbelief at some of the creative things he did. No one could think with the puck like Gretzky. Only a few had ever shown similar skill: Orr, Lafleur, Mikita. All of them had that special touch, that hockey sense and instinct, the ability to be at the right place at the right time, to move before thought but still think, a gift for the game. But even then — Gretzky was in another realm, another league of understanding and perception.

In 1981–82 Wayne put on a show that was unparalleled to that point. Like most of the sports world, we sat in the press boxes and TV control vans across two nations and stared in amazement.

The incredible 21-year-old centre scored a record 92 goals,

shattering Espo's 76, and set another record with 120 assists for an astounding third record of 212 points. Holy Jumpin' Jehoshaphat, ya can't beat that folks! Suuuupperrr! That's hockey!

Wayne scored a stupefying 50 goals in just 39 games that year and set a record for three or more goal performances of 10 games. His team jumped from 15th spot the year before to second overall at the end of the season, making him the first ever unanimous choice as the Hart Trophy winner for the league's Most Valuable Player.

On another level was the remainder of the NHL scoring parade that saw Mike Bossy finish second overall on 64 goals and 83 assists for 147 points and Peter Stastny third with 139.

The Islanders repeated as the powerhouse in the regular season, finishing atop the league with 118 points. Edmonton was second overall at 111 and led the Smythe Division with Montreal finishing third overall and on top of the Adams Division at 109. Minnesota topped the Norris with 94 points.

Oilers' left winger Messier certainly earned his spot on the first All-Star team alongside Gretzky and Bossy. I think that's the best forward line ever on a first All-Star team, even though two of them had not yet fully matured on blades. At that time Bossy was in the prime of his career, but both Messier and Gretzky were still two or three years away from being their best. All three had excellent skills with the puck and the brain. All could play in a crowd, score at will, and set up perfect plays.

Bossy had excellent timing, great hands, and a good shot and could score and contribute in any kind of game.

Messier was just a teensie-weensie bit behind Wayne and Mike in the above skills, but he had two things needed by the others to make them work. He was tough and mean. Because he was powerful, unpredictable, unforgiving, a fierce competitor, and played to win in any way, shape, or form you wanted, Mark was feared. He created an atmosphere in which the other two would excel and he didn't do too badly over the years in the atmosphere he mainly created.

Despite the heroics of Gretzky and Messier, the league dominance still belonged to the guys from Long Island. In fact, the Oilers never got started in the playoffs, getting upset in the first round by Dionne and the Kings. The Islanders defeated Pittsburgh, the Rangers, Quebec, and finally the Vancouver Canucks on their way to a third straight Cup.

The final series in Vancouver was particularly exciting not only because it was in my backyard (just a puddle jump from Parksville on Vancouver Island, where I was living), but also because of the white-towel frenzy. In the second game of the Blackhawks' series, coach Roger Neilson, incensed at the officiating, waved a white towel on the end of a hockey stick in mock surrender to the referee. The gesture and symbolism caught on with the Vancouver fans and led to a sea of white towels in the finals. It became known as the White-Towel Series, and in no time the Canucks had indeed surrendered.

In a take-no-prisoner mannerism, Bossy, Trottier, and crew marched through the Canucks in four straight games with Bossy earning the Conn Smythe Trophy. Three Islanders set playoff records with Bossy getting seven goals in the final four-game series, Trottier earning 23 assists in 19 games, and Smith tying his own record of 15 playoff wins. The Islanders also became the first U.S. team in history to win three consecutive Stanley Cups.

BEST PLAYER: Wayne Gretzky — Edmonton
BEST LINE: Wayne Gretzky, Jari Kurri, and Dave
Semenko/Mark Messier — Edmonton
Bryan Trottier, Mike Bossy, Clark Gillies —
New York Islanders
Peter Stastny, Marion Stastny, Anton Stastny —
Quebec

1982–83

The Boston Bruins continued to be a strong club in the early 1980s, led by Barry Pederson, Ray Bourque, Rick Middleton, and others. Not dominant but strong, and that season they topped the league after the regular season with 110 points on the year. Philadelphia topped the Patrick with 106. Chicago with 104 won the Norris, and Edmonton with 106 were leaders of the Smythe.

Once again it was the amazing Great One who ran wild in his own little world, outdistancing the next nearest player in the scoring race by 72 points. Wayne amassed 71 goals and 125 assists for 196 points. Peter Stastny was second at 124 while Chicago's fiery little centre Denis Savard (much in the Mikita mould) finished third with 121 points. Those three centres just amazed me all year.

Bossy picked up 60 goals, while Dionne finished in fifth with 56 goals and 107 points. It was Dionne's seventh season in a row in which he broke the 100-point mark, and that was a new league record. Three other Edmonton Oilers crashed the top 10 in scoring: Messier, Glenn Anderson, and Jari Kurri.

It was also a bounce-back year of sorts for Charlie Simmer, who finally appeared to have recovered from his serious broken leg of two years before. Simmer tallied 80 points.

It was a different goalie, however, who earned my laurels and glory in the part of the year that really counts. "Wild" Billy Smith turned around a bad ending to the year and cleaned up in the play-offs, setting the league on its head in the process. Billy won the Conn Smythe Trophy after allowing just six goals in the final series' four-game sweep of Wayne and the Oilers. Smith actually shut the Oilers out in the opening game, something no one had done since the previous year. He also held them pointless in seven of 12 periods of play. Wayne was held without a goal in his first Stanley Cup finals but he earned four assists on the club's six markers.

The Cup victory marked the Islanders' fourth straight, putting them in a unique category (with only two Montreal teams) to have won that many consecutive Cups.

BEST PLAYER: Wayne Gretzky — Edmonton

BEST LINES: Wayne Gretzky, Jari Kurri, Glenn Anderson — Edmonton

Peter Stastny, Anton Stastny, Michel Goulet — Quebec

1983–84

The season clearly belonged to Wayne and the Oilers. Gretzky won the scoring title (naturally) and set an incredible continual point streak of 51 games. In that time, he amassed 153 points, including 61 goals. Wayne also reached the 100-point mark in just his 34th game of the season, a phenomenal feat.

When the dust settled, Gretzky had scored 87 goals and 118 assists for 205 points. This time he outdistanced his nearest scoring competitor, teammate Paul Coffey, by 79 points. The guy just never quit.

I remember many a night after a game in Vancouver, Toronto, or somewhere on the road, when a few of the guys from the broadcast team would be having a couple beers at the end of the night, and invariably the topic would turn to a Gretzky goal or three on the night. Game after game, night after night, we would simply shake our heads in amazement. He was hockey poetry in motion.

Superstar Oilers defenceman Coffey finished second in the league-scoring stats with an impressive 40 goals and 86 assists for 126 points. Broadcasts became more exciting from my perspective that year as a five-minute sudden-death overtime was re-instituted after more than 40 years. Teams no longer settled for a tie so easily. In sudden death, the first goal to break a draw wins, so no one plays boring hockey.

Edmonton led the league and the Smythe Division with 119 points on the year while Boston and the Islanders led the Adams and Patrick respectively with 104 points each. Buffalo was second behind Boston in the Adams with 103 while Washington, led by U.S. star centre Bobby Carpenter and sniper Mike Gartner, finished second in the Patrick with 101.

In the playoffs, it was the mirror image of the previous season with the Oilers and the Islanders meeting in the final. In dramatic fashion, the Oilers won the first game 1–0 and then won the Cup in five games. Gretzky, Messier, and Coffey were just too much for the Islanders, with Gretzky gathering 35 points during the finals. Messier was spectacular and received the Conn Smythe Trophy for his playoff heroics.

Eighteen-year-old American netminder Tom Barrasso jumped straight out of U.S. high school hockey to the Buffalo Sabres and won both the Vezina and Calder Trophies that year. The incredible puck-stopper played 42 games with a 2.84 goals against average, making the first All-Star team to boot. Barrasso, a stand-up goalie with a quick stick and feet, seemed to re-open the U.S. floodgates, which had slowed down after several of the 1980 U.S. Winter Olympic gold medal team joined the NHL. Barrasso proved to have a competitive nature and skill, and even in 1998–99 was showing great backstopping ability with the Pittsburgh Penguins in a solid playoff performance.

The league lost another great player at the end of the season as Bobby Clarke hung up his skates following 15 tremendous years with the Flyers.

BEST PLAYER: Wayne Gretzky — Edmonton
BEST LINES: Wayne Gretzky, Jari Kurri, Glenn Anderson — Edmonton
Bryan Trottier, Mike Bossy, Clark Gillies — New York Islanders

1984–85

In the NHL, finishing last often has its perks and for the Pittsburgh Penguins their perk turned out to be Super Mario the Magician, scoring sensation Mario Lemieux.

It's rare that such an amazing talent and genius shows itself in sport, so to suddenly have two incredible superstars playing the same game at the same time was fantastic. That's what happened when Mario Lemieux joined Wayne Gretzky in the NHL that season.

From the very start (just as it had been with Wayne) it was obvious Mario's arrival meant more amazing moments and lessons for fans. Indeed, the giant star who ripped apart the Quebec Major Junior Hockey League with 282 points the year before lived up to all his advance hype. In his first season in the big league, Mario scored 43 goals and added 57 assists for 100 points. He became just the third rookie to hit the century mark with the other two, Peter Stastny and Dale Hawerchuk, having set the mark within the previous couple seasons. In the case of Mario, however, he was playing with a weak line-up of teammates. Aside from Rick Kehoe and Mike Bullard, the Penguins were thin. So thin in fact they finished with just 53 points despite Lemieux's heroics. At the end of the year, Mario grabbed the rookie award without much question.

Gretzky was simply amazing again, which sadly some of us began to mistake as ordinary. The Great One netted 73 goals and 135 assists. On the way to his total, Wayne also passed the 1,000 point in his brief NHL career. Unreal!

Aside from Wayne and Mario, Jari Kurri also had an impressive year as he racked up 71 goals making him only the third player ever, aside from Wayne and Phil Esposito, to score more than 70 goals in a season. The Finnish Flash also garnered 64 assists for 135 points and finished second overall in the individual scoring race. Several players, including Mike Gartner, broke the 50-goal plateau. Holy smokes, that Gartner was some hockey player. He made the game look so easy. Skate? Could he ever. Shoot? You bet. He was durable, an iron man who made plays with the best of 'em. Only he finished 'em better as his 19-year average of 37 goals per season attest.

Stop it there, back it up! *Nineteen years* at 37 goals per season? Yep, 708 goals in 432 games with 612 assists. He isn't in the Hall of Fame yet, folks, but jeepers, they can't keep him out. For years, he was a premier player, fun to watch, and a great guy too.

The Flyers wound up the top club on the regular season with 113 points.

Regardless of their showing in the regular season, and their impressive climb to the Stanley Cup finals, the Flyers did not have enough stuff to take the Cup away from the Oilers. Their physical play had taken its price and a fresher, faster Gretzky, Coffey, Fuhr, and crew steam-rolled over them in the playoffs. The Oilers lost the first match of the finals in Philadelphia but then took the next four games for their second Cup. In the process, Gretzky tallied a record 30 assists and 47 points while Kurri equalled the most-goals total of 19 in the playoffs. Fast-skating, accurate-shooting Paul Coffey

shattered a couple of Orr records as well, but in the end it was
Wayne Gretzky who won the playoff MVP.

BEST PLAYER: Wayne Gretzky — Edmonton
BEST LINE: Wayne Gretzky, Jari Kurri, Glenn Anderson —
Edmonton

1985–86

Just when I thought I'd seen Gretzky do it all, he did more.

In 1985–86 Wayne racked up points at a boggling pace and
ended the year in top spot with a breath-taking 215 points,
including 163 assists. It was the sixth season straight that Wayne
had won the scoring championship. This time he was 74 points
ahead of the second-place scorer, sophomore Super Mario.

Lemieux had 141 points, including 48 goals, but his Pittsburgh
club still floundered near the bottom of the Patrick Division. Coffey
finished the year with a new record for defencemen of 48 goals,
beating Orr's old mark. He also added 90 assists for 138 points,
one shy of Orr's total point record. The impressive sum put Coffey
in third place in overall scoring. I marvelled night after night not
just at Wayne and Jari, but also at Paul. Jumpin' Jehoshaphat, what
a show!

The New York Rangers had a young free agent "walk on" attend
camp and crack the line-up. His name was Mike Ridley and he
quickly became a fan favourite, picking up 65 points. My oh my,
what hands he had and what a face-off man.

Despite the amazing work of Gretzky and others that year, a dark
cloud hung over the league most of the season, and for good reason.
In November that year, Flyer goalie sensation Pelle Lindbergh
crashed his sportscar into a wall and died instantly. The death left
his teammates and fans stunned. Amazingly, the Flyers rallied and
finished second overall (110) in team standings at the end of the
year, dedicating their gallant effort to their fallen friend. Edmonton
topped the league and Smythe with their 119. Quebec won the
Adams seasonal race with 92 points ahead of Montreal while

Chicago edged Minnesota by one point in the Norris with 86.

Like my 1949–50 Leafs, overconfidence sneaked up and knee-capped the Oilers that year in the playoffs. After eliminating Vancouver in the opening round of play, the Oilers were bounced from the playoffs by their Alberta nemesis, the Calgary Flames. Calgary was led by rookie netminder Mike Vernon and won the seventh game when Edmonton defenceman Steve Smith scored on his own net. The Flames then skimmed past St. Louis four games to three in the conference final.

The Montreal Canadiens, meanwhile, were led by the hot goaltending of rookie Patrick Roy. The Habs dumped Boston, Hartford, and then the Rangers in order to meet Calgary for the Cup.

The Flames may have been hot, but the Habs were too cool to be easily rattled and took the final series in five games. Calgary sneaked the first match 5–2 in Calgary led by Lanny McDonald and Mike Vernon, but Roy and Montreal closed the door after that. Montreal won the second match in overtime 3–2 to tie the series. The Habs won the next three, including a game four 1–0 shutout by Roy at home. Roy posted 15 wins in the playoffs and an impressive 1.92 average in earning the Conn Smythe Trophy.

The series had marked the first all-Canadian final since Toronto met the Montreal in 1967. The cup marked the 23rd ever won by the incredible Canadiens.

BEST PLAYERS: Wayne Gretzky, Paul Coffey — Edmonton
BEST LINES: Wayne Gretzky, Jari Kurri, Glenn Anderson/Mark Messier — Edmonton

1986-87

Prior to the 1986–87 season, a few more players were shuffled about, including Vancouver sending rugged winger Cam Neely to Boston for young Barry Pederson. What a robbery that was. Someone should have called security. Every time I hear the name Neely, I can't help but shake my head and think about Tyee salmon fishing. It's always the "big mean ones" that get away and break your heart. I cringed at the trade, not because Pederson was not a skilled player, but because I knew Neely was going to be a real gem no matter where he played and would glow in Boston. Likewise, I suspected that Pederson would not flourish in Vancouver the way he did in Boston because of the Canuck team make-up. For once, unfortunately, I was right.

For a season under coach Tom Watt, Neely had little chance to play, and to this day I still have no idea why. I was doing some broadcast work for BCTV and the Vancouver Canucks at the time and saw a great deal of the lanky winger from Comox. Golly gee, I liked the kid. He was big, strong, and hard-hitting, had good hands, could score, and hit consistently. To me he clearly looked like money in the bank. But Tom Watt, more mindful (I think) of his coaching reputation than he was with winning and developing talent for the Canucks, just wouldn't give Neely the necessary ice time to develop.

People in the hockey broadcasting business get to know most people involved in the game, including players, training staff, officials, NHL staff, referees, writers, public relations people, and scouts. One day when Vancouver was playing the Rangers in New York, I met and talked with the Boston scout, former goalie Gerry Cheevers. On the same road trip, but in Philly, I ran into him again and had a beer with him, and then three days later on the same trip there he was in Toronto. We go home with two losses and a tie and a week later the Oilers are in town. So is Cheevers. Finally, at the next game with Calgary, during the pre-game skate, the Boston scout slips in to the seat beside me, and before I can ask who he's looking at, he blurts out, "This kid, Neely . . ." Before he could go on I cut in with, "Get him, play him regularly next year, and he will get you 30 goals, and eventually 50."

Cheevers looked at me for a second, grinned, and said, "See you after the game — we'll have a beer."

When Cam was on his way to 40 goals for Boston two years later, Gerry slid in beside me one night and said, "I didn't think it [the goals] would happen so quick. Thanks."

Neely proved to be a terrific leader for Boston not only in goals but in guts, leadership, and heart. In his first year there, he popped 36 goals, the second season 42. Before his 10 years in Boston were done, he would hit or surpass 50 goals three times. He scored 395 goals and 694 points in 726 games before hip, knees, and back injuries ended his career.

Barry Pederson, meanwhile, had his career go the other way, flourishing early in Boston and dying later in Vancouver. When he was healthy over his three years in Boston, he was awesome, racking up 92 points in 1981–82, 107 points the next season, and 116 in 1983–84.

I've often talked about players needing to work as a group to create an atmosphere in which others can display their talents. I think the expression "feed off the opportunities created" fits the bill. In those years (oh hell, in most of their years), the Boston Bruins were a hard-working, hard-hitting, hard-checking, hard-fighting, tough, mean hockey club. Except in the Orr-Esposito days, the Bruins have mainly been a lunch-bucket motley crew. It was part of their trademark style and it worked well, especially in the playoffs, year after year.

When any team played the Bruins, especially at home in Boston Garden, better known as "The Zoo," the players knew it was going to be a long, tough night and they'd better not drop their head. Most of the night the opposition was being harassed regularly and if they did anything physical, it was to go back at their attacker. Players didn't have time to go looking for anybody else, including Barry Pederson.

I'm sure that before the game the opposing coaches all said, "Look, boys, this Pederson is killing everybody with his passing, shooting, and skating skills. Let's make him pay." But it seldom happened, because the Bruins kept the other team too busy checking their own rearview mirror. When Pederson was traded to Vancouver, the team at that time played soft (as they still do today) and the opposition found out two things: they could run Pederson and wouldn't have to pay the price; and that two guys could go after him and even if he did complete the pass, the receiver couldn't put the puck in the ocean off the wharf. In short, Vancouver never created an atmosphere in which Pederson could display his skills. Whether they couldn't or wouldn't, I don't know, but either way it was too bad because he did have very good skills.

Finally, Barry just faded in Vancouver, quickly went to Pittsburgh, Hartford, back to Boston . . . and disappeared from the hockey world. In 701 games, however, he managed a very impressive 654 points.

I liked Barry Pederson and think it's too bad he never hit his full potential or stride. In the end, this trade looked far more lopsided than it should have been, and that is largely not Pederson's fault.

The Edmonton Oilers went to work from the first face-off in the first game of the 1986–87 season to prove they deserved the title of champions again. There was a fire within the club all season, even though it had some rough times. At year end, the Oilers topped the league and the Smythe Division with 106 points. Philly was best in the Patrick with 100, while Hartford edged out Montreal 93 to 92 for the Adams Division title.

The weakest division overall was the Norris, however it also played host to an intense competition that year as the St. Louis Blues, in first with 79 points, finished just nine points ahead of fifth-place Minnesota. Detroit was second with 78. The season marked probably the closest the teams had come to parity at that time.

Once again Gretzky claimed the scoring title. This time he racked up 62 goals and 121 assists for 183 points, which was 75 points ahead of second-place linemate Jari Kurri. The sharp-shooting Finn scored 54 times and totalled 108 points. Marvellous Mario was third overall with just one less point than Kurri. Lemieux also scored 54 goals.

There have been many combinations of players who, when playing together, were almost a perfect match. Lach and Richard, Kennedy and Sloan, Howe and Lindsay, Sittler and McDonald, Esposito and Hodge, Trottier and Bossy. However, from both my playing and broadcasting days I can't remember any better duo than Gretzky and Kurri.

Like Lemieux, Gretzky could play with anyone and was spoiled by having Anderson, Messier, Coffey, and Lowe on his club. All of them were able to take full advantage of Wayne's various moves, but Jari read him best. Kurri also had the best timing and change of pace of any player to work regularly with Wayne, and Kurri was also a superior goal scorer.

Holy cow, was it fun to watch that Edmonton Oilers machine play hockey. It was a once in a lifetime experience watching a once in a lifetime team.

Kurri was a great sniper and after 10 years in Edmonton, 32 goals was his lowest on a season and 71 his highest. He totalled 474 regular-season goals in Edmonton, averaging 47 goals per year, with 569 assists. By the time Kurri finished five more NHL years with L.A. and the Rangers, he had with 583 goals, 758 assists for 1,341 points in 1,099 games, well over a point a game through 15 years.

The flying Finn wasn't bad in the playoffs either. Kurri netted 105 goals and added 125 assists in the 185 games by the end of the 1996 playoffs. Super. Another sure-fire Hall of Fame player. Gretzky once said of his winger that if he did not make the Hall of Fame, "they should just board the place up."

When the regular season ended, the answer to the question everyone was asking started to become clear. Were the Oilers for real or not? Would they take back the Cup or were they just dynasty pretenders after all?

In one of the early rounds, Washington and the Islanders engaged in a long, gruelling seventh-game overtime classic. The game went on until 8:47 of the fourth overtime when Pat LaFontaine slammed in a goal off the post for the Islander win. It was the longest game in more than 40 years.

The Islanders continued to look like a comeback club as they fell behind Philadelphia in the series again, three games to one, then rallied to tie the series. Game seven belonged to the Flyers, though, and the Islanders were sunk.

The Flyers kept up their intimidation tactics in playoffs even late into the '80s and it seemed to work not too badly. It certainly worked for them in the series against the Habs, which the Flyers won in six bruising, punishing games. After tenderizing the opponents with their tough guys, Philadelphia would send out the snipers to pot a few goals and win the game.

Edmonton went through L.A., Winnipeg, and Detroit before facing the fierce Flyers. The final round was a physical session, though not as wild as some predicted, especially after Hextall viciously chopped down the Oilers' Kent Nilsson. The fighting, determined Flyers took Edmonton all the way to the seventh game before finally bowing out 3–1.

Hextall was given the MVP even though his club did not grab the coveted Cup. Gretzky scored 34 points in the playoffs. For the Oilers their third Cup in four years was sweet.

The Kings' Luc Robitaille, who showed great potential, was named Rookie of the Year.

BEST PLAYERS: Wayne Gretzky — Edmonton; Mario Lemieux — Pittsburgh

BEST LINE: Wayne Gretzky, Jari Kurri, Mark Messier — Edmonton

1987–88

The Canada Cup '87 presented one of those "what if" scenarios at the beginning of the 1987–88 season. The tournament brought together the best of Canada's players and meant Wayne Gretzky and Mario Lemieux, among others, could play on the same team.

But it got better. The two magicians wound up playing together on the same line. And the world watched as they scored some amazing goals together. When the series was over, Lemieux had posted a leading 11 goals, including four game winners and 18 points, second in total only to Wayne, who had 21.

To every thing there is a season, and for the Great Gretzky his autumn as NHL regular-season scoring leader was 1988. Mario Lemieux took advantage of an injured and then playing-while-wounded Wayne. Even so, Mario well earned his title. Lemieux was spectacular as he banged in 70 goals and helped out with 98 more for a tremendous 168-point year. Wayne finished second, missing 16 games with eye and knee injuries but still snagged 149 points, including 109 assists. On March 1, Wayne notched his 1,050 assist to surpass the old record held by Gordie Howe.

No doubt Wayne missed (and Mario enjoyed) the skills of superstar defenceman Paul Coffey. The skilled rearguard held out on the Oilers in a contract battle at the beginning of the season and in late November of '87 was traded in a big seven-player deal to Pittsburgh.

In December Ronny Hextall intentionally scored a goal during a game. Meanwhile, Grant Fuhr set a new record for most games played in a year by a goalie at 75.

Despite Lemieux, the Penguins failed to make the playoffs.

In the extra season, when things really count, the Oilers turned it on and won the Cup with little effort. Edmonton put down Winnipeg in five games, Calgary in four, Detroit in five (in the semi-finals) and then eliminated Boston in the Cup finals in four games — which actually took five to play. A power outage in Boston in game four resulted in a fifth game, called game four (again), which was played in Edmonton. The Oilers took the Cup in front of a home crowd and Gretzky earned his second Conn Smythe Award.

BEST PLAYERS: Mario Lemieux — Pittsburgh; Wayne Gretzky — Edmonton

BEST LINES: Wayne Gretzky, Jari Kurri, Esa Tikkanen — Edmonton

Jimmy Carson, Bernie Nicholls, Luc Robitaille — Los Angeles

Peter Stastny, Michel Goulet, and Anton Stastny — Quebec

1988–89

In early August of 1988, the entire hockey world was knocked on its butt when Wayne Gretzky was traded to the Los Angeles Kings. Even in the media circles when the long discussed possibility of Wayne leaving Edmonton began, no one seriously thought it would happen. It was one thing to trade Coffey, but Wayne the Boy Wonder? Never.

But it did happen.

Canada stuttered, Edmonton stumbled, and Oilers fans were stupefied.

Reactions to "the trade" varied but there was enough anger to legitimately warrant security protection for Oilers owner Peter Pocklington, who'd been instrumental in the move. Pocklington was some $50 million in debt and the banks had forced the trade to get some cash. Some questioned the logic in selling a national institution and hero, while others ranted and raved that it was just Wayne gladly going as the hired gun to the highest bidder. Los Angeles owners said they made the move for the sake of improving the club on the ice but certainly the trade/purchase would not hurt marketing of the hockey team either. In L.A. you had to have stars and glitz if you wanted to be anything and the L.A. Kings now certainly had a king in their hockey castle.

While Canadians moaned, and rightfully so, at the loss of their Canadian boy-hero to a U.S. city, the move helped to sell the game in the U.S. market. For that and much more, hockey owes a lot to Wayne Gretzky. With Gretzky in the west and Lemieux in the east, the United States was now a lot better exposed to the game.

In the end, the deal was Gretzky, Marty McSorley, and Mike Krushelnyski to the Kings for sniper Jimmy Carson, first-round draft pick Martin Gelinas, three first-round draft picks, and around $15 million plus other goodies.

After all the fuss, the deal did not give the Cup to either Edmonton or L.A. that year. Though the Oilers would win one more Cup the following season, many suggest that trade and earlier loss of Coffey marked the beginning of the end of the Oilers' dynasty.

Other significant moves early that year saw the immortal Guy Lafleur return to the game. After a three-and-a-half-year retirement, Lafleur made a comeback, but rather than sign with the Canadiens, Lafleur inked a deal with the New York Rangers just after he'd been selected to go into the Hall of Fame. By the end of the year, Guy had played in 67 games and earned 45 points. He notched 18 goals, including one in his return game in Montreal.

Mario Lemieux enjoyed a full year of having Paul Coffey on the point and a hot right winger named Rob Brown. Lemieux won his second straight scoring championship with 199 points, including 85 goals and 114 assists.

Gretzky finished in second despite his change of uniforms. Wayne scored 54 goals in L.A. and added 114 assists for 168 points. Meanwhile, another of my favourite players, Steve Yzerman, showed all his skills leading a developing Detroit club with 155 points, including 65 goals for third place in the scoring parade.

All the players shuffling about made for some interesting changes in the team standings. Montreal continued to dominate the Adams with 115 points for top spot, while Washington was the best in the Patrick with 92. Detroit stayed on top of the Norris.

In the Smythe Division, Calgary was the benefactor of the Gretzky shift as they finished on top of the division and the league with 117 points. The Flames had been building a solid nucleus for a few seasons with Lanny McDonald, Hakan Loob, 1987–88 Rookie of the Year Joe Nieuwendyk, and others. They also added goalie Rick Wamsley from St. Louis the previous season and he helped considerably.

Hard-shooting Al MacInnis went 17 straight playoff games with at least a point each game, winding up with seven goals and 24 assists for 31 points and won the Conn Smythe Trophy as his Calgary Flames won all the marbles that year.

Calgary was a deep club with goalie Mike Vernon starting and MacInnis and Gary Suter on defence. Up front they had Joey Mullen, tenacious Doug Gilmour, and Joel Otto, in addition to McDonald and Nieuwendyk. But it still took them until overtime of game seven to eliminate the feisty Vancouver Canucks.

Next up was L.A., who'd ironically met and defeated Edmonton in the first round. Calgary dumped L.A. in four games, a series that seemed over before it really started. Calgary then disposed of Chicago in five before meeting Montreal in the finals.

Montreal made it to the finals after defeating Hartford in four,

Boston in five, and Philadelphia in six. The Canadiens were led by the amazing young goalie Patrick Roy, who never lost all season at home during the regular season (25–0–3). While Montreal had a tough defence, they were not deadly up front and that was their Achilles' heel. It took the Flames just six games to earn their first Stanley Cup.

Fittingly, Lanny scored a goal in what was the final game of his career. It was his first Stanley Cup. What a classy finish for a classy guy.

BEST PLAYERS: Mario Lemieux — Pittsburgh; Wayne Gretzky — Los Angeles

BEST LINES: Wayne Gretzky, Bernie Nicholls, Luc Robitaille — Los Angeles

Mario Lemieux, Rob Brown, Bob Errey — Pittsburgh

THE DECADE

BEST PLAYERS: Wayne Gretzky, Peter Stastny, Paul Coffey, Mario Lemieux

BEST LINES: Wayne Gretzky, Jari Kurri, Glenn Anderson/Mark Messier — Edmonton

Bryan Trottier, Mike Bossy, Clark Gillies — New York Islanders

Marcel Dionne, Dave Taylor, Charlie Simmer — Los Angeles

DYNASTIES: **New York Islanders, Edmonton Oilers**

New York Islanders 1980, 1981, 1982, 1983 (finalist in 1984)

LEADERS: Bryan Trottier, Mike Bossy, Clark Gillies, Denis Potvin, Billy Smith, Butch Goring

BLEEDERS: Chico Resch, Duane Sutter, Bob Nystrom, John Tonelli, Bob Bourne, Stefan Persson, Ken Morrow, Brent Sutter, Pat Flatley, Pat LaFontaine

FEEDERS: Gord Lane, Dave Langevin, Bob Lorimer, Wayne Merrick, Gary Howatt, Lorne Henning, Anders Kallur, Billy Carroll, Mike McEwen, Tomas Jonsson, Greg Gilbert, Paul Boutilier, Mats Hallin, Gord Dineen, Roland Melanson, Jean Potvin, Steve Tambellini, Hector Marini, Alex McKendry

Edmonton Oilers: 1984, 1985, 1987, 1988, 1990

LEADERS: Wayne Gretzky, Paul Coffey, Grant Fuhr, Mark Messier, Jari Kurri, Glenn Anderson, Kevin Lowe

BLEEDERS: Andy Moog, Randy Gregg, Charlie Huddy, Mike Krushelnyski, Ken Linseman, Willy Lindstrom, Esa Tikkanen, Marty McSorley, Craig Simpson, Kevin McClelland, Joe Murphy, Adam Graves, Bill Ranford, Reijo Ruotsalainen, Kent Nilsson, Craig MacTavish

FEEDERS: Dave Semenko, Lee Fogolin Jr., Tom Roulston, Ray Cote, Pat Hughes, Don Jackson, Dave Hunter, Dave Lumley, Pat Conacher, Jaroslav Pouzar, Larry Melnyk, Billy Caroll, Mark Napier, Craig Muni, Kelly Buchberger, Steve Smith, Keith Acton, Normand Lacombe, Jeff Beukeboom, Geoff Courtnall, Mark Lamb, Petr Klima, Martin Gelinas, Geoff Smith, Dave Brown, Dave Hannan, Pokey Reddick, Moe Lemay

THE EUROPEANS
ARE COMING!

■ ■ ■

I started the decade already working for CBC and BCTV at the same time, when Gordon Craig called me up and said, "Howie, I've left CBC and some friends and I are starting up a TV sports network station owned by Labatts Brewery called TSN out of Toronto. We need you for hockey. Will you come and work for us?"

I don't know of anyone else who's ever worked for three different networks at the same time. It was sure great fun, very interesting, and kept me busier than a ferret in a chicken coop. I'm very glad Gordon called and that I took him up on the offer, because, goodness gracious, what a decade of hockey it was in the 1990s.

Once again the flip of the calendar into the new decade seemed akin to flicking a light switch, because a quick shift in the power structure of the league took place. The difference was that no single club was ever dominant over the others for more than two years.

Just when I figured some club looked good, there would be a trade, contract dispute, free agent walk away, retirement, or injury that would ding the team good. Only Pittsburgh early in the decade and Detroit in the latter parts would show any monopoly on the Stanley Cup, and even then they were continually challenged by more than a couple of teams. Edmonton, Montreal, and Minnesota chased Pittsburgh with Colorado, Philadelphia, New Jersey, and Dallas knocking on Detroit's door.

The 1990s may not have produced a plethora of powerhouse teams, however it certainly was rich in player talent. A real bundle of tremendously gifted players, stars, and superstars donned the blades to dominate during the decade, including Jaromir Jagr, Sergei Fedorov, Peter Forsberg, Eric Lindros, Paul Kariya, Pavel Bure, Teemu Selanne, Theo Fleury, Martin Brodeur, and Dominik Hasek. Players continued to come forth who were bigger, faster, stronger, and many of them were smarter.

Certainly, Canada produced its share of great players but without a doubt the European influx was now a significant component of the game. Clearly the statistics, awards, All-Star team selections, and international competition inside and outside the NHL proved that. No longer were the line-ups of the All-Star teams or scoring statistics owned by Canadians. American and European players routinely began to contribute greatly to the NHL's highlights and successes.

The United States regularly produced significant numbers of players showing great growth, particularly in the college and university programs. Emerging U.S. stars included Tom Barrasso, Mike Richter, Chris Chelios, Craig Ludwig, Brian Leetch, John Vanbiesbrouck, Craig Janney, Jeremy Roenick, Tony Amonte, John LeClair, Keith Tkachuk, and Doug Weight.

Thank goodness for that non-Canadian player influx because the '90s continued to see the number of teams in the league increase. With 21 clubs in the league in 1989–90 and 27 by 1998–99, there was the demand for talented players . . . wherever they came from.

High-scoring stars continued to dominate the standings, especially during the first two-thirds of the decade. In 1989–90 the top 11 scorers finished with 102 points or more, and until the strike year of 1994–95, the top 10 was always filled with players of 99 points or more. During the 1995–96 season, the phenomenal high scoring returned with the 10th place scorer Sergei Fedorov sitting at 107 points.

During the 1996–97 season, the scoring tapered off dramatically, partly due to injuries, but also due to a shift in the game toward more holding, interference, and stickwork. Stars like Lemieux complained about it plenty but to little avail. Also, a defensive system of zones and trap plays was perfected by some clubs such as New Jersey, Florida, and Buffalo, much to the frustration of fleeter, perhaps more gifted teams. Finally, the philosophy that teaching good defensive skills to young players, especially defencemen, helps you win games was sinking in.

There was (and is) another major contributing factor to the low scoring statistics of late 1990s NHL games, and that's the number of truly magnificent goaltenders, especially in the latter half of the decade. There had been a time when only a small percentage of clubs had superb netminders, but as the new millennium arrives, despite the huge number of clubs, there are numerous extremely talented puck-stoppers including Dominik Hasek, Ed Belfour, Chris Osgood, Curtis Joseph, Martin Brodeur, Patrick Roy, John Vanbiesbrouck, Arturs Irbe, Byron Dafoe, Mike Richter, Ron Tugnutt, and even Old-timers Tom Barrasso, Bill Ranford, Ron Hextall, and Grant Fuhr.

During the 1990s I spent a great amount of my time covering the Vancouver Canucks and clubs in the Western Division, which suited me just fine, especially since Wayne had moved to L.A. and hockey was getting hotter by the season on the west coast.

1989–90

The NHL season was barely under way when the Boy Wonder (who was now a man) became the NHL's all-time top point-scorer. Typical Wayne, he even seemed to control the timing on when he would establish records, including the NHL all-time total point record of 1,850 points originally set by his idol Gordie Howe. On October 15 during an L.A. Kings visit to the Edmonton Coliseum, the returning Great One put on yet another demonstration of why he was considered the best player in the world. Going into the game, Wayne had 1,849 points but his teammates had plans on helping Wayne with his moment of glory in Edmonton. Early in the first period Bernie Nicholls, the natural sniper, stuffed the puck into the Edmonton net after a nifty feed by Gretzky, and the mark was tied. The Edmonton fans gave Wayne a suitable roar of approval, saluting the player they still held as their own.

In true Wayne style, just when it seemed that he would miss the opportunity to set the record in front of his old hometown fans, he pulled it off. With less than a minute remaining in the game, Wayne snagged a pass and beat Bill Ranford to tie the game and set the new record. As his final touch to a classic night, Gretzky then drained the winner in overtime for a spectacular performance. The Edmonton fans went nuts, and I doubt if any arena ever rocked as loudly when their own team had just lost an overtime game. It was a marvellous moment.

Other players also had tremendous years. Brett Hull, son of Bobby, displayed his inherited and refined sniper skills, blasting in a remarkable 72 goals for St. Louis. His performance made the Hull trade by Calgary look even worse than it had when completed two seasons before.

I heard about Brett Hull long before I ever saw him. Word around the scouts and media was that "Bobby's boy" had been quite a junior star in Penticton, and then later in college. I was not surprised. When I first saw Brett Hull at the Canadian National team training camp in Calgary a number of years back, he interested me. More, obviously, than he had interested the coaches and club personnel who told me Hull "probably won't make the team. He can't skate, can't keep up." But he had great goal-scoring ability — 50 in the minors.

I saw him a year or so later, also in Calgary, trying to make the Flames. Once again it was suggested to me that Brett wouldn't make the team. "Too slow to get into position to shoot the puck."

Well, Hull sort of made Calgary, barely, and met exactly the low expectations that some Flames' management and coaching staff had unfairly stuck in everyone's mind (except Brett's). He played four games with Calgary during the 1986–87 playoffs, and I thought he did fairly well. The next year he played a bit more regularly in the early season and, despite showing some good goal-scoring potential, was traded to St. Louis. The tag on Hull, according to some, was that he couldn't skate and was lazy, undisciplined, and uninvolved.

Well, in St. Louis he may have been a pain in the butt for some management and coaching staff, but he sure as hell was not lazy or uninvolved on the ice. As far as disciplined, I only know that Brett Hull plays the game as well as or better than most players in the league, is very smart, and has many hockey gifts.

So it was off to St. Louis, where by the end of the season Brett had managed 64 points in just 65 games. Over the next 10 years in St. Louis, he averaged more than 50 goals and 85 points a year.

Geeze, I wish I couldn't skate like that. Needless to say, he was a quick fan favourite in St. Louis.

In 1989–90, Brett scored an electrifying 72 goals on the season and 113 points and the next year amazingly topped that show with an unbelievable 86 goals and 131 points. Another 70-goal year followed, and then seasons of 54 and 57 goals. Wow. Can you imagine bagging 86 goals in a year? Golly gee, he makes it sound as easy as shooting fish in a barrel.

There are three particular attributes I find amazing about Brett: his timing, wrist shot, and the ability to lose himself in a crowd (or alone) on the ice. How many times over the years have I watched him come from nowhere into open ice, arrive there at the same time as the puck, and swish it into the net?

I used to tell my camera operators, "Stay as wide as possible, I want to see where that sucker hides." I came to the conclusion it was a calculated manoeuvre. Hull utilizes his ability to read an unfolding play and then time his arrival for just such an attack pattern. Brett loves to burst out of nowhere and quickly whip the puck in to the net. His father used to simply create that space like a locomotive with the puck.

Brett probably has the most accurate and hardest wrist shot of anyone who played the game, ever. His father was famous for his

118-mile-an-hour (plus) slap shot, yet somehow Brett has failed to gain a similar legendary respect for his amazing wrist shot. Just ask any goalie and he will attest to Brett's shot and strength. Most times he just overpowers the goaltender or blows the puck by him, and almost always on a wrist shot or a short wind-up slap.

Over the years, from excellent sight lines, I've seen Hull shoot from the top of the face-off circle area and pick spots maybe 12 to 18 inches in diameter high over the goalie's shoulders. The goalie will do everything right, come out square to the shooter, and stand solid with no five-hole. But just like Gretzky (only his is a slapper), Hull pulls the trigger and bull's eye!

For a lazy, uninvolved guy who can't skate, he's done pretty well, eh?

Hull's 72 goals in 1989–90, however, set a new record for right wingers in the league, beating Jari Kurri's previous total by one, and everyone sat up and noticed. It was about time.

Due to continued back problems, Lemieux played in just 59 games but still amassed an incredible 123 points. I shook my head in amazement.

Clearly no particular club was in domination that year, but ironically much of the power had shifted to the Smythe Division, which had regularly been the dregs of the league. When the season ended, Calgary had 99 points on top of the Smythe, and in the Norris Division, Chicago finished on top with St. Louis second. The Boston Bruins were the top team overall, and their strong 101 points put them atop the Adams Division as well. In the Patrick Division, it was the Rangers in first, two points ahead of New Jersey.

At the end of the season, Gretzky claimed the individual point-scoring championship with 142 points, including a boggling 102 assists. Messier was second at 129 points with Yzerman third at 127, including 62 goals. Lemieux was fourth. There was some irony to Gretzky reclaiming the scoring crown from Lemieux. Mario had won the title two years before partly due to Wayne being affected by injuries, and now two years later it was Lemieux who was out for several games and Gretzky who was the benefactor.

Sergei Makarov, a smooth-skating veteran right winger from the

Soviet Union, was the Calder Memorial Trophy winner while Bourque won the Norris again and Patrick Roy grabbed the Vezina. Hull, Robitaille, and Messier were named as the forward unit to the first All-Star team with Bourque and Al MacInnis of Calgary on defence. Once again the first All-Star team was dominated by Canadian-born players, but that hold was waning.

The playoffs held special interest for fans because the teams were so close in the standings. Truly, it seemed to be anyone's game. The Cup was up for grabs. There were no four-game sweeps in the eight opening-round series, and only two of them were decided in five games. When the ice chips settled, Boston, Montreal, the Rangers, Washington, Chicago, St. Louis, Los Angeles, and Edmonton were still standing.

Boston, Washington, Edmonton, and Chicago advanced through the next round, where the hard-hitting, hard-working Bruins wasted no time dispatching Washington in four straight while Chicago came up dry against the mighty Oilers. Led by players such as Mark Messier, Randy Gregg, Glenn Anderson, the Oilers rolled over a bruised and battered Chicago in six.

The final series was set to be a dilly, because most fans agreed the teams were similar in their composition. The Oilers, with their history and depth, however, were given the nod, and correctly so. The teams had also swapped netminders two years before. Former Boston netminder Bill Ranford was outstanding for Edmonton and would prove to be his old team's real nemesis. Gosh, he was quick and acrobatic.

Both teams started off hitting hard and often, and went at each other most of the night in a classic game of old-fashioned hockey. At the end of three periods, however, the clubs were tied at two goals apiece, and I already had an evening full of highlight footage. Most of it included Ranford or Moog making tremendous saves.

As the night went on, and on, and on — so did the saves. Finally, former Red Wing, then Oiler Petr Klima pocketed the puck in the Boston net and the night was done. When the Oilers finally rolled into the sack that night, they were up one game to nothing.

In game two Edmonton found the holes in Moog and Lemelin

and pounded the Bruins 7–2 to take a series lead and psychological advantage. When the bumping and skating was done, the Oilers edged Boston in five and won their fifth Stanley Cup. Ranford was magnificent the entire playoffs, claiming all 16 Oilers playoff wins and the Conn Smythe. Glenn Anderson, Grant Fuhr, Randy Gregg, Charlie Huddy, Jari Kurri, Kevin Lowe, and Mark Messier all had their names on the Stanley Cup for the fifth time.

BEST PLAYERS: Wayne Gretzky — Los Angeles; Steve Yzerman — Detroit

BEST LINE: Adam Oates, Brett Hull, Rod Brind'Amour — St. Louis

1990–91

The summertime blues hit the Pittsburgh Penguins when Mario went under the knife in a big way. Doctors removed a herniated disc, and recovery basically wiped out two-thirds of the season for the talented man from Laval.

My final year as a Leaf had been plagued with pain from a lower back injury I received in a game. (In the old days the bottom six to eight inches of the boards extended out about one inch from the rest of the boards, and I'd landed on that lip after getting nailed.) The pain never really quit until years after I did. I can relate in a small way to the pain that Mario must have played under and can only marvel at his tenacity and ability to perform under such horrendous pain. Amazing.

Once again, however, the absence of Mario left the regular-season scoring championship uncontested for Gretzky. Wayne had another tremendous season with 41 goals and 122 assists for 163 points and added another scoring championship to his name.

When the year began, Brett Hull started off again at a deadly scoring pace and simply never slowed down. When the year was up, the St. Louis winger had rifled in his amazing 86 goals on the year — the third highest tally ever behind Wayne's 92 and 87. I watched Hull fire goals in every way possible that year including deflections, dekes, backhands, a feared slap shot much like his father's, and a wrist shot that was even more deadly and the league's most powerful.

The days of dynamite duos rather than three-player regular forward lines seemed to dominate in the late '80s and '90s, and few better combos appeared than Hull and his slick centre Adam Oates. Always a smooth passer and playmaker in his college days, Oates showed his gift aptly again in the 1990–91 season, setting up 90 goals for teammates, mainly his right winger, Hull. Combined with 25 goals, his 115-point performance earned him third place overall in the individual player scoring race.

Pittsburgh was expected to tumble without Lemieux, however no one anticipated the tremendous season that forward Mark Recchi would have. Recchi scored 40 times and added 73 assists to take fourth spot overall with 113 points.

A young, diminutive netminder in Chicago named Ed Belfour turned in a phenomenal showing that year playing in some 74 games and winning 43 of them. Belfour, along with forward Steve Larmer and Chris Chelios, led Chicago to top spot in the Norris Division (and the league) at the end of the season, just squeezing past St. Louis.

Things were just as competitive in the Smythe Division, where I generally hung out, as Los Angeles finished just two points ahead of Calgary in the division race with 102 points. Boston also hit the even century mark as they claimed the Adams crown, while Recchi, Kevin Stevens, Bryan Trottier, Tom Barrasso, Paul Coffey, and Larry Murphy helped Pittsburgh finish first in the Patrick.

Lemieux returned with around 30 games left in the year, and his presence gave an additional lift to the already flying Penguins. I could not believe that he was actually back. I never imagined the impact he would have after such a long break.

In their opening series, Pittsburgh dropped the first games to the defensive New Jersey Devils and had to battle it out the full seven before eliminating them. Washington won the opening match in the Division Final match-up, but again Pittsburgh woke up and turned things around, winning four straight.

The Conference Finals brought on the tough and determined

Boston Bruins and it looked like it was all over but the crying after Boston took a 2–0 lead in the series. However, the Penguins rallied again to win the series in six games. The Penguins had to blink when they realized not only had they reached the Stanley Cup finals, but their opponents were the unlikely Minnesota North Stars. It marked the second time the Stars had ever reached the finals. During the 1990–91 regular season, Minnesota had mustered only 68 points on the year for fourth in the Norris Division and were the second last club to qualify. Under new GM Bobby Clarke, their roster was thin but had plenty of spirit.

All that aside, Pittsburgh again blew the first game in the final round to Minnesota 5–4. It took Mario, Paul, and company six games to finally eclipse the North Stars and hoist their first Stanley Cup. It seemed appropriate to watch Mario skate around with the Stanley Cup, in light of all the obstacles he'd overcome to get there.

In the final round Lemieux played just five games but picked up 12 points, while Murphy tallied 10 points in six games. Lemieux won the Conn Smythe as the playoff's top star, notching 44 points, including 16 goals. What an absolutely thrilling performance he gave, and goodness gracious, what a display of guts.

Hull rightfully earned the Hart Trophy for regular-season MVP, while Bourque won the Norris again.

BEST PLAYERS: Wayne Gretzky — Los Angeles; Eddie Belfour — Chicago; Brett Hull — St. Louis

BEST LINES: Adam Oates, Brett Hull, Rod Brind'Amour — St. Louis
Wayne Gretzky, Tomas Sandstrom, Luc Robitaille — Los Angeles

1991–92

Just a few months later, all the laughter died in sorrow in Pittsburgh when we learned that Penguin coach Bob Johnson had incurable brain cancer, which had been discovered soon after the Cup win. Badger Bob died in November.

It was a strange season for player moves, trades, and conflicts. The number one draft choice that summer was the strapping, bruising centre Eric Lindros, who was happily snagged by the Quebec Nordiques. Their joy ended quickly when Lindros announced he would not play in Quebec. His rebuff caused one hell of a commotion that still has ripples today. No one in their right mind would want to play in Quebec. No one gets national exposure — no exposure, no multimillion-dollar promotional contracts.

Eventually Lindros would wind up in Philadelphia, exchanged for six players including Peter Forsberg, Mike Ricci, Ron Hextall, Kerry Huffman, Chris Simon, and Steve Duchesne, two first-round draft picks, $15 million, and some other goodies. I figure Quebec (Colorado) cleaned up on the deal and have a Stanley Cup to show for it.

No matter how good Eric Lindros turns out, it would have been a bad deal for the Flyers to have just traded Forsberg and Duschene for Lindros. In 1998–99, even prior to Eric's serious lung injury, I bet the Flyers would have gladly swapped Lindros for Forsberg straight across. In making that original deal, Philly gave up too many first- and second-line players to maintain a healthy and vibrant operation or a solid club for Lindros to grow with. At the time of the trade, the deal did not seem as lopsided, but in light of Forsberg's brilliant career and the subsequent excellent seasons by Steve Duchesne in Quebec, St. Louis, and Ottawa, and Ron Hextall's short but successful adventures in Quebec and New York, well . . . it was a steal.

Mark Messier became the next famous Oilers player to leave the Alberta city as he was dealt to the New York Rangers in early October for Bernie Nicholls (who'd been bumped about) and others. You just knew that things were going to happen in New York with that move. The breakdown of the once-dominant Oilers only made me think again of how Conn Smythe dismantled the mighty Leafs team of the early '50s. The winters would seem much longer in the northern Alberta city.

The season of 1991–92 was the initiation year for the San Jose Sharks. My oh my, what a great city for the NHL to add to the league, if for no other reason than the joy of going to that part of the world on business. Who'd have thought that someday we'd be playing NHL hockey in places like sunny San Jose?

Even if I was just a half-hearted hockey fan, though, I'd still buy seasons tickets in San Jose just to hang out in the arena. Yup, they're still a pretty lousy hockey club, but the building they play in is by far the most people-friendly I've ever seen.

Regardless, that first year the Sharks and their striking logos and uniforms were a big hit in the league even if the club was terrible on skates. At the end of the year, the toothless Sharks had won just 17 games, including only three road victories, but San Jose and others loved them anyway.

At the end of the tumultuous season, a blockbuster trade saw Pittsburgh send Paul Coffey to L.A. and Mark Recchi to Philadelphia, receiving Rick Tocchet and Kjell Samuelsson in return. Another stinker deal or what?

With only a week left in the schedule, the NHL Players' Association went on a 10-day strike (and were locked out) over a number of issues including free agency, salary arbitration, and pension concerns. Out of that skate-off came some new collective bargaining agreements, including less restrictive free agency. Ted Lindsay must have had a grin on his mug from ear to ear that day.

With the year resumed and completed, some new teams led their divisions. In the Smythe it was the Vancouver Canucks, complete with new sensational Soviet speedster Pavel Bure, who dominated the division. The Canucks had been building again the past few years with Trevor Linden and goaltender Kirk McLean, and now with Bure it seemed they had a superstar and might just start to do some serious damage. Vancouver finished 12 ahead of L.A. The Detroit Red Wings were back in top spot in the Norris Division with Chicago in second. Montreal earned status as division champion in the Adams, while Mark Messier and his newly inspired New York Rangers were top dogs in the Patrick Division. It marked the first time in some 50 years that the Rangers, with 105 points, had qualified as the best team in the entire league during the regular season.

Big Mario the marvellous won back his scoring title notching 87 assists on route to a 131 point season. Not bad for a player who missed another 16 games on the season.

The competitiveness of the league was displayed in the playoffs. After the first round, Vancouver, Detroit, Pittsburgh, Montreal, the Rangers, Boston, Chicago, and Edmonton had survived. Not one of the eight series went less than six games with six going the full seven.

The second round was far more decisive, as Boston joyfully swept Montreal, and Chicago did the same to the Red Wings. Pittsburgh took the Rangers in six as did Edmonton over Vancouver. Pittsburgh lost the services of Mario Lemieux in game two of that Ranger clash after his hand was broken by a reckless slash. Jaromir Jagr, however, continued to sparkle for the Penguins, and they eventually rolled over the Blueshirts.

In the Conference finals, Pittsburgh buried the Bruins in four straight. Edmonton also ran out of legs and bodies against Chicago and went down in four.

The writing was on the wall when Mario returned at the beginning of the final series and goaltender Tom Barrasso continued his solid play. Both Pittsburgh and Chicago set new records for consecutive playoff wins at 11. Chicago did it early in the playoffs, while Pittsburgh cinched their 11 straight by dumping the Blackhawks in four to win their second consecutive Stanley Cup.

Lemieux won his second Conn Smythe award in a row, garnering 34 points including 16 goals. Rookie of the year was Vancouver's tremendously explosive Bure. The little speedster was not only exciting and talented but rugged. Messier won his second Hart and rightfully so as the Rangers had a brilliant turnaround year, while Brian Leetch won the Norris.

BEST PLAYERS: Mario Lemieux — Pittsburgh; Wayne Gretzky — Los Angeles; Patrick Roy — Montreal

BEST LINE: Mario Lemieux, Jaromir Jagr/Ron Francis, Kevin Stevens — Pittsburgh

1992–93

The roller-coaster Rangers proved the theory that what goes up must come down as they plummeted from the top of the Patrick Division in 1991–92 to the bottom in 1992–93.

It was another year of change and odd occurrences, including the arrival of commissioner Gary Bettman as the league's new guru. Mr. Bettman may be a fine man, but he knows absolutely beans about hockey, as do most of his owners. A basketball brain perhaps, very good at negotiations, and an expert in the marketing field; he must have considerable skills to keep 27 owners from his throat. How many of his questionable decisions originate from his office or from a committee of owners we will never know.

Mr. Bettman, folks, has one tough job and it's going to get tougher, with the available player talent (and no more Gretzky to showcase) to keep all 27 balls up in the air at the same time. If he can do that, he is not only quick of mind but he has hands to match. If he can skate, too, for goodness sake someone should sign him and give him a stick.

Ottawa finally received another NHL team (the Senators), as did the most unlikely of spots, Tampa Bay (the Lightning). The Senators wisely drafted a young team for future growth; however, the immediate results proved pathetic that year as they sported an amazingly inept road record of one win and 41 losses. In that terrible tally, they set a record of 38 straight road losses. At year end, Ottawa had 10 wins, 70 losses, 4 ties for 24 points. The Lightning, however, sported a better record of 53 points. Their instant relative success, however, did not set them on the same bright future course as Ottawa. That first year, Ottawa drafted a potential star, the Russian Alexei Yashin, while Tampa Bay took defenceman Roman Hamrlik.

The leader of the pack that year was again the Penguins, who appeared to be establishing a hold on the league's top position.

Most unbelievable to me was that Mario missed 24 games yet still won the scoring title with 69 goals and 91 assists for 160 points. Even more amazing was that he missed the 24 games largely due to treatment for Hodgkin's disease, the same disease that had killed his cousin. Lemieux underwent heavy treatment, overcame the cancer that year, and played on. His amazing strength and perseverance are storybook stuff.

Another sensational story that season was the crop of outstanding rookies and new players in the league. At the top of the list was Winnipeg rookie Teemu Selanne. The unbelievably slick forward from Finland had been picked 10th overall in the 1988 draft and was terrific on skates and handling the puck. Holy jumpin', I was thrilled whenever I got to do a broadcast involving the Jets, and believe me, that was not something I had looked forward to greatly in the past. Selanne was brilliant and scored 76 goals in his first year, a record at the time. He tallied 132 points, good enough for fifth overall in the individual point race.

When I look at that list of 1988 draft picks, I see it was a pretty good year. Mike Modano, the hotshot U.S. star went number one (Minnesota) and Trevor Linden number two (Vancouver) followed by Curtis Leschyshyn, Darrin Shannon, Daniel Dore, Scott Pearson, Martin Gelinas, Jeremy Roenick, Rod Brind'Amour, and *then* Selanne. Yikes, that's a lot of dumb GMs and scouts after the number one pick. There isn't one of those players I'd take over Selanne and only Modano and Roenick are even close to being in the same league. Linden, Brind'Amour, and Gelinas are gifted, though not necessarily consistent, and the rest are workers and journeymen players at best. I just can't believe Selanne went number 10. (Someone get me in a poker game with those GMs.)

A total of 10 teams finished the year with 93 points or more including Pittsburgh, leading the league at 119. Boston won the Adams; Vancouver, led by the marvellous Bure, soared to 101 points and top spot in the Smythe; and Chicago squeezed past Detroit for tops in the Norris.

Once again a goaltender proved the hero for the Habs in the playoffs as Patrick Roy led the team to the finals and eventually the club's 24th Stanley Cup.

Roy's battle began appropriately enough in La Belle Province in the opening round against the fast-skating Quebec Nordiques. It was a hell of a series to cover. In many ways the Nordiques were like a traditional Canadiens club because they were playing fire-wagon–style hockey. Things did not look bright for the Habs after opening night when the provincial upstarts defeated Montreal in game one 3–2 in overtime in Quebec City. Quebec followed that up with a solid 4–1 pounding in game two and seemed to have their opponents well in hand. Which, of course, is always a mistake to assume with Montreal. True to form, Montreal rebounded with four straight victories, including two more overtime games, to take the series. The two OT victories began a remarkable string for Montreal, who set a playoff record of 10 straight overtime wins.

After Quebec came Buffalo who'd upset Boston. The Habs dispatched the Sabres in four straight with identical 4–3 scores in every game, the last three in overtime. The Islanders were their next meal in the Conference Finals, but it took five meetings to do it, including two more overtime matches. The New York boys tried valiantly but Pierre Turgeon was playing with only one good arm after he was horribly hit by Dale Hunter in the previous round. Hunter's shot was one of the cheapest I recall and came from behind several seconds after Turgeon had scored and had his hands in the air. The Islanders had startled everyone and upset the Penguins in seven games, including a final overtime game in the previous round, but their luck had run out.

The Canucks had a solid year and seemed poised to do some playoff damage. With Bure flying and Linden looking good, the Canucks were on a roll. Vancouver dropped Winnipeg in six tough games but unfortunately met L.A. next and went down quickly. L.A. then edged a determined Maple Leafs club in seven robust affairs, including two overtime games.

Suddenly Roy and Montreal were back on familiar, though unexpected, turf — the Stanley Cup finals. Across the ice was Gretzky and the hungry L.A. Kings. All season and into the playoffs, Wayne, joined by Tomas Sandstrom and Luc Robitaille, were a formidable unit. Gretzky led the playoff scoring race that year and the Kings had made it to the final round for the first (and only) time.

Once again the Habs started off slowly as the Kings took game one 4–1. The shift came late in the second game with L.A. leading by one goal. The Habs called for an illegal stick measurement on Kings' defenceman Marty McSorley, and sure enough he was guilty of having too big a curve. Of course Montreal tied the game on the ensuing penalty and then won the important match in overtime.

Quite a few players in the NHL use an illegal stick for 50 minutes, then if the score is close late in the game, they switch to the legal size because they don't want to take the chance of being called for it. But Marty blew it big time. The Kings were in complete control of the game, with Gretzky all fired up. Trust me, if the Kings had gone home leading 2–0 in the series, they would have won the Stanley Cup.

If I'd owned the L.A. team, I'd have fired them all. Likewise I'd probably have traded McSorley. I can't believe that management would allow any player in a crucial series to use an illegal stick or even have one on the stick rack. I'm sure Marty never finished kicking himself for that one.

You had to give the Montreal Canadiens credit, though; they sure took advantage of every break. The famous Montreal machine went into action and won the next three games in a row, including two more overtime wins for the Cup.

Patrick Roy won his second Conn Smythe and deserved to, earning 10 overtime victories. I've never seen any goaltender play better over an extended period than Patrick did during their run to the Stanley Cup. I'm not a fan of the butterfly guessing goaltender, and in his early years in the league, Roy stood up much more than he has in recent years. A dipper, diver, flopping, butterfly netminder gets beat at least once a game on shots any peewee goaltender could stop, but some (a rare few) make it work. Most (almost all) break your heart in the playoffs. Of the 10 overtime games won by the Habs, Roy was the reason the games went into extra innings, and in half of those games he was sensational before his teammates notched the winner.

BEST PLAYERS: Mario Lemieux — Pittsburgh; Teemu Selanne — Winnipeg

Best Lines: Pat LaFontaine, Alexander Mogilny, Dave
Andreychuk — Buffalo
Wayne Gretzky, Tomas Sandstrom, Luc Robitaille
— Los Angeles

1993-94

Many fans anticipated Teemu Selanne would challenge for the scoring title after his brilliant previous year, but his season was snuffed out quickly when he severed his Achilles tendon.

Three more southern ports joined the league including two new teams, and the movement of another. Financially troubled Minnesota became the Dallas Stars, while the league expanded to include the Florida Panthers and the Anaheim Mighty Ducks. I thought the league already seemed like some sort of Disneyland without having the actual place as a part of the league. In my mind, the last thing the NHL needed to do to improve its image as a serious league or sport was to have a team named the Mighty Ducks.

Once again, how wrong I was.

The owners provided one of the best arenas on the continent and today have a couple of the best players in the world in tow. The club finished fourth in the Pacific Division with an impressive 71 points, ahead of both L.A. and Edmonton. Their 33 wins set a record for expansion teams.

Calgary topped the Smythe, Vancouver, with Bure in the saddle, finished second and San Jose, in a remarkable jump, was third.

Sergei Fedorov had a brilliant season and helped Detroit to a first-place finish in the Central Division with 100 points.

In the Eastern Conference, the Rangers were the big story. With new coach Mike Keenan at the helm, New York rebounded from their plummet into the basement in 1993. Mark Messier, Mike Richter, Brian Leetch, Adam Graves, and Sergei Zubov helped put the Rangers back on top as the best team in the regular season.

The Florida Panthers also had a tremendous first year, notching 83 points and finishing ahead of both Philadelphia and Tampa Bay. The Penguins were on top of the Northeast Division at 110 but it was a dogfight after that. Boston was second at 97, Montreal had 96 and Buffalo 95. What a tremendous race that was in the final two months.

In late March, just weeks before the season ended, Gretzky scored his 802nd goal against Vancouver to beat Gordie Howe's former goal-scoring record. At year's end, Gretzky was back on top of the scoring stats again with 92 assists and 130 points.

Sergei Fedorov was just brilliant all season and earned second spot with 56 goals and 120 points. What a marvellous magician he is with the puck. When he first entered the league with Detroit in 1990–91, he scored 31 goals then had seasons of 32, 34, and then 56 goals. I think he's floated since 1992–93 but Sergei consistently hits the 30-goal plateau and averages 40 assists with ease every year. He is an amazing skater, passer, and stickhandler and sees the whole ice. Fedorov can play any position including defence, and for a while the Wings even played him there — though lord knows why. But oh my, does he move the puck out of his own zone well.

Over the last few years Fedorov has aptly gained a reputation as a playoff player or money player, and certainly he seems to rev his engines up another level come the extra season. Maybe, because of the big bucks he makes, he figures to pace himself for when it counts. In fairness, Fedorov has been used as a second-line centre behind Yzerman, and very often in the role of a defensive centre, which he apparently does with little or no complaint. It goes to show how fortunate (or wise) Detroit is to have the luxury of a quality forward like Fedorov as their *second* centre. Most teams would sell their mother to have Fedorov in their line-up — period.

I have friends who see most Red Wing games and they can't believe how little Fedorov is doing for the money being paid during the regular season. However, when it comes to chasing Lord Stanley's mug, he has proven his value. It's hard to argue with those results.

Slick Adam Oates earned third place with 112 points while feisty Doug Gilmour added to his hero status in Toronto with 111 points and fourth overall.

That tremendously exciting little Russian speedster, aptly nick-named "the Russian Rocket," Pavel Bure, lit up the board for the

Canucks with a club record 60 goals and 107 points. A former Soviet teammate of Fedorov, Pavel's tremendous production gave him fifth spot in league scoring. What a pleasure it was over the years to watch game-day morning skates in Vancouver and witness Pavel weave his magic. It was during those workout sessions that Pavel would practise nifty moves and literally play with the puck. Some of the things he would do were unreal. And skate fast? Lord t'un-derin' Jesus b'y, can he move! I'd swear the little sparkplug speeds up when given the puck. It was too bad for Vancouver and a bonus for Florida that Pavel never felt at home in the Canadian port city, and that for whatever reasons he joined the Panthers in 1998–99. With his departure went the Canucks' Cup dreams.

Early in the season many suggested that either the Red Wings or the Rangers would snag the Cup, something neither team had done in decades. Come the beginning of the playoffs, those two clubs were indeed still considered among the top contenders.

That's when the Sharks bit Detroit's ass.

In the opening round, Sergei, Stevie Y, and the boys were taken aback by a hot Shark team and could never get unravelled in game one, which the Sharks won. Detroit rebounded, winning two straight, and it looked like it was all over but the crying for the Sharks; however, they continued to battle back in the series. The Wings pasted the Sharks 7–1 in game six to tie the series and everyone agreed that finally Detroit was back in control.

But wrong again.

Latvian Arturs Irbe stoned the Wings and the Sharks won the clincher 3–2. The Sharks' celebration was short-lived, however, as they were gaffed in seven games in round two by Toronto.

The Canucks pulled off an equally fabulous playoff showing in rallying from a 3–1 game deficit with Calgary to win the series. It was Bure who scored a dramatic second-overtime goal in game seven that sent the Canucks to the Conference semifinals. What a helluva series that was. In the next round, the Canucks took on the transplanted Dallas Stars, whom they eliminated easily four games to one. Finally the Canucks were on a roll. In the Conference finals, the Canucks faced the Shark-devouring Leafs and once again the

Canucks won the set four games to one, led by Bure. Suddenly the Canucks were in the Stanley Cup finals.

In the eastern sector of the hockey world, the New York Rangers, the Boston Bruins, Washington Capitals, and New Jersey Devils all advanced through their Conference Quarter-finals, though New Jersey was pushed to seven games by Buffalo. The Rangers predictably then dispatched the perennial playoff flunky Capitals in the Conference semi-finals while New Jersey edged Boston.

It was a classic clash in the Conference finals with the defensive Devils and the explosive New York Rangers as they vied for the berth in the Cup finals. The series was a perfect set-up for some great sports moments, including a memorable prediction by Ranger Mark Messier after his team lost game five and faced elimination in game six. The veteran centre told our TV cameras and media, "I guarantee there will be a game seven."

True to his word, Messier gave a remarkable performance and made his prediction come true, scoring three times and assisting on the fourth Ranger goal in a 4–2 win.

In the final seven seconds of the seventh and deciding match of the Conference title, held at Madison Square Garden, the Devils, with their brilliant netminder Martin Brodeur on the bench, scored to tie the game and force overtime again. Talk about a heart-stopper! It took two overtimes before Stephane Matteau netted the winner and the Rangers moved ahead.

The Vancouver Canucks jumped out to a surprising one-game lead in the thrilling finals, but New York soon took charge, winning the next three straight and putting a choke hold on the boys across the Strait of Georgia from my house. Vancouver, led by Trevor Linden, goalie Kirk McLean, and Bure, rallied in game five, dumping the Rangers in New York 6–3, and then, inspired by Geoff Courtnall, won game six as well. Suddenly the series was deadlocked at 3–3.

In the classic final, New York led 3–1 after two periods, and even though Linden scored five minutes into the frame to make it 3–2 and then pressed the rest of the night, the Blueshirts finally won their first Cup in 54 years.

Watching Messier skate around at centre ice with the Cup in his hand and a Ranger sweater on his chest was a memorable moment. How ironic that relatively soon after he would wind up sporting a Canuck jersey.

BEST PLAYERS: Wayne Gretzky — Los Angeles; Dominik Hasek — Buffalo; Pavel Bure — Vancouver
BEST LINES: Mark Messier, Glenn Anderson/Mike Gartner, Adam Graves — New York Rangers
Doug Gilmour, Wendel Clark/Nikolai Borschevsky, Dave Andreychuk — Toronto

1994–95

On the positive side, the players' strike/lock-out that shortened the 1994–95 season to 48 games meant a reduced amount of work. On the other hand, it also extended the playoffs well into prime fishing season.

And in the end, it was boring hockey that won the day.

The sore spot of players' rights, and the controversy that had been going on ever since the days when I was playing, finally festered to the bursting point. When the poisoned feelings finally let fly, the wounds were ripped open pretty wide on both sides. Some players relocated because of the battles they'd had or would soon have with management. It was not a good year, but one that had been coming for a long time. We may have another year like it in the near future if the current pendulum shift does not slow down.

Regardless, the key issues between the NHL Players' Association and franchise owners in 1994 included free agency, increasing the draft age from 18 to 19 (though a player could waive his protection at 18), and a salary cap on players entering the league.

In late January the two sides finally came to terms and the league began play with a reduced 48-game schedule. For many players it seemed they never got back on track in the shortened year, while others flourished.

What filled the remainder of the season was largely boring, defensive hockey using defensive traps, dump-chase-hit, hold, hook (mostly hold and hook), and icing the puck. It was a slow, low-scoring, stifling style of shinny less invigorating by far than even the regular defensive hockey.

The 26-team league was dominated by one of the original six clubs as Detroit finished top overall. The Red Wings were fleet-footed and led by Fedorov, Yzerman, Coffey, Dino Ciccarelli, Doug Brown, Viacheslav Fetisov, and Nicklas Lidstrom.

St. Louis, with Mike Keenan now coaching there after a contract battle with the Rangers, finished second in the Central Division. The Calgary Flames edged Vancouver for the Pacific Division title.

The real story of the year aside from Detroit, however, was the talented teams atop the Eastern Conference divisions. Quebec was the boss of the Northeast Division and sported amazing Swedish rookie Peter Forsberg. Quebec fans were thrilled with their new star and had already started to forget (but not forgive) the snubbing by Lindros. Pittsburgh without Lemieux finished just four points behind Quebec. In the Atlantic Division it was the Philadelphia Flyers who topped the totem, while the Devils finished second.

Czech forward Jaromir Jagr showed that he was a superstar in his own right in the Steel City and took top spot in the individual scoring race with 70 points. It marked the first time that a European player had ever won the NHL scoring title.

Holy cow, is he big and strong! In the early years with Mario Lemieux around, no one was quite sure just how good Jagr really was. But Lemieux would miss long stretches of games and the team wouldn't collapse. Somebody kept them going, and anyone paying attention knew it was largely Jagr.

When I reduced my TV appearances (and eventually quit), I gained a lot more time to watch hockey games on my satellite dish. Detroit is now my number one priority to watch, then the Ducks — only because of Selanne and Kariya. A close third is trying to find a game with Jagr in Steel Town. My oh my, is he something else or what? Great moves laterally and shifts to the left or right with the same ease. Jagr is a gifted stickhandler, nifty passer, and remark-able shooter — he has the whole package!

The Wings, when flying, give you four or five big plays a period.

On rare occasions when Selanne and Kariya get together, they give you one or two bright spots a period, but the huge guy — Jagr — gives you one or two highlights a shift. One on one he's deadly and turns more guys inside out than anyone else. He forces a team's defence to send two guys after him every time he touches the puck. He beats one guy alone so easily you're immediately in trouble because he's so good with the puck. Jagr makes every kind of pass there is tape-to-tape, or he can beat your goalie with a great shot from the top of the circle. Yikes.

I think he's head and shoulders the best entertainer in the league today, and he's just hitting his prime. If the Penguins can play defence and get good goaltending, they could be a rough team in the next decade. I am sure Pittsburgh management in 1998–99 took a page from Detroit's plan book and surrounded their young Czech star with other Europeans (Martin Straka, German Titov, Robert Lang, Alexei Kovalev . . .) and is it ever working. But the grease, oil, and power is Jaromir Jagr. Hopefully Pittsburgh's financial woes will not stop them from giving Jagr enough support to do a winner's job again in the future. With Mario in charge, it should be very interesting.

Eric Lindros, the can't-miss-but-just-won't-play kid, finally showed what he could do in Philadelphia, where he scored 29 goals and added 41 assists. His 70 points left him equal with Jagr's total but Jagr won the title on most goals scored. Either way, big Lindros was certainly the spotlight of the short season, along with his line-mates Mikael Renberg and John LeClair, the latter acquired early in the year from Montreal. The line was dubbed the "Legion of Doom" and was a powerhouse unit in the brief season with both of Lindros's wingers making the top 10 in scoring.

The impressive Alexei Zhamnov of Winnipeg surprised everyone and finished third with 65 points while talented Joe Sakic of Quebec was fourth. Dominik Hasek and Jim Carey were the shining stars between the pipes that year with Hasek posting a 2.11 goals against average. Carey was brilliant for Washington and sported a decent 2.13 average. Hasek the sprawler, flopper, roller, diver . . . eventually won the Vezina and made the first All-Star team.

The playoffs were simply an extension of the same kind of play, only worse. In the quest for the Cup, the teams increased their defensive play as is normally the case in the playoffs. However, after a dull defensive season, the additional shift toward further closing up the box made for fairly dry hockey. A lot of stars continued to express their frustration with the hooking, holding, and other such silliness they had to put up with in the game.

It was a perfect template for the Devils, Flyers, Blackhawks, and others to play within that year, even though everyone had virtually given the Cup to either the Red Wings or the Flyers. That's the beauty of the Stanley Cup playoffs — you just never know what might happen.

In the dull 1994–95 season, it was the feisty little San Jose Sharks who again brought some salvation to the late-spring early-summer event. The Sharks never paid attention to the fact that the hot division rival Calgary Flames were their first-round opponents and simply went to work. It turned into a little feeding frenzy and Sharks ate the Flames in a seventh-game overtime thriller.

Vancouver pulled off an equally interesting seven-game battle with the St. Louis Blues with the Canucks winning the final game 5–3 in St. Louis.

In the Conference semi-finals, the Rangers were dumped even more easily than most thought by the Flyers, going down four straight. Lindros and team were certainly on a roll. The upset of the round, however, was the Devils, who choked the Penguins to death in five games. Their zone clamp-down plays and checking system simply eliminated the Penguins' ability to put the puck in the net. It was dull, frustrating, and hurt the excitement of the game — but it worked. The Red Wings gaffed the Sharks in four, while the Hawks destroyed Vancouver, also in four, in the Western Conference.

In the Conference finals, the media and armchair experts once again figured the Flyers would take care of the Devils, and once again we were all wrong as Claude Lemieux, Martin Brodeur, and others went to work. The Flyers were grounded in six. Detroit, according to script, eliminated Chicago in five.

At the start of the Cup finals, the smug media grins were back in place and, bloody but undaunted, they continued with the predictions. For New Jersey the speed-bumps and roadblocks on their road to glory had suddenly become a mountain, and that mountain was called Detroit. "Without a doubt, it was all over but the crying now for the Devils," the experts prattled.

The irritating and very effective Claude Lemieux took home the Conn Smythe trophy as playoff MVP after he and the Devils dumped the Wings in four straight games and drank champagne from the Stanley Cup.

The critics and hockey experts cried in their beer.

BEST PLAYERS: Jaromir Jagr — Pittsburgh; Eric Lindros — Philadelphia

BEST LINE: Eric Lindros, Mikael Renberg, John LeClair — Philadelphia

1995–96

If the previous season had been disappointing for fans and players alike, the 1995–96 campaign certainly was a turnaround. The Penguins gleefully announced that Mario Lemieux would play in about 40 or 50 matches "at the most" throughout the year, pacing himself as he went. Instead, Mario played in 70 games, scored 69 goals, added 92 assists, and totalled 161 points for top spot overall in the individual point-scoring parade.

In my mind, that phenomenal return ranks as one of the most amazing sports comeback stories of all time. I long admired and marvelled at the Magnificent One prior to that season, but after that truly outstanding display of determination and dedication . . . well, it's humbling to say the least.

Quebec finally (sadly) collapsed and moved to Colorado, where the reborn team was dubbed the Avalanche. The name would prove prophetic as the club eventually buried all the others that year. The Lindros experience, some other trades, and the shift from Quebec marked the start of the franchise's domino-like steps toward hockey's Holy Grail.

The next big snowball in the mounting Avalanche threat took

place in December when Montreal Canadiens' netminder Patrick Roy stormed off the ice after an embarrassing nine goals were scored against him by Detroit. His Hab teammates were pathetic that night, and Roy was left helpless much of the evening. After finally getting yanked far too late in the game by coach Mario Tremblay, Roy let it be known to several folks nearby, including team owners, that he was done in Montreal. Roy demanded a trade and a couple of days later he wound up in Colorado. He was just the medicine the doctor ordered.

Superstar Wayne Gretzky added to the season's drama by announcing that he also wanted a change of scenery. He was obliged by the L.A. owners in a big trade in late February that sent him to St. Louis, of all places.

It was a season with few dull moments, especially around the nets. Young Jagr continued to flourish and shine in Pittsburgh with the return of Lemieux, and though the two often played together on the power play and in other situations, Jagr played the right side most of the year with centre Ron Francis. Either way, the young Czech was second overall in scoring behind Mario with 149 points including 62 goals. Smooth Joey Sakic finished third with 51 goals and 120 points for Colorado while Frances was fourth at 119. Sophomore Swede sensation Peter Forsberg finished fifth with 116. Lindros had 115 and the small but slippery Paul Kariya had 108 points including 50 goals. Kariya had been joined part way through the season by talented Finnish forward Teemu Selanne from Winnipeg, who also finished in the top 10. Vancouver had picked up Alexander Mogilny from Buffalo, and the talented Russian scored 55 goals and 107 points for ninth place overall.

Working in the west was turning into a real joy for me as I now got to regularly watch dynamite duos such as Bure and Mogilny, Selanne and Kariya, Fedorov and Yzerman, Forsberg and Sakic. Gee, what a tough job.

At season's end, Detroit again dominated the league with an amazing 131 points, including 62 wins in the 82-game season. Colorado was second overall and first in the Pacific Division with 104 points.

In the Eastern Conference, Philadelphia led the Atlantic with 103; Pittsburgh topped the Northeast Division with 102. Once again, everyone was prepared to hand the Cup to Mike Vernon, Chris Osgood, Paul Coffey, and other Red Wings, and once again it just didn't happen. The Detroit curse was holding true.

The Florida Panthers and Colorado Avalanche surprised everyone, making it to the finals, though in reality no one should have been shocked with the rise of the Avalanche. Up to that season, the Nordiques had been building steadily, and suddenly were that much stronger with developing players acquired through the Eric Lindros deal. Leading that list was the tremendously talented Forsberg. Not only did the super Swede continuously show tremendous hands and skating agility, but he was also big, tough, not easily knocked down, intimidated or pushed around. I love to watch the talented slot man play, and from the first instant I saw him on skates I knew he was a real jim-dandy. If anyone is (or was) stupid enough to buy the bunk about Europeans not being tough enough or playing well in heavy traffic, Forsberg certainly silences them. He seems to thrive in the tough going.

The Avalanche's addition of three-time Vezina winner Roy seemed to be the important missing piece in their success puzzle; however, their journey to the top of the hockey mountain was not easy. They started with an opening-round six-game victory over Vancouver before taking on a tough Chicago team for six more gruelling battles. As their reward, they earned the right to take on the mighty Wings.

Detroit, with absolutely no right nor reason to be smug, was not prepared for the Avalanche, and it showed in game one when Colorado took an opening overtime win. The Wings woke up for game two, but by then Roy was in a groove and they couldn't touch him. Every puck looked like a beach ball to him. He stopped everything, including 56 shots in game two and closed up the store. Joe Sakic, superb defenceman Sandis Ozolinsh, tenacious Claude Lemieux, and Forsberg played great hockey and the series ended in six games. Sakic and Forsberg — my, oh my, what talent!

The surprising third-year Panthers had pawed and clawed their way past Boston in five games, and then devoured the star-studded Flyers in six. It took the Panthers seven games and a bungled 60-foot slap shot to defeat the Penguins. Pittsburgh netminder Tom Barrasso simply misplayed the dipping shot by Panther Tom Fitzgerald, and the Penguins never caught up.

At the end of the warm-up playoffs, Florida and Colorado were the final two teams standing. After defeating Detroit, the Panthers were much easier pickings for Colorado, though it took three over-time periods in the fourth game to finally drop them. Forsberg set the pace early in game two of the crushing sweep as he scored three times in the first period and the Avalanche won the game 8–1. The fourth game featured brilliant netminding by Roy and the Panthers' John Vanbiesbrouck. Uwe Krupp eventually scored the overtime winner for a 1–0 win for Colorado.

For Roy, skating about holding the Stanley Cup aloft once more was sweet revenge, while for Hab fans in homes and pubs across the continent it was a heartbreak.

BEST PLAYERS: Mario Lemieux, Jaromir Jagr — Pittsburgh
BEST LINE: Ron Francis, Jaromir Jagr, Tomas Sandstrom — Pittsburgh

1996–97

During the off-season, the Great One moved again, this time signing a deal with the New York Rangers. The new scenery seemed to better suit the star, however Gretzky and many other players didn't score a lot of goals. Solid goaltending had a lot to do with the reduction of goals but the clutch-and-grab, holding, hooking, hacking hockey that New Jersey, Buffalo, and a couple of other clubs had perfected the past few years returned in a flourish. The results were pretty obvious, except the final one, which in hockey is all that really matters.

Detroit finally ended its curse and won the Cup a couple of years after they probably first should have. I admired their team, coach Scotty Bowman, and all the players. Wings fans well deserved their celebration and the city went nuts, but that was at the end of the year, and a lot happened before that magic moment.

The Winnipeg Jets became the second former WHA team in a row to finally fold. Like the Nordiques, the Jets said goodbye to their devoted fans and went to a wealthier place — in the Jets' case, to that hockey hotbed of Phoenix.

To many fans, the idea of the NHL relocating in the middle of the desert state of Arizona seemed bizarre. Of course, they either didn't know or didn't care that Phoenix had hosted pro hockey for many years with their famous Roadrunners. The Jets became Coyotes and Phoenix instantly had a respectable club with players such as Keith Tkachuk, Mike Gartner, and young defenceman Oleg Tverdovsky.

Two teams made significant shifts in the standings at the end of the year, with Dallas the talk of the league. The Stars had done a compete 360-degree turnaround from the year before when they finished on the bottom of the Central Division with 66 points. In 1996–97, the club leaped to 104 points and first place in their division — second in the league.

Buffalo made top spot in the Northeast Division. New Jersey and Philadelphia battled all season long, and when time ran out, New Jersey finished first in the Atlantic with 104 points. Philly had 103. What a tremendous rivalry that kindled. Defending Cup champs Colorado led the Pacific Division and the league with 107.

Despite more problems and pain, the marvellous Mario tried once again to bring the Stanley Cup home to Pittsburgh, but his effort fell short. He did, however, recapture the Art Ross. Mario netted 50 pucks and assisted on 72 others for a 122-point season while Teemu Selanne was second, happy in his new Anaheim home with 109 points, including 51 goals. Linemate Paul Kariya finished third with 99. That marked the first time since 1969–70 that the player in third spot had finished with less than 100 points during a full regular season, and was an indication of things to come.

Rugged and talented Brendan Shanahan had found a happy new home in Detroit halfway through the season. The trade seemed to do for Detroit what the Roy deal did for Colorado the year before —

it provided the key player to fill that important missing piece. Detroit was ready to strike. Did they ever!

It was crystal clear from the very beginning of the playoffs that Detroit had their mind on nothing less than the Stanley Cup, and though Colorado, Dallas, Philadelphia, and New Jersey were all determined to take it instead, they never stood a chance. The general feeling in the Red Wings dressing room was that they had come close too many times the past few years and it was simply time to complete the quest.

After a solid battle all the way to the finals, both the Wings and the Flyers clashed in what many thought might be a full seven-game battle. But the Wings disposed of the Flyers in four quick games. Eric Lindros led the playoffs in points with 12 goals and 26 points in 19 games when it was over, but it was the guys on Detroit who had the biggest grins at the end.

Detroit had finally won the Stanley Cup, their first since 1954–55, and the city went bonkers.

I will never forget the look of pleasure on Steve Yzerman's face as he kissed the Cup and skated about the ice. It was great to see such a classy guy and his teammates so happy, and to see the fans, many of whom had never seen their team win the Cup, go wild.

But heartbreak was hiding just around the corner once again. Soon after the Cup celebrations, a couple of Red Wings were in a terrible limousine crash. Vladimir Konstantinov was put into a wheelchair for life as a quadriplegic; Slava Fetisov was also badly hurt. The terrible crash muted the celebrations quickly.

There had been times before their first Cup that the Wings were heavy favourites to win, but in the playoffs lost to teams they should have beat. During the season, I'd watch every Wing game I could get on the dish and, geeze, were they good entertainment — the very best.

Detroit had two units of five who were beautiful to watch. They included Sergei Fedorov, Nicklas Lidstrom, Igor Larionov, Viacheslav Fetisov, Vladimir Konstantinov, Slava Kozlov, and Anders Eriksson. When you coupled any four of these Soviet or European players with Coffey, Yzerman, or Larry Murphy (when he later came over from Toronto), they fit like a glove. In my time I don't think I've ever seen a team with a unit of five, let alone two, with such mental skills. The first fivesome was all Russian, though — amazing! I've been saying for years that to advance the puck, you pass it backwards. Geeze, do I get some queer looks from hockey fans. The main Red Wing fivesome that drew most raves was nicknamed the "Wizards of Ov" and included Fedorov, Konstantinov, Fetisov, Kozlov, and Larionov. They were magic. They would make five passes — three of which were drop passes or passes back to unchecked teammates, never challenging anyone physically. The player would simply lead the opponent to the boards, creating open ice. The players would continue to drop the puck back three or four times until centre ice was suddenly wide open for the teammate coming late and he'd cruise unchallenged into the other team's defensive zone.

Shoot the puck in? Never. They played the game like chess and all were highly skilled with the puck, and all on the same wavelength. Anticipation and the main key, timing, were well within all their capabilities. My oh my, what a treat it was to watch.

The Wings heading into the year 2000 have one and a half units now with the same skills, but when one complete unit followed the other back then, it gave you time to recognize the pattern. Holy Jumpin', wouldn't it be super if every team in the NHL had one or two units like that? Well, I can dream, can't I?

Oh — Chris Chelios will fit right in with the Soviet machine in Detroit, and will he ever appreciate their skill level. He'll think he's died and gone to hockey heaven.

BEST PLAYERS: Mario Lemieux — Pittsburgh; Teemu Selanne —
Anaheim
BEST LINE: Steve Rucchin, Teemu Selanne, Paul Kariya —
Anaheim

1997–98

The third of four former WHA teams disappeared from the NHL with another franchise shift that summer. The Hartford Whalers became the Carolina Hurricanes, and at year end the relocated squad missed the playoffs by just four points.

Much of the hockey focus that summer remained with the tragic car accident involving the Red Wing players. Many wondered how the Wings would respond to the incident.

It didn't take too long to find out.

Dallas, Detroit, Colorado, and St. Louis had a battle going all season within the Western Conference, and when the season was settled, Dallas had edged the Wings for top spot in the central Division. Dallas, led by Mike Modano and Joe Nieuwendyk, were tops in the league as well. Peter Forsberg and his Avalanche teammates earned top spot in the Pacific.

New Jersey continued to win with their defensive game and solid scoring. It worked well enough to garner them the top in the Atlantic Division and Eastern Conference.

Hotshot marksman Jaromir Jagr led Pittsburgh to the Northeast title. Jagr continued to prove he was a superstar all on his own and dominated the league scoring race. He finished first with 102 points, 11 more than second-place Peter Forsberg.

The overall player point totals were remarkably low that season considering how players had been racking up points at the beginning and even middle of the decade. For the first time since 1967–68, the second place scorer did not reach 99 points in a full season.

I believe the dramatic reduction in scoring was reflective of the game's new defensive systems, stick interference, and clutch-and-grab hockey as many suggested, while others blamed goal-crease changes, bigger players, better goalies . . . In fact it probably was (and is) a bunch of all the above, but certainly the hooking, holding, and bigger bodies have a lot to do with it. For whatever reason, the scoring numbers plummeted that year.

Forsberg dazzled many with his astounding play and deserved his second place but was hard pressed by both Pavel Bure of

Vancouver and Wayne Gretzky of New York, both of whom finished with 90 points. The Russian Rocket was brilliant for Vancouver, scoring 51 goals.

Injuries and other issues took their toll, and a couple of key players missed significant action. Lindros played just 63 games, Hull 66, and Turgeon 60. Sergei Fedorov came back after a long contract holdout in time to be effective in the playoffs; Paul Kariya had virtually the entire year off due to a prolonged holdout and to recover from his series of concussions.

Dominik Hasek was again the story between the pipes as the amazing little flopper, dipper, diver did his thing to near perfection. He won the Hart Trophy as most valuable player and also the Vezina and made the first All-Star team.

Boston boasted an outstanding rookie in the form of winger Sergei Samsonov.

When the teams lined up for the annual spring strutting rites to the Stanley Cup, the only question was who, if anyone, would knock off the Red Wings. Colorado was a willing combatant and so was Dallas. Some suggested it was the clingy Devils. In the end, it turned out to be the perennial chokers of modern hockey — the Washington Capitals, who played final-round sacrificial lambs.

The Red Wings were kind and ended it in four quick games.

By making it to the finals, led by the brilliant netminding of Olaf Kolzig (just down the road at Union Bay on Vancouver Island) the Capitals finally rid themselves of the choker label (though they didn't win the Cup, did they?). Ironically the Capitals would slip out of playoff sight the next year.

A tearful Steve Yzerman told the Detroit fans that the second Cup was dedicated to Konstantinov and the other Red Wings hurt in the car crash the spring before. Konstantinov was wheeled onto the ice, complete in a Wing jersey, for the Cup celebrations. It was a special, highly emotional moment in hockey.

Best Players: Peter Forsberg — Colorado; Dominik Hasek — Detroit; Jaromir Jagr — Pittsburgh

Best Lines: Ron Francis, Jaromir Jagr, Stu Barnes — Pittsburgh

Steve Yzerman, Doug Brown, Brendan Shanahan —
Detroit

1998–99

Many fans and hockey folks figured the new Nashville entry
would get chewed up by the rest of the league their first year. But
in the end it was the Predators, living up to their name, who bit off
a good hunk of other teams' backsides. The Predators finished out
of the playoff race but with a respectable showing.

Pavel Bure turned out to be the year's best pouter as he refused
to return to the Vancouver Canucks. Sadly, the talented player was
fed up with Vancouver management and their alleged broken
promises, and said he wanted to play elsewhere. Eventually he went
to Florida late in the year, was injured twice, and played just 11
games for this new club. His departure, Alexander Mogilny's total
loss of talent, and injuries to Mark Messier and other Canucks contributed to a dismal and pathetic year for the club.

Former financial holdout Petr Nedved returned to the league
from a season's self-banishment and signed with the struggling
Rangers. He looked awesome for the first 10 games and then went
into the tank. The Rangers, even led by the brilliant Gretzky who
set the all-time, all time of all time, total goals mark for players in
late March, could not help his club into the playoffs. Gretzky scored
a game-winning goal against the rival New York Islanders on March
29 for his 1,072nd goal. The record edged Howe's by one for the
all-time goals including playoffs and WHA play.

At the end of the season Jagr had once again clearly claimed the
scoring crown as he racked up 127 points. Selanne finished second
with 107, Kariya third at 101, and Forsberg fourth at 97.

The regular season ended on two sad notes. Eric Lindros sus-
tained a collapsed lung just a few games before the season ended.
Though it shelved the talented man for the playoffs, it was anticipated that Lindros would return for the 1999–2000 season. Then,
with two games left in the Rangers' season, superstar Wayne Gretzky
announced he was hanging up his skates.

A couple of teams promised to battle Detroit for the Cup, including Dallas and Colorado in the Western Conference and Ottawa and New Jersey in the East. Detroit and Dallas swept their first-round opponents while Buffalo upset Ottawa and Pittsburgh edged New Jersey. Earlier round eliminations had included Boston dumping Carolina in six games. After the deciding game, Carolina defenceman Steve Chiasson was killed in an single-vehicle automobile crash, which dampened the playoff passion for all involved.

The Wings were upset by the powerful Avalanche, complete with a tenacious Theo Fleury in the line-up from a late-season deal with Calgary. The series began with Peter Forsberg taking Brendan Shanahan heavily into the glass, and cutting him (accidentally) for 40 stitches. (That damn new seamless glass will kill some player soon. There is no give, which is insane for 225-pound men colliding with it at high speeds.) After a brutal series, the Avalanche ran into the tough Dallas Stars.

Led by Ed Belfour, Joe Nieuwendyk, and Mike Modano, the Dallas Stars eliminated the Colorado Avalanche and then manhandled Buffalo in six games to win the Cup. It was the first win for the franchise in league history.

BEST PLAYER:	Jaromir Jagr — Pittsburgh
BEST LINES:	Steve Rucchin, Teemu Selanne, Paul Kariya — Anaheim
	Martin Straka, Jaromir Jagr, and Alexei Kovalev — Pittsburgh

DYNASTIES:	**Detroit Red Wings 1997, 1998**
LEADERS:	Steve Yzerman, Sergei Fedorov, Larry Murphy, Chris Osgood, Nicklas Lidstrom, Igor Larionov, Brendan Shanahan
BLEEDERS:	Mike Vernon, Victor Kozlov, Doug Brown, Kris Draper, Viacheslav Fetisov, Tomas Holmstrom, Vladimir Konstantinov, Slava Kozlov, Martin Lapointe, Darren McCarty, Tomas Sandstrom, Doug Brown, Norm Maracle

FEEDERS: Mathieu Dandenault, Kevin Hodson, Joey Kocur, Kirk Maltby, Bob Rouse, Jamie Pushor, Tim Taylor, Aaron Ward, Dimitri Mirinov, Brent Gilchrist, Anders Eriksson, Michael Knuble, Uwe Krupp

4

■ ■ ■

THE
PLAYERS

A BOUT

THE PLAYERS

■ ■ ■

Over the years I've been asked a couple of key hockey questions repeatedly, such as who's the greatest player of all time, and who would I name to my All-Time All-Star team? I've also been asked such questions as who would I list as the top 50 players ever, who was the toughest, fastest . . . and so on.

While none of those questions is as tough as explaining the meaning of life, why there is air, or Einstein's theory on relativity . . . they still call for a lot of thought to answer. Even for someone like me — a scholar of the game, a player, coach, and broadcaster involved in hockey for more than 50 years — such answers are not at all simple.

There are many factors to consider, including how the game has evolved. Even within the past 50 years, the sport has altered drastically in equipment, rules, and popularity, not to mention speed, player size, and other significant aspects of the game itself. When I look back at the number of players and teams, and the plethora of stars who've played during the last half century, even picking the top 50 players is damn tough, let alone naming the best at anything.

Still that was one of the challenges I said I'd take on in writing this book. I just never thought it would be so goldarn cotton-picking tough.

In this section I not only attempt to name my top 50 players and top three All-Time All-Star teams, I also acknowledge a few of the many players and people that helped make the past 50 years of hockey memories special for me. They were real characters of the NHL's past half decade.

Take note — there is a difference between the top 50 players and the All-Time All-Star teams. Different question, different answer.

And so . . .

ALL-TIME
ALL-STARS

14

■ ■ ■

Every hockey fan in Canada, United States, Europe, and the rest of the world seems fixated with picking all-star teams, and especially the "All-Time" All-Star hockey team. When I was first asked to pick a super squad from 1949 to 1999 my immediate thought was, "Give up, you can't win!"

My next reaction was a personal oath to give my list verbally only. I figured if I avoided writing it on paper I could always deny anything and everything, and simply say I was misquoted.

After many, many hours analyzing this hockey question over the years, I finally was forced (by this book project) to sit down and take a stab at creating my own all-star list. The latest epic effort began some three hours and three glasses of wine into a very, very long plane ride from Vancouver to Boston. I actually dragged out the pencil and notepad, and some old notes I'd made years before, and started to make my list. That's when I began to fight with myself.

Ever do that? Ever argue with yourself and then lose? It's

frustrating and I do it all the time, especially when it comes to hockey and politics. I started creating lists of players, but after tearing up and throwing away dozens of new attempts and experiencing many bouts of cussing and discussion with myself, I sat back in frustration and took a break. Aimlessly sifting through the old hockey notes I'd brought along for background info, I discovered a crumpled list I'd made about a dozen years before, attempting the same all-star task.

I looked over the list closely and agreed that, indeed, they were the best six players I'd seen perform. On the list were Terry Sawchuk in goal, Bobby Orr and Doug Harvey on defence, Wayne Gretzky at centre, with Gordie Howe and Bobby Hull on the wings.

That was easy.

Or was it?

Looking at the six names in the starting line-up, I realized I'd left off Jacques Plante, Tim Horton, Brad Park, Jean Beliveau, Maurice Richard, and Mike Bossy. Even if those superstars only made the second team, that meant for my third roster I had a choice of Ken Dryden, Glenn Hall, and Grant Fuhr in goal, Ray Bourque, Paul Coffey, Red Kelly, Chris Chelios, and Denis Potvin on defence, while up front I still had Guy Lafleur, Ted Lindsay, Teeder Kennedy, Michel Goulet, the Pocket Rocket, and Mario Lemieux . . .

"Aaaaggghh," I roared loudly to no one in particular, though a number of passengers reacted to my groan (and pencil-breaking antics), and the stewardess scurried over in a flash. After assuring her that I was not having a heart attack I settled back down with my notepad and a new pencil to try to resolve the dilemma.

When I looked at my top three all-star line-ups from a dozen years ago I realized that in 2000 I'd make a couple of changes. I immediately scratched out Bossy as the right winger on the second line and scribbled in Lafleur.

Why?

Good question, and one I had to ponder myself. For another half hour I stared out the window in space, literally, and contemplated why I'd made the change. I sought a valid reason. Then it hit me. I asked myself, "If I was the owner, general manager, and coach of the team (all rolled into one) and both Bossy and Lafleur were available, who would I pick?"

No problem — Guy Lafleur.

Why?

Lafleur was not just a great player but also a tremendous leader. Guy had all kinds of pizzazz, was tough, and had a real mean streak in him. He absolutely loved to play the game and was a fierce competitor. Lafleur loved life and sold lots and lots of arena seats across two countries. Guy had to be on my second team.

Then I wondered, "Why not Lafleur on the first team?" Certainly he could not replace Howe, but what about Hull? Why not? A winger is a winger is a winger. Left or right doesn't mean a hill of beans to many players. It's true the hand you hold your stick in has an effect, but for some playing the off-wing is an advantage. To each his own . . . a wing is a wing is a wing.

The choice was between Hull and Lafleur, and after much deliberation, I went with Lafleur again.

Some Hull fans will (and should) heartily argue differently but — "Stop it there — back it up" — I asked myself the same question as I had with Bossy and Lafleur. If I was an NHL owner/GM/coach and had the choice between Bobby Hull and Guy Lafleur, who would I take? Guy — in a New York minute.

I'll tell you what, folks, put Hull in Montreal and Lafleur in Chicago and over the years the Hawks would have won more than the single Cup they did with big Robert there. Guy Lafleur playing lots with Mikita at centre would have scored more points than he did in Montreal.

But aside from all his scoring talent and hockey skills, Lafleur's greatest asset was his desire to win. His tremendous focus rubbed off on anyone who came close to him. He made you want to win, inspired you to play hard and tough for every shift of every game.

How'd he do it? I don't know, but I can guess because I was on some teams with some great leaders. There were the quiet, gentle types like Syl Apps and the hardworking, tough, loud, and cussing Ted Kennedy types. No two stars did it the same way. Guy, as usual, did it his way.

Suddenly Lafleur had jumped from the third line to the first and I could see a whole new piece of paper about to start. As I drew up the second unit forward line, I started to wage mental war over the choices of Hull or Lindsay for left wing and Richard or Bossy for right, and that's when my brain kicked in with an additional question. Since the ultimate goal, the Holy Grail of hockey, is the Stanley Cup, perhaps the real question should be "As an owner/GM/coach whose job it is to win a Stanley Cup within three years, who would my All-Time All-Star team of 15 players be since 1949?"

And that means a bit of a different answer.

My first unit would stay the same with Sawchuk, Orr, Harvey, Gretzky, Howe, and now Mr. Lafleur. The second line again takes a lot of thought but has Jacques Plante in goal with a defence pairing of the great Tim Horton and Brad Park. I now had Hull penciled in above Ted Lindsay's name in the second-line left-wing position. The dilemma continued until I considered the playoff factor, and once again Bobby took another bumping. Terrible Ted earned his nickname as a fierce competitor, particularly in playoff games when the going was rough. The expression "When the going gets tough, the tough get going" was coined, I'm sure, for Terrible Ted. Not only was he fierce but he was talented and had a knack for big goals.

I got the same results when I held up Bossy next to Rocket Richard. For all his sniper skills and talent, Bossy could simply not hold a candle to the Rocket for intensity and fire to win no matter what. The Rocket would go through walls, burning hoops, and cut glass to win, and he proved it over and over. Few competitors better than the Rocket ever lived. Bossy could dent the twine as well as or better than the Rocket and was just as talented for big goals, but on fire and brimstone Richard earned the nod. Bossy played the game in pain in the latter stages of his career; however, so did the Rocket, who also inflicted a hell of a lot on others in the process.

Then I made the change I never thought I'd make, which was to rub out the name Beliveau at centre ice on the second line and insert the name Mario Lemieux. After staring blankly out the window at the night sky about 35,000 feet somewhere over Michigan, I underlined Lemieux's name in confirmation of my choice. Beliveau ranks as one of the finest players and men I have ever known in the game, but when I seriously consider the career Lemieux had, short as it was, I realize he must be the second-line slot man. Mario was a Beliveau but bigger, stronger, and more skilled (though not a lot more). His tremendous output, domination of the league, dexterity, and smoothness for such a large man, and his will to overcome incredible odds to win, give him that honour. I would argue that for five years of his career he was as good as or maybe better than anyone else who played the game. In 1997 when he finally hung up the blades for good, he'd averaged .82 goals per game, ahead of Gretzky's average of .65 (then). They are the only two NHL players with more than 500 points to have averaged more than two points per game in their careers. I looked at my revised second line: Lindsay, Lemieux, and Richard. Holy smokes, that's one talented, tough trio.

Even with the third-team selections the decisions remained tough. In goal I had four possible names at the top: Grant Fuhr, Ken Dryden, Glenn Hall, and Turk Broda. The long haul and grind of today's regular season would probably have been too much for Broda, and in a hard squeeze and based on his years of continual winning play, I give the third between-the-pipes position to Fuhr. I'd be thrilled to have whoever was left over as my netminder, and Glenn Hall was always one of my favourites.

Defence was now a problem as well, because whoever I eliminated was simply not in the club. The choices were numerous and plentiful. Who to pick from Ray Bourque, Red Kelly, Eddie Shore, Larry Robinson, Chris Chelios? Without much hesitation, I put Bourque in first spot. What a pleasure to watch this young man. Not only has he tremendous skating, passing, and stickhandling skills, but he's also probably the most accurate shooting player in the league, slap or wrist. After staring out the window a few more minutes, I finally gave the final position to Kelly, largely due to his skills in both ends of the rink. His offensive skill was largely due to his excellent years as a centre man later in his career. As a defenceman, he was superb, controlling the play and passing with precision.

Up front, Bobby Hull and Jean Beliveau finally get their long-overdue honours while the right wing position goes to the also-bumped Mike Bossy. Beliveau, Bossy, and Hull . . . not a bad line, eh? Jumpin' Jehoshaphat, that Team Three is a regular dream team all on its own and pretty impressive for a bunch of double cast-offs. Probably two of the finest and hardest shooters ever in the league on the same line? Yikes.

So there you are for what it's worth. I've picked my 15 guys and the selection was not easy. Left out in the cold are marvellous players such as Teeder Kennedy, the Pocket Rocket, Michel Goulet, Chris Chelios, Glenn Hall, Peter Stastny, J.C. Tremblay, Syl Apps, Frank Mahovlich, Milt Schmidt, Denis Potvin . . .

Disagree all you like. You could be right.

THE TOP PLAYERS

TOP GOALIES

- Terry Sawchuk
- Jacques Plante
- Grant Fuhr
- Glenn Hall
- Ken Dryden
- Turk Broda

TOP DEFENCEMEN

- Bobby Orr
- Doug Harvey
- Tim Horton
- Brad Park
- Ray Bourque
- Red Kelly
- Larry Robinson
- Chris Chelios
- Eddie Shore
- Paul Coffey
- King Clancy
- Denis Potvin

TOP FORWARDS

- Wayne Gretzky
- Mario Lemieux
- Gordie Howe
- Guy Lafleur
- Jean Beliveau
- Maurice Richard
- Ted Lindsay
- Bobby Hull
- Mark Messier
- Mike Bossy

- Stan Mikita
- Michel Goulet
- Harvey Jackson
- Jaromir Jagr
- Teeder Kennedy
- Henri Richard
- Frank Mahovlich
- Eric Lindros
- Phil Esposito

LEFT WING
- Lafleur
- Lindsay
- Hull

CENTRE
- Gretzky
- Lemieux
- Beliveau

RIGHT WING
- Howe
- Richard
- Bossy

LEFT DEFENCE
- Harvey
- Park
- Bourque

RIGHT DEFENCE
- Orr
- Horton
- Kelly

GOALTENDERS
- Sawchuk
- Plante
- Fuhr

Top 50
All-Time Players

■ ■ ■

When *The Hockey News* recently polled hockey people for their opinions on the all-time best players, I was one of the so-called experts they asked. A very detailed list arrived with tons of statistics about each player, and those from the earlier years with shortened schedules had their stats increased and pro-rated to 70 games. My package arrived late, four days before my holiday to Palm Springs. I must have spent eight to 10 hours listing who I thought were the best goalies, defencemen, centres, and wingers. Then I called in little brother Tom, who played top-flight university hockey for Clarkston College in the mid-1940s.

"Here's the problem, b'y," I said. "Here's who I think is best at each position. I've also listed my top 10 with Gretzky in first, but I'm not sure on anything yet, so do as you want. It should be a piece of cake to finish the project and list the top 50 from there."

More than 20 hours of anguish later (so I'm told), brother Tom sent my/his/our list off to the patiently waiting *Hockey News* folks.

Tom chose Orr as number one over Gretzky, and I have no real problem with that, because in some ways he was better.

In order to list the top 50, I ask myself the number one hockey question I get asked frequently: "Who is the best player I ever saw?" My answer, which is another question, remains the same: When and for how long?

Over a five-year period, Bobby Orr; over a 10-year stretch, Wayne Gretzky; over 20 years, Gordie Howe. Each of them was marvellous, specially gifted at the game, with a sense for the puck and the play. They each shaped and changed the game for the better and were wonderful ambassadors to the greatest sport in the world.

When I'm trying to choose the best player ever, I again put myself in the position of owner, general manager, and coach and I come up with four players of equal consideration: Orr, Gretzky, Howe, and Lemieux.

I saw Wayne play live at least 50 times, Orr 30, Lemieux 20, and I played at least 70 games against Gordie Howe and saw him in another 25 games live, and all four men time after time impressed me with their physical and mental talents. Gretzky had the best mental ability and Mario the most physical skills. Bobby Orr was the greatest skater, best accelerator, and made the best passes coming out of his own end, while Big Gordie had the strongest body, best elbows (I have three missing teeth to prove it), meanest temperament, and set the best all-star standards over a 20-year period.

As a GM/coach faced with choosing one of those four players, I would quite happily say to the other three GMs, "Please pick first." I would be absolutely tickled pink with whoever was left.

Still, the question is "Who is the best?"

After taking the four names and shaking them up in a hat, the answers are as follows. (I have listed, in fact, my entire top 50 and added the names of some other players deserving mention as well. Some justification for my decisions are found within the individual player snippets later in this section.)

TOP 50 ALL-TIME PLAYERS

1. Wayne Gretzky
2. Bobby Orr
3. Mario Lemieux
4. Gordie Howe
5. Guy Lafleur
6. Jean Beliveau
7. Bobby Hull
8. Doug Harvey
9. Terry Sawchuk
10. Mark Messier
11. Jacques Plante
12. Mike Bossy
13. Stan Mikita
14. Eddie Shore
15. Maurice Richard
16. Ken Dryden
17. Ray Bourque
18. Harvey Jackson
19. Chris Chelios
20. Jaromir Jagr
21. Turk Broda
22. Ted Lindsay
23. Phil Esposito
24. Ted Kennedy
25. Henri Richard
26. Bill Durnan
27. Bobby Clarke
28. Frank Mahovlich
29. Dickie Moore
30. Larry Robinson
31. Eric Lindros
32. King Clancy
33. Bryan Trottier
34. Marcel Dionne
35. Charlie Conacher
36. Elmer Lach
37. Glenn Hall
38. Peter Statsny
39. Steve Yzerman
40. Syl Apps
41. Jari Kurri
42. Gilbert Perreault
43. Howie Morenz
44. Patrick Roy
45. Milt Schmidt
46. Paul Coffey
47. Denis Potvin
48. Michel Goulet
49. Dit Clapper
50. Nels Stewart

HONOURABLE MENTION

Peter Forsberg, Paul Kariya, Brian Leetch, Joe Sakic,
Cal Gardner, Brad Park, Red Kelly, Andy Bathgate, Tony Esposito,
Bernie Parent, George Hainsworth, Grant Fuhr

P R O F I L E S O F S E L E C T
T O P 5 0 P L A Y E R S

■ ■ ■

As a player, coach, and broadcaster, I have come to know many incredible hockey people over the years. As well, thousands of hockey fans have asked me about various players or coaches, some household names or stars, others lesser known players who simply stand out for one reason or another. I've taken a few pages here to comment on some of those characters in my life.

There is no rhyme or reason to the collection other than they are people often asked about by fans.

WAYNE GRETZKY

Wayne Gretzky was born to play hockey.

I'm sure in God's big picture, He had lots of other plans for Wayne, but playing hockey had to be high on the list. If ever a player had a God-given feel and ability for the game, it was Wayne.

His knack for hockey was immediately obvious as an outstanding minor hockey player. At age 11 he scored 378 goals and 517 points in less than 82 games. As a 16-year-old Tier One OHA junior in Sault Ste. Marie, Wayne drew attention and created plenty of discussion. Gretzky was a well-known hockey name long before ever lacing up his skates as a pro. In his final junior year, he finished second (behind Bobby Smith) in the Ontario Junior Hockey League scoring race with 70–112–182 and was the leading scorer at the World Junior Tournament. At 17 he was too young to be eligible for the National Hockey League, so he joined the World Hockey Association's Indianapolis Racers. The rest is history.

While Gretzky was admired and sought after by many scouts, coaches, and hockey experts, not all the hockey writers or broadcasters (especially some Americans) had a clue how good Wayne would be. During research on this book, we stumbled on some gems, including a December 1978 Sports Special Hockey Annual, which analyzed teams for the 1978–79 season. In the World Hockey Association analysis of the Racers were various references to the "Great Gretsky [sic]" including the following: "He may or may not become a superstar but he is for sure a rich kid . . . . Gretsky [sic] is almost six feet in height, although a shade on the skinny side, and is a super stick-handler with good speed and a quick shot. He might make it as a star." Right.

It's appropriate to say that Wayne Gretzky was the greatest player to ever lace on a pair of skates, and difficult (though nice) to imagine that someday there may actually be someone who is even better.

Lemieux and Orr qualify in the running for the title of Greatest Player Ever, but when push came to shove for this book and I was forced to choose between Orr and Gretzky, I finally gave it to Wayne, by a hair. Time, of course, was a factor because Orr was gone so quickly, while Wayne dominated and turned in 20 years of phenomenal hockey before retiring at the end of the 1998–99 season.

I keep looking over his amazing statistics, year after year, and shake my head. He racked up 196 points in 1982–83, 72 points ahead of the nearest scorer, Peter Stastny. In 1983–84 he had a remarkable point streak of 51 games when he accumulated 153 points, including 61 goals. He tallied 100 points in 34 games, and at season end had a phenomenal total of 205 points, 79 ahead of teammate Paul Coffey. But he wasn't done and in 1984–85 racked up another scoring title with 208 points, including 73 goals.

Broadcasters, hockey writers, oh heck — everybody — figured that no one was ever going to eclipse Gretzky's amazing total that season. And no one did — except the Great One himself, the next year. In 1985–86 he stunned us all with 215 points, 74 points ahead of next best, Mario Lemieux at 141 points.

Wayne had 163 assists, 22 more points than he needed in total to win the scoring title. Incredibly, he could have won on his assists alone. No one has ever dominated any sport the way that Gretzky dominated hockey, and he did it year after year after year. Howe, Orr, Lemieux, Beliveau, Bossy, Trottier, Bentley — all marvellous but none of them dominated hockey the way Wayne did.

When critics tried to find some flaw in the gem, they would often suggest his skating was a little slow or awkward. The night before his final game in a salute by a former teammate, Marty McSorley pooh-poohed the suggestion saying, "If that was the case, how come no one caught him or stopped him?"

Quite simply, Wayne's hockey skills were at a level very few others might ever attain. One can argue that so-and-so was a better shooter, or someone else a better stickhandler or skater, but Wayne had the complete package.

He holds or shares 61 NHL records, which is probably another record in itself. During his 20 years, he won the Art Ross Trophy as scoring champion 10 times, the Most Valuable Player nine times, and for 13 years in a row he led the league in assists. He had four seasons of more than 200 points!

Wayne never stopped giving his all, and his competitiveness drove him to go full out every night. That spirit helped make him the phenomenal scorer he was when he finally retired. His scoring legacy is amazing and shows 830 multiple-point games, including 50 three-or-more-goal games and an unbelievable 95 games in which he scored five or more points.

In the 1997–98 season, after more than 20 years in the NHL, Gretzky finished fourth overall in scoring despite his New York Rangers missing the playoffs.

What made Wayne so good, so special, is that you never saw him take a game, a period, or even a shift off. There might be four minutes left in a game, Edmonton ahead 6–2, and there would be Wayne, working his butt off. He probably had two goals and two assists already but he was looking for his fifth point and working just as hard as he had in the first shift. He never quit and the results showed it.

It was the same thing when he played for the Kings, the Blues, and the Rangers. The guy took the greatest pride in his performance of anyone I know, and every fan at home or away got to see his best effort and performance every night, right down to the last second. Even in his last game at home in New York against the Penguins, Wayne never stopped. In typical Wayne fashion, he managed to help tie the game with just 29 seconds left in the second period, setting up Brian Leetch. It marked Wayne's 2,857th point. It turned out to be the last Ranger goal of the year as the Penguins won in overtime 2-1.

Wayne's next best asset, though, was his mind. His anticipation, timing, knowledge of where everybody was, and at what speed they were travelling were baffling. I believe he even knew what other players were thinking. Watching him was sometimes scary, realizing how in tune he was.

On a scale of 1 to 10, Wayne's mind was a 10 plus. Thankfully, there are a few other players close to that today: Selanne, Yashin, Kariya, Jagr, and Forsberg are some of the ones who are either a 10 or close to it. The problem is they play a much different game than their teammates, who have a game mentality of 5 or 6. Few of them have even one or two teammates who are a 9 or 10 to work with.

Part of Wayne's tremendous success was his exceptional luck in playing in Edmonton with at least five other guys who played at or near his hockey intelligence; Paul Coffey, Kevin Lowe, Glenn Anderson, Jari Kurri, and Mark Messier were all bright, talented players in their prime. Jeepers, what fun it must have been any time those five got on the ice together.

Almost every game I worked in Edmonton, I'd pick an exceptional play by Gretzky and cast, and after explaining it with the help of the telestrator would finish with something like "That's it, folks, that's hockey! And you will never see anything better."

But the next week the same thing would happen, another incredible play by the cast or part of the cast. It was like that week after week after week, and it was sure lovely to watch.

Wayne's phenomenal skill and touch were such that even alone he stood out as a superb player, never mind blended with other similar talent. Game after game he did things that astounded and amazed us all. He was so incredible he did things that almost made me speechless.

I've been in and around the game of hockey for 70 years and I can remember plays and goals scored (some by me) on the pond, on the river, in the backyard, in my first indoor arena, at organized games, at overseas matches at Richmond, Wembley, Paisley, and Brighton arenas, some in the NHL, and quite a few from 45 years of teaching and coaching, but there is one that I think stands out above all others. I can it recall anytime, anywhere, in slow motion in vivid detail. It was a goal engineered by Gretzky but scored by Kevin Lowe.

It started when teammate Charlie Huddy beat a forechecker to the puck in the corner and passed it behind the net to Lowe, who was facing the boards to pick up the pass. Watching this play develop was Gretzky, slowly returning along the fence at the red line toward his own end. The second Lowe touched the puck, Wayne broke into the centre ice area near the blueline and picked up a tape-to-tape pass from Lowe, who had to know Gretzky would be there because he just turned and shot the puck. I thought his play would be icing until Gretzky appeared like magic out of nowhere to take the pass.

"Great play," I thought as the pass beat one player, but now it was four against Gretzky — which turned out to be no contest. Wayne easily beat one man going through centre ice close to the right wing boards, then as the defenceman and checking winger closed in on him as he crossed the opposing blueline 10 feet from the boards, he cast the fly upon the water.

Gretzky greatly reduced speed and started to go diagonally

across the ice, and both checkers, thinking they had him cornered, started to chase him. What happened in the next 10 seconds was the greatest exhibition of creating open ice I've ever seen. With two checkers already chasing him, Gretzky headed for the right-side defenceman, got his attention, and lured him into taking up the chase as well. The backchecking winger also got caught in the maze, and by this point Wayne was near the top of the circle. He beat the winger, lost the other three by making a sharp turn toward the boards and, while fighting off the fifth checker, softly floated a 60-foot pass across the ice to a hard-skating Lowe. When Kevin picked up the puck, he didn't have a player within 20 feet of him except the goalie, and he simply snapped the puck home.

During the entire time Wayne had the puck in that play, he was under constant attack, he beat every checker on the ice at least once, but he, Lowe, and at least two other Oilers on the ice knew what was going on. The thing that stunned me was the pass. Never once did I see him look where his teammates were. He knew by instinct where everyone would or should be as a result of what he was doing. He knew where Kevin Lowe was, and at what speed he was travelling. How else can you explain such a perfect play? Folks, that fellow was plain scary. Jeepers, what talent.

Even today I still bump into occasional non-believers who say that in the old-six team league they would have eaten Gretzky up. Baloney! In any era Wayne would have dominated the game like he did in his spectacular years during the 1980s. It scares me to think what would have happened if Gretzky had played centre between Gordie Howe and Ted Lindsay, Sid Smith and Tod Sloan, Max and Doug Bentley, Rocket Richard and Toe Blake, or Bobby Bauer and Woody Dumart. It would have been no contest.

The same doubters also say we would have "run him" — hit him, in other words — in the old days. Once again, baloney. We weren't that big, we weren't that tough, and we weren't in any kind of condition to run anybody in the 1940s and '50s. During the 1960s the players started to be bigger and tougher, stronger and faster. Wayne Gretzky would have had no problem leading the league in scoring by 50 points playing with Hull and Wharram, etc.

In any era, Gretzky in his prime would have been number one by a country mile. During the 1997–98 season playing with a very weak Ranger club, Wayne scored 90 points and finished fourth overall. Later, Colin Campbell, who coached the Rangers for most of 1997–98, told me, "If New York had had anybody who could put the puck in the water off a wharf Gretzky would have had 125 points minimum."

When Wayne announced his retirement, many of us felt an emptiness in the pit of our stomachs. We were fully aware that the greatest player in the game was going to leave. But we should be thankful for what he gave us, and thankful for the memories.

BOBBY ORR

The top defenceman ever and number two player on my All-Time list is the wonder-kid from Parry Sound, Bobby Orr.

I've been a lucky man much of my life and can say that along the way I've had a number of honours and thrills to enjoy. Ranked high on the list is the joy and pleasure I had of watching Bobby Orr play this wonderful sport. No other player could dramatically change the tempo or flow of a hockey game, or the outcome, quite like Bobby Orr. Amazing hands, amazing skater, amazing talent.

Tragically, Bobby never had the opportunity to play the game for as long as we all would have liked. Crippled by knee injuries, repeated surgeries, and constant pain, he left the game long before his time should have been up. But Bobby possessed too much pride to play the game at only 70 or 80 percent of his ability.

I first saw him as a junior playing for Oshawa in the Memorial Cup finals and he was just recovering from knee surgery. Orr was obviously operating on half a leg but he was still clearly the best player on the ice. Over the years I've played with, and coached, quite a few players who had operations on their knees, and even those who stayed out of the game for the proper healing and rehab period, without exception, have told me that it takes at least a year before the knee returns to normal. Sure, the player gets back sooner but they're always thinking, "Another knock and I'm done." They usually have sub-par years. Oshawa's obvious desire to win that year pushed them into playing Orr before they should have, and quite probably was the start of his career-ending knee problems.

But holy cow, in his best five years in the NHL was he a somebody or what?

Orr had the greatest acceleration, especially in coming out of a turn, of anyone I ever saw play the game. When he picked up the puck anywhere deep in his zone, he would usually face his own end, then cut into a sharp short power turn, usually to his left. It would be right foot, inside edge, power left foot, outside edge, more power then again almost completed the turn, inside edge, right foot again, and as quick as 1, 2, 4, he'd be at full Bobby Orr speed. Then he'd take two short strides and with his straightaway acceleration he was gone, headed up ice. No one could catch him, no one even came close. I'd often get his power turns for my telestrator to show fans.

I am very familiar with skating posture — in fact I teach balance on skates. The power and speed Orr could develop in three strides was amazing, mind boggling. The inside-outside-inside blade power skill is easy to teach but to develop the power Orr did took great leg strength and good posture.

As beautiful to watch as his skating and stickhandling was his precision passing ability. He constantly went tape to tape on 99 out of 100 passes. And he was graceful in the way Beliveau was. You got your money's worth just watching Bobby skate with the puck; slow or full speed, he was just syrupy smooth. He seemed to float along effortlessly while everyone around him seemed herky-jerky in trying to keep up. And he did it all with a sly grin on his face. He was so good because he simply loved playing the game.

In the end Orr played just 657 games, amassing 915 regular-season points. In that short time, he won the Stanley Cup twice for the previously hapless Bruins, won the Calder Trophy in 1966–67, the James Norris a record eight times, the Hart Memorial Trophy three times, the Art Ross Trophy twice, the Conn Smythe Trophy twice, the Lester B. Pearson Award, the Lester Patrick Award, was named to eight First All-Star teams and one Second Team selection.

But those are all cold recorded numbers, amazing as they are.

More amazing than his totals was the various, versatile, and creative ways in which he scored or set up plays. What Bobby did best was electrify the crowd by picking up the puck deep in his own end, circle his net, and then begin an amazing trip to the other end of the frozen battleground, where he would seemingly at will deposit the puck in the other team's net. If a teammate had kept up, he'd gladly set him up with a perfect pass instead of scoring himself. I can close my eyes and replay this picture time and again. He truly was a hockey poem on skates.

And along the way he changed the game of hockey — forever. Few players have had an impact on any sport the way Bobby did, and his skills and style brought a whole new approach to the greatest game in the world. Without Bobby, it is hard to imagine how the game would have evolved to its current level. Every time I saw him play he seemed to do something phenomenal, something new. With his tremendous skating and puck-handling skills, Bobby seemed to simply outplay the others on the ice.

My good friend Don Skoyen (who's been with me for 30 years in the hockey school business) is the consummate Bobby Orr fan. When I picked Gretzky ahead of Orr in the "best players ever" list, Don jumped all over me. Whenever I even suggest Gretzky is in the same class as Bobby O, he admonishes me. How many times have I, over a half-empty bottle of London Dock, had to listen to Don say, "Orr was the dictator, the dominator of every game he ever played in. He forced you to try and play the game at his speed and when he upped the pace, no one on any team could keep up. When he played at normal speed of the average player, he killed them with deadly passes and great moves in order to beat anyone one on one. He had no such thing as top speed, he simply went as quickly as he had to in any given situation, and when he kicked it into gear — swoosh, he was gone. Orr had a very late panic point, and simply put, Howie, Bobby Orr was the greatest hockey player ever."

The league may have expanded in numbers a year after he arrived on the pro scene, but it was Orr who expanded the popularity of the game. His flash and dare excited even the newest fan and drew thousands to the game. Without a doubt, no player had the impact on changing the game the way Bobby did, and over a five-year period no player was better.

Folks, if you never saw Orr play, was like seeing Babe Ruth hit one downtown, seeing Joe DiMaggio run one down, watching Arnie Palmer drain a golf ball from 150 yards out, Michael Jordan dunking one with no time on the clock, Ali doing the butterfly shuffle, like Johnny Unitas tossing the bomb, or Sammy Sosa knocking one home. And if you missed him, well, golly gee you really missed out.

GUY LAFLEUR

When Montreal coach Jacques Lemaire drove Guy Lafleur to retire in 1984–85, at least six years before he should have, at age 33, I said, "It's too bad Guy Lafleur never learned how to play hockey like everyone else does." My comment got a lot of play, especially in Quebec papers. The phone never stopped ringing.

"Are you nuts or what?"

I watched Guy play for years, talked skills with him for hours, and also hired him many times at my hockey school in Stanstead, Quebec. He also worked with me filming *Pro Tips* and on my own CBC television hockey school show, so obviously Guy and I were good friends and spent a fair bit of time together.

Besides being a great physical talent, Guy was mentally similar to Gretzky. Lafleur always knew on offence what was happening and, as a result of what he was doing, what else would take place. He knew how to create openings, and how to anticipate or dictate how a play was about to unfold. Guy could see the game and would often put the puck to the spot where the action was going, but unfortunately, more times than not, nobody was there. He was too far ahead of his teammates in thinking and reacting — and that was what I meant by my comment. It was too bad Guy never learned to play the game at a normal level like other players.

Lafleur, like Wayne, played the game in another atmosphere. When you have one, two, or three other people on the ice who comprehend, read, and understand what you're trying to do and take advantage of it, it's super! Gretzky had many teammates in Edmonton, but Guy, for the most part, was alone on the ice in his thinking.

Oh, there were teammates who fit in pretty well with his brilliance; Lemaire was the best, and Shutt, Savard, and Robinson at times could read and understand his moves, but he was never blessed with too many people who were at his mental or skill level.

When Lemaire took over the Canadiens as coach, he wanted Guy to play to systems of defensive and offensive hockey. To do so takes patience and discipline, of which Guy had none. Other coaches such as Bowman had said, "Guy, go play, do your own thing, and we will feed off you." Lemaire wanted to control Lafleur's mind and body — not a chance!

During his retirement years, Lafleur played Old-timers hockey, learned how the game was played by mortals, came back to the NHL, and had three very good years.

I've heard some suggest that the booze, smoking, and other such things slowed Guy down at the end of his career, but I don't buy that. Rather, I believe Guy came back to the Rangers and then Quebec Nordiques for a couple of reasons, including that he missed the game and did not like the way he had left. Also, he said himself that he wanted to "retire comfortably."

Others suggest that when Guy returned from his more than three-year retirement and recent selection to the Hall of Fame, he'd lost a lot of his shine and that his mesmerizing skills were gone. I simply think he learned discipline, patience, and how to take advantage of other players' skills, and he squeezed out a few good years of enjoyable hockey with reasonable results.

Guy was a tremendous athlete and wonderful talent on the ice, and as readers will have noted, he ranked higher in my top 10 the more I thought about his skills and contribution. Over 17 seasons he made the playoffs 14 times. In 1,126 regular-season matches, he scored 560 goals and 1,353 points and won the Stanley Cup five times, a half-dozen major trophies, six first All-Star team selections, and the hearts of thousands and thousands of hockey fans.

Of the many attributes The Flower had (aside from his swooshing down the right-wing boards with his blond hair flying in the Forum air, and the puck cradled on his stick), his most outstanding was his insatiable desire to win. Guy could not tolerate losing. He took nothing as seriously as his hockey. Some condemned him for that, others applauded.

Either way, it was his fierce, competitive streak that makes him one of the true champions of hockey for all time.

BOBBY HULL

You know you've been around the game a long time when you can talk about great players, and then about that great player's kid.

When it comes to goal scoring it's "like father like son" with the Hull clan. Brett Hull comes by his flair for goal scoring with good bloodline connections, for his dad was likely the hardest shooter ever in the history of the NHL. There have been some big boomers like Boom Boom Geoffrion, Andy Bathgate, Al MacInnis, brother Dennis Hull, and Bobby Schmautz — but none placed the fear in goaltenders that the Golden Jet did when he wound up for his famous slap shot.

Personally I would have just got the hell out of the way. You couldn't have paid me enough to be a goalie and have that man fire at me all night long.

Depending on who you talk to, Bobby's shot has been recorded at various top speeds. The official fastest one I'm aware of is 113 miles an hour, though I heard he reached 118. Does it matter? That's about 30 miles an hour faster than the average player.

It's a safe bet to suggest there will never be a harder-shooting father-and-son duo than the Golden Jet and his son, whom I call the Stealth Bomber.

However, the elder Hull was more than just a wind-up scoring machine. In fact he was capable of playing a complete game when he wanted. Bobby was another example of a supremely fit hockey player whose additional strength and power gave him an edge. He tossed plenty of hay (not a lot of cows like some reporters have suggested!) and worked very hard all his life. He came by his build and fitness based on hard work, and it worked for him big time.

When Hull wound up in his end with the puck, or broke up the wing looking for a pass, his legs started churning like pistons and the ice crunched beneath his skates. The immovable force had been placed in motion. Bobby was the virtual bull in a china shop, but with grace and control. Opponents seemingly bounced off the Golden Jet as he roared toward the net. A few feet either side of the blue-line, Hull would wind up and blast a shot, or burst for the net and drive home a backhand. Either way it was power, art, excitement!

Bobby was an outstanding junior player, and it didn't take a rocket scientist to figure out he was going to be a good pro player as well. Indeed, even I saw the lad's potential. Once again, back during my Maple Leaf "management" career, I had cause to seek out a junior match and spotted young Bobby among the crowd of wanna-be's. On April 4, 1957, I wrote to Leafs owner Conn Smythe:

"Saw last night's junior game in Guelph between St. Kitts and Guelph. Guelph winning easily 6-2.

"Bobby Hull was the outstanding player for St. Kitts. He is a strong skater, has an excellent shot, a good competitor and seems to have better than average hockey brains. I think he is a good NHL prospect.

It's good to know that I didn't miss all of the obvious future stars.

Bobby was also a strong passer and stickhandler and, in fact, spent most of his junior (and first couple of seasons with the Hawks) at centre ice before making the shift to the left side. I wonder how his career would have altered had he stayed in the slot. Somehow it seems hard not to imagine Bobby roaring down the left wing boards, hand on the stick, shovelling the puck just ahead of the "immovable force" in motion.

Gosh he was exciting.

Bobby's power, however, was often best displayed under collision conditions. The force in motion when it hits a wall — that was Hull versus a couple of other players, including Terry Harper, Gordie Howe (can you believe that, gosh, nice old Gordie), and Bobby's most famous rival of all, John Ferguson. Next to Hull's blazing speed and shooting skills, his infamous run-ins with big John were something else many folks remember. Two freight trains, one track. Ouch! Yikes!

Bobby was fierce as a player in a competitive and mental way. With Bobby there was no long route or shortcuts, it was up and down his wing and to the net. Sometimes around people, sometimes through them. No easy nights. Even when Bobby floated he was there in a physical way.

I will never forget the beatings he took in two different playoff years in the 1960s and yet never quit working. He was amazingly tough, playing with a broken jaw one year, needing a football helmet in order to be able to play.

Bobby won the Stanley Cup only once for all his years in the league, and that somehow seems unfair. The game of hockey owes a lot of thanks to Bobby Hull for helping give the game some real excitement during key years. When I hear the term "power play," I think of Bobby Hull.

TERRY SAWCHUK

I always figured Terry Sawchuk was an arrogant son of a bitch. I never did like him, still, he was one hell of a netminder.

Sawchuk would come on the ice for the pre-game warm-up and skate slowly past you on the ice or the bench and look like King Tut. He'd give you a snobbish look as if to say, "What the hell do you want and what are you doing here? I'm getting a shutout tonight so pack your bags and go home." If he didn't get the shutout, odds are he held us to two goals.

Hah, but how many games did we win in Motor Town 1–0 or 2–1?

Plenty! The Wings would play 50 of the 60 minutes in our end and yet sure enough we'd win. We hated each other as hockey clubs and as players.

I don't think I was the only one who disliked Terry, if for no other reason than his haughty arrogance on the ice. I'm sure he was as cut up and ugly as he was because some of the guys intentionally fired at his head. I wasn't that good a shot or I might have tried.

I guess I also hated the guy because he made stopping the puck look so damn easy. He was a great standup goalie and as quick as a cat with his hands and feet. Though he always played in that crouch, he never flopped around. Very exciting to watch, but snarly during the game and mean with his stick. He cut me at least once.

In his first years in the league, from 1950 to 1955, Sawchuk allowed fewer than two goals per game! Enough said. Yes, he could certainly stop a puck, and an even bigger feat was that he posted a 2.57 goals against average in his two years in Boston, where he saw more rubber than he had in the previous five years at Detroit.

I remember him well while he was playing for Imlach in Toronto. He and Johnny Bower won the Stanley Cup for the Leafs in 1967. He flopped a lot more then, but in the pressure-packed games he kept the biscuit out of the basket.

He was a different kind of a guy — even for goalies.

Sawchuk played in 971 games in 21 amazing years. He leads my All-Time list of goalies, with most shutouts at 103 (no one else is close), owns four Stanley Cup rings, and is in the Hall of Fame.

And I still hate the SOB.

MARK MESSIER

Geeze, how time flies. Seems just like yesterday that I saw Mark Messier holding his fifth Stanley Cup in his arms, with a smile as big as all outdoors and saying, "This one's for you, Wayne." Knowing hockey players, I wouldn't be a bit surprised if Gretzky contributed to Edmonton's cause almost as much as a Los Angeles King as he did while a teammate.

The odds before the 1989–90 playoffs that the Oilers would even be in the Stanley Cup finals had to be better than 100 to 1 — to win, 500 to 1. Having been there three times myself, and only once (1947–48) did we have the best team, I know there are many things that make it possible for your team to beat the skilled players. The Oilers had great pride, and I'm sure Messier and management worked Gretzky's great love for Edmonton into one of their motivational reasons for winning.

Most of the best Messier stories go back to his Ranger years including his classic leadership prediction, in the finals against New Jersey. However, there was one series with the Oilers when Messier was truly outstanding — against the New York Islanders in Edmonton, in their second Stanley Cup series.

In the post-game TV interview between Messier and Dave Hodge, both Glen Sather and I were there, standing just off camera, with tears in our eyes because we were so pleased for Messier. Messier's other finest moment was the 1989–90 surprise run to the Cup. Sure, Bill Ranford was everybody's hero and rightly so (he won the Conn Smythe) but hardly any team wins Lord Stanley's Cup without the goalie being the best player on the ice.

Although Edmonton had a great goalie in Bill Ranford, in this particular run for the roses, Messier's size and strength, skill, leadership, work ethic, and mental toughness led his team to a great victory. Oh, the rest of that famous gang — Anderson, Gregg, Kurri, Lowe — should all be proud too because holy smokes they were something special.

Messier left the Rangers on a quest to lead another lost club, Vancouver, out of the hockey wilderness. However the brave, good Sir Mark may have finally met even his match, for the daunting quest seems to grow darker each day.

Fittingly, Messier managed to surpass Gordie Howe to fourth place overall in the all-time NHL regular season assist standings. Messier set up teammate Alexander Mogilny for the club's final goal in the final game of the 1998–99 season. The assist gave Messier 1,050 in his illustrious career. Marvellous.

However, Mark saved a little bit for the 1999–2000 season, remaining tied with Bobby Hull in seventh spot in all-time NHL goals scored with 610. By the time this book hits the shelves, he will have broken that tie as well.

A tremendous competitor with tremendous skills, Messier was and is the kind of player you are damn glad to have on your team and not the other guys'.

STAN MIKITA

Early in Stan Mikita's NHL career, he carried a big chip on his shoulder and he and others paid for it. Stan was as good a stick man as any, and it didn't help that he was mean as a rattlesnake. My oh my, could he hack, slash, hook, and cross-check with the best of them.

However, he also had tremendous skills with a stick in other ways. Nobody (other than maybe Gretzky) could work the magic with the puck as well as Stan.

The first game I broadcast for *Hockey Night in Canada* at the Forum was a match between the Hawks and the Canadiens in 1968. All the talk was about curved sticks and while when I was chatting with Danny Gallivan and Dick Irvin before the pre-game warm-up, I said, "It doesn't help their game. How can they stickhandle with a blade curved like a 'No U-Turn' sign?"

Honest, folks, that's how Mikita and Bobby Hull had bent their stick blades, and Mikita's had a bigger hook than Hull's. It was more like a boomerang.

"And for sure," I prattled on in lecture mode, "they won't be able to make a backhand pass or shot." I may as well have just smashed an egg on my face because, sure enough, they made me look dumb. Ten minutes later, the Hawks were on the ice warming up netminder Denis DeJordy. I watched as Mikita skated in on the off-wing against the netminder and dropped his shoulder to fake the shot. DeJordy dropped to his knees. Stan went from forehand to backhand, hesitated for a half second, and then roofed the puck. I thought to myself, "Well, so much for that curved stick theory."

When they did the regular three-on-two drills, Mikita was between Ken Wharram and Bobby Hull. Geeze, did they remind me of another older fabulous puck-handling line of Max and Doug Bentley and Bill Mosienko. Mikita and his wingers moved the puck like it was a hot potato, and when a defenceman got in the way, Stan and Bob (both with their curved blades) moved the puck by and around them like a hoop around a barrel.

So late in the first period, the Hab goalie made three or four big saves when the Canadiens were locked in their own zone. As one Hawk attack on the net broke up and the puck headed out of the Canadiens' zone, the goalie slashed Mikita across the shins as he skated by the net on his way out.

No penalty.

Stan stopped at the top of the circle, stared at the netminder, got his attention, then raised his stick, and pointed it at his head. He took off one glove and pointed his finger at his head, a gesture that I interpreted as "I'll get you for that."

In the second period, Hawks defenceman Pierre Pilote hit Hull with a pass while Hull was under a full head of steam coming out of his own zone. The big guy went one on one against Serge Savard, took him wide, and then hit Mikita wide open at the Montreal blueline with a perfect pass. Stan took two strides to the top of the circle and fired a bullet at the goalie's head. The puck hit him on the left cheek with such force that it cut his eyebrow for six stitches. If he hadn't had a mask on, the shot would have killed him. I was definitely left in no doubt about the accuracy that could be obtained from that curved blade or about Mikita's meanness. Dollars to doughnuts says the Montreal goalie never again took a swing at the Blackhawks' nasty little centre.

But Mikita mellowed, and when he stuck to hockey, my oh my, was he a dandy. He was one of the finest centres to ever play the game and showed not only the skills but the smarts to be a leader for many years. For his stick stills, he's one of my all time favourites for sure.

MAURICE "ROCKET" RICHARD

Very few players have ever had the same intensity for the game, or for life, than the Rocket.

On the ice, the man was a menace, plain and simple. Many a big, tough, respected player in the league gave the Rocket a very wide berth on the ice because he was totally unpredictable. For all of his marvellous skills and contributions, he was a madman on skates whose volatile temper often got the best of him.

No other player can list off the resumés of riots, brawls, fights, and suspensions that the Rocket racked up in his career. From choking referees to clubbing players in the head with his stick . . . the Rocket could explode anytime, anywhere. One of his more famous incidents was attacking a referee in a hotel lobby. But his antics gave him plenty of room on the ice and probably 10 points more on the season.

Like several other players, off the ice Richard was another person, and few finer gentleman are to be found. Just don't give him a pair of skates and a stick.

There are only two guys in the game of hockey that ever seemed to have sparks come out their eyes; one is Mark Messier and the other, the wilder of the two, was the Rocket. When he was in full flight and totally involved in the game, his eyes were black — rock black and they seemed to be flashing. If you looked him in the eyes just then, you'd swear there were sparks coming out of them. I was on the receiving end of that flared-eye, lightning stare a few times, and it was unnerving as hell.

The Rocket didn't make my top four or five all-time players list but that only had to do with the tremendous talent of the players ahead of him.

Injuries, bad luck, and his own temper stopped Maurice from ever winning the individual scoring title. He was a natural scorer, quick with the stick and hands. Tic-tac-toe and bang it was in the net. When the Rocket flew in from his right-wing position, it was like watching a tornado come down on you. He was just as deadly on the forehand as he was on the backhand and many say he was ambidextrous, just like Howe.

All I know was I'm glad he played the right-wing slot on his club as well, because that meant we seldom had to meet head to head on the ice. I was always battling whoever he had on the left wing, which was bad enough.

Richard was a strong skater but not tremendous, a smooth passer, and great stickhandler. Like most great scorers, he had the ability to find or create open ice. He had the knack of hiding in a crowd and then at the perfect split second, burst through a maze of players with the puck to stuff it in the net.

His greatest two advantages, however, were his strength and his lust for winning. Despite his average skating skills, Maurice was great at shifting either way, left or right, and undressed many an all-star defenceman night after night. The Rocket was much like a bull on skates and would regularly have one or two players trying to drag him down as he burst for the net. They seldom stopped him. It was simply amazing to watch.

When it comes to competitiveness, no one ever matched the Rocket. No player showed more fire during the spring quest for the Stanley Cup than the Rocket. The proof is etched on the Cup itself.

RAY BOURQUE

Most very good hockey players do something with flare, something special that catches the eye of the fans and writers. They might be an outstanding skater, have great speed, be an accurate passer or shooter, a good fighter, a mean player, have a booming shot, or be a punishing body-checker.

Then there's the rare dude you find who can do all those things very well, yet also has other gifts. Ray Bourque is one of those.

A tremendous skater and passer, Ray's accurate shot from the point has not only resulted in volumes of goals over 20 years as a Bruin, but is well documented in the popular Skills Competition that is now part of the annual NHL All-Star weekend. For several years Bourque cleaned up in the shot accuracy contest, picking targets in all four corners of the net with deadly accuracy.

Bourque also knows how to play defence, how to play the game without the puck, how to make the offence work, and has another very key ingredient — timing. Of even greater importance are his amazing recuperative abilities. Bourque takes his lumps, bumps, and injuries yet he is seldom out of the line-up.

Ray plays within his talents, and plays well consistently game in and game out. He has always helped the Bruins offensively, often being the focal point on the power play, and yet over the years there have been few defencemen any better at guiding their team out of their own zone. After many years of watching Ray play the game, it suddenly dawned on me how brilliant he is at setting the tempo, and the play, and at moving the puck out of his own end.

What makes Bourque so consistently effective and valuable is his almost flawless ability to beat at least the first forechecker coming after him. He loves to play coy, waiting around behind his net, or just off the goal post, or temptingly dawdling around in the corner. Almost always Bourque draws the first checker deep, deep into his zone, and preferably even gets the checker to chase him behind the net. When that happens, Bourque will nearly always manage to beat at least two forecheckers, either with a good pass or great acceleration, before or by the time he hits his own blueline. The first forechecker simply chases him behind the net or swings off into the corner in pursuit and puts himself behind Bourque (and few can catch Ray if he doesn't want to be caught). The second forechecker is then drawn in by his own and his teammate's stupidity. Seeing the huge open ice in the slot area (which his teammate should not have gone past), the second checker moves in to fill the void, and Ray beats him as simply as he would have the first checker — if he'd stayed in position. Voilà, two down — three to go, and Ray still has four open teammates to pass to.

With all due respect to the effective lunch-pail work ethic the Bruins have almost always shown, they have had only a handful of stars or superstars during Bourque's two-decade career. I can only wonder what sort of success and numbers Ray would have had if he'd been surrounded with a really solid club for a few years, like Orr enjoyed during his years in Beantown.

Success has not spoiled Ray Bourque. The kid from Montreal who dropped out of school at Grade 10 to chase a dream remains humble in his success. What a talent and what a pleasure to watch and to know him.

It's a shame he never lifted Lord Stanley's mug. Ray's another classic example of a player who never won, but certainly deserved a Stanley Cup ring, because of sure effort, skill, and leadership.

PETER STASTNY

When I first started my hockey school business on mainland Canada in Stanstead, Quebec, it wasn't a sellout. However, that summer, *Hockey Night in Canada* boss Ralph Mellanby and crew filmed a short segment of a hockey clinic I ran there, edited it down to five minutes, and played it between periods of a Canadiens–Leafs game. Ralph was interested in what sort of response the viewers might have.

For the next eight years my hockey school was sold out, and the film clip was the spark for a regular *HNIC* feature on skills and pro tips. I'd been after *HNIC* to let me do that series on hockey skills for years and they saw the light and agreed.

Most clubs said yes, most players said yes, and most technical people came aboard, including Jack Vandermay, who had saved our ass hundreds of times when he filmed the Howie Meeker Hockey School in St. John's, Newfoundland. Vandermay had a great understanding of the game of hockey. His quick grasp of what I was trying to accomplish, knowledge of the best way to film it, and determination and persistence until he was sure he had what I wanted, was amazing. To Jack, time meant nothing. He'd work 14 or 16 hours a day until it was right. Vandermay was as important to the series as any player.

One day when filming the series, I spied Marcel Aubut, the major shareholder of the Quebec Nordiques, standing along the boards with two young men talking to Ralph Mellanby. Ralph called me over and, after exchanging greetings with Marcel, introduced me to Peter and Anton Stastny. When I asked if they would join us for a show and do some passing demonstrations, they had smiles on their faces a mile wide. Even at that time, early in the 1980s, Europeans had considerably more and better stick skills than most Canadian and U.S. players. Their demonstration was done in just a few takes, because they were practically flawless.

Peter and Anton were among the significant leaders of the European jump into the NHL, and their play was as exciting as their arrival into the league. They were the youngest of three talented brothers and heroes in their homeland of Czechoslovakia. Anton played nine years at left wing for the Nordiques, had 636 points and 252 goals, and got nearly 30 goals per year. He was a solid winger who hit, checked, and had a great positional play dedication.

Peter was the NHL star of all the brothers. He was the focal point when he and quiet Anton arrived in Quebec for the start of the 1980–81 season. Peter endured the rigours of the league for 14 seasons. He starred with Quebec for nine years before being swapped to New Jersey. He played 23 games with St. Louis over bits of his 14th and 15th seasons in the league and then retired due to injuries. In 977 regular-season games, Peter netted 450 goals and set up 789 others for 1,239 career points. He was an amazing passer, skater, and stickhandler.

The third and oldest Stastny was Marian, who many said was the best of them all. I don't agree, but he was in his twilight when

I saw him. Oddly, I do not recall a lot about Marian, though surely I must have been aware of his skills as he was a legendary international European and Czech player. In his homeland, Marian was regarded like Howe or Lafleur here. He joined the NHL a year after his younger brothers had paved the way and he could leave his Czech playing commitment. In five NHL seasons and 322 games, Marian scored 121 goals and had 294 points. His first four years were spent in Quebec and in his final year he was a Leaf. Taken together, that's 2,169 points for the three brothers from Czechoslovakia. Talk about a ground-breaking trio.

Peter ended up in the Hall of Fame. I got to know him a little bit better in November 1998 when Leah and I met him and his charming wife at the Boys' Club of New York Hall of Fame dinner. A couple of weekends later, we met again when we were both inducted into the Hall of Fame and were able to spend a few days together. I learned a lot about hockey watching and talking with Peter Stastny, a first class guy both on and off the ice.

OTHER IMPORTANT
PLAYERS (AND A COACH)

■ ■ ■

MICKEY REDMOND

Many years ago, a superb minor league hockey player by the name of Rollie McLenahan ran the biggest and best hockey school in the country, at St.-Andrews-by-the-Sea, New Brunswick. Rollie was built like a miniature tank — 200 pounds of muscle on a 5' 8" frame — and was also a brilliant defenceman.

During the late 1960s, Rollie was director of sport and recreation for New Brunswick. He was in the Montreal Canadiens chain, so half the instructors were from the Canadiens. The other half were from Scotty Bowman's St. Louis team. Rollie and Scotty were good friends when Bowman first worked for the Habs.

I got lucky and was given an invitation to become an instructor. I thought I'd died and gone to hockey heaven. What a staff — Bowman; Jacques Plante; Donnie Marshall; Camille Henry; Barclay, Bob, and Bill Plager; Doug Harvey; Eddie Bush; Gus Bodnar. Every Saturday night we had a lobster barbecue, all you could eat. Saturday night Rollie and I would sit up drinking dark rum (London Dock, naturally) while eating and picking all the very best eggs, and meat everyone else had left in the lobster body.

That year we had a young instructor in camp named Mickey Redmond. He was about six feet, 190 pounds and really built solid. Redmond knew nothing about teaching skills to kids, and wasn't anxious to impart what little knowledge he had to our paying customers. He was too busy developing a new kind of shot. It was the early days of the hooked blade, and naturally Mickey sported a good bend in his, but in a different place. On a normal 12-to-14-inch blade, his was straight until the last three inches and then it was hooked or bent.

One day I was talking my way through a demonstration, showing how to hold the stick when carrying the puck, how you drop the bottom hand an inch or two using your wrist when shooting, that you only go down another one or two inches when you slap-shoot the puck. All the time I was talking to the group, there was a continuous boom, boom noise, like cannons going off and rebounding off boards and glass. Geeze, it was like working in a riveting shop. I couldn't hear myself talk and I knew the kids couldn't either. Finally, I'd had enough and asked Donnie Marshall to demonstrate the three positions of the hands when shooting. I headed for the kid, prepared to tear a strip off his ass.

Redmond was at the opposite end of the arena with a pile of 20 or 30 pucks. He reached out, rolled the hooked toe of the stick over the puck, and pulled it toward the centre of his body. This action forced the heel of the stick 12 inches off the ice, and when the stick and puck reached the normal shooting position, he uncoiled, rolled his wrist, and followed through with his arms and shoulders. The puck left the stick blade like a rocket.

I stopped, mouth open in awe, and waited for him to do it again. Where'd he get the velocity? I wondered.

I watched again as he reached out, turned the stick blade over, the toe of the blade nestled beside the puck, heel off the ice. He pulled the stick and puck toward him, unwound the wrist, the heel of the stick hitting the ice behind the puck. He bent the handle that unwinds on follow through. It was a mini slap shot with almost all the power of a full slap shot — but with no big wind-up. And it was done almost as quick as a wrist shot.

"Hey kid, who taught you that shot?"

"Nobody, Howie, it's just something I've been fooling around with for years."

"Do you know where the thing is going?"

"Sure. Watch the far post." *Klonk*. "Five-hole centre net, post." *Clink*, "low short side." *Thunk*, "crossbar centre net." *Clang*!

By now I was practically dragging him over to Donnie and his group of shooters. I put a goalie in the net and Mickey deep slot. "Hey kids, watch Mickey shoot the puck," I ordered.

And did he put on a show. Jumpin' gee whillikers, never in a month of Sundays did I ever see such a shooting display.

It didn't take long for every kid in camp to get on the outdoor shooting galleries we had. And it didn't take Mickey very long to become a 52-goal scorer in the NHL. Geeze, what a shot. To the best of my knowledge, Redmond was the first to use it — the snapshot.

Another youngster with real scoring promise at that camp picked up on the Redmond technique. His name was Danny Grant and like Redmond, filled the net a bunch in the big leagues.

KEN WHARRAM AND PIERRE PILOTE

Any time I get a little uppity, thinking I know quite a bit about anything and everything, I think about Ken Wharram and Pierre Pilote. Did I screw up.

After my eight seasons playing for the Leafs, I wound up in 1953–54 coaching senior hockey in Stratford, Ontario, then in 1954 Hap Day hired me to coach the Leafs' farm team in Pittsburgh, Pennsylvania. The American Hockey League in those years had six teams, including Buffalo, Cleveland, Hershey, Providence, and Springfield. Part of my job was to send Day a description of every goal scored against us in every game; who was on the ice, and who did what or didn't do what. Geeze, now when I look back I realize what a tremendous task it was, especially after a 6–5 loss in Springfield and then the next night to get blown away 7–4 in Providence. It didn't happen often but a lot of my players had friends in both cities and some of them lived high on the hog for a few days on the road. It made for a lot of writing. (Years later that ability to see the game develop kept me in TV, especially when the telestrator came along.)

Ex-goalie Baz Bastien, who lost an eye while at training camp in Port Colbourne in 1949, was our general manager. Although Baz attended most road matches he couldn't sit and watch any close game, so with no place to walk in the seating area, he'd head for the Zamboni entrance and walk the hallways. As he paced about, he would always take out his glass eye, shine it up, and put it back in. It was a scream to watch. Back of the Zamboni entrance, he would take a look at the score, 2-1 Buffalo with two minutes left to play — "Oh God" and take another walk, pop out the eye, shine it, in with the eye again, and back to the Zamboni door . . .

So over a beer and ribs after one game, I asked Baz (just for fun), "Who was playing for us when Buffalo scored the winning goal?"

"How the hell would I know?"

Another important part of my job was to keep an eye out for potential NHL talent. I had to name the best three players in the game, including players from the opposition. Lots of times my choices were not named one of the three stars on the night.

Ken Wharram and Pierre Pilote both played for Buffalo, who we met in the finals that first year (we won four games to two). That means I saw Kenny and Pierre play 18 times during that season. The next year we played them 12 times, which means I'd probably seen them each play 25 to 30 times — yet I never saw their potential.

Three years later, in 1958 (after my one brief season as Leaf coach and Pilote's two seasons in the NHL), both Wharram and Pilote were together in Chicago, and well on their way to being ranked among the cream of the crop. One day when I was living in Newfoundland, I said to myself, "I wonder if they ever made my list as potential NHL players?" After searching for a day and a half, I finally found my Pittsburgh folder containing my game books and anxiously went from game to game. When I was done, I was shocked to discover that not once had I noted them as possibles for the NHL.

How had I missed these guys? After a few minutes, I managed to scrape up a reason, and a pretty damn lame one at that. If you've ever coached, you know that you're so wrapped up in your own team's performance during the game — power play, killing penalty, best unit on last minute of a period, getting the next shift ready — that you can't see straight. There is very little time to assess the talent or potential talent of the opposition, let alone your own club.

Our team, the Hornets, were big, strong, tough, and talented. We finished or almost finished every check and we created an atmosphere where our small, skilled talent could perform unmolested.

Buffalo's Kenny Wharram could motor. No doubt he had the legs because he later became a member of the famed Blackhawks' trio dubbed the Scooter Line (Wharram with Doug Mohns and Stan Mikita). If you gave Wharram open ice — something we never did — he'd kill you. I'd just put Andy Barbe and Gerry Foley on him and it was game over. So it's not surprising I didn't see his promise.

For an average-size defenceman back then, Pierre Pilote played endurance hockey. He wisely stood up to block shots and cleared the net regularly with cute moves and sly stickwork. He was not dirty or even mean, but he was effective. He played defence with his head, very little body. Pierre was also good on the point — and would make a shot on net most times. He was not a terribly talented man on the blades, but he never wandered from his post either. Pilote was steady with the puck, seldom fancy, and a so-so passer. In his own zone, if you got to him quickly as possible, you could make him move the puck, and often he'd give it away.

But Wharram and Pilote learned and learned, and in 1963–64, they both made the first All-Star team (Wharram for the first time), along with Hull, Mikita, and Glenn Hall — amazing! Five of six from Chicago.

Over the years, Pilote learned how to handle and pass the puck, and Kenny Wharram learned how to handle the tough game. (Hell, that's a laugh because come to think of it the American League in those days was much tougher than the NHL. If a kid could survive and perform in our league, he was a cinch to make it in the NHL.)

Wharram played all his 11 regular seasons (and three partial seasons) with Chicago and scored 252 regular-season goals and 533 points in 766 games. Pilote shone even brighter, making numerous trips to All-Star games while picking up 498 points in 890 games. Both players sport a Stanley Cup ring.

I could excuse myself for missing one guy on a team like that, but missing two — what a dummy! I wasn't a complete failure in the scouting role, however. I did recommend a few other players to the Leafs. I implored them to get Johnny Bower from Cleveland.

Still, whenever I get to thinking I know quite a bit about anything, I try to remember to advise myself, "Keep your eyes and ears open, and your mouth shut."

CRAIG LUDWIG

Defencemen come in all sizes, shapes, and styles, with a variety of physical and mental skills. But the ones I like the most are the slow yet steady, big guys who are as tricky as an alley cat. When I played I didn't appreciate such superb blueliners as Bob Goldham, Babe Pratt, Jack Stewart, and Pat Egan. I didn't realize then how little mobility was needed to play defence. If a player understood how to play the game and what his duties and responsibilities were, and if the player could make a 180-degree turn (it didn't matter how fast, just make it) and come out of it faster than he went in, then he had a chance to be a decent defenceman.

While I was coaching in Pittsburgh, I had Frank Mathers playing defence. He had good mobility, not great, but probably was still the best defenceman in the league, and he got me looking at the game through a defenceman's eyes — at the philosophy, duties, and responsibilities.

Mathers also suggested I watch other AHL defencemen, including Pete Backer, Rolly McLenahan, and Keith Allen, and that I talk with Eddie Shore. What an education I got in the next two years. Shore spent hours with me talking hockey. Although he had some nutty ideas, he had others that were years ahead of anyone else in the game.

Like most other sports, you win championships on defence. The winners almost every year in basketball, football, baseball, soccer

— any team sport — usually are the ones that are hardest to score on. Playing defence is a group, unit, or team philosophy and effort, but the ones most responsible for turning the puck over and retrieving it are the two defencemen.

Today, the "D" men are handling the puck much more than they did the majority of time between the 1950s and mid-1980s. That's because in today's game, the team with the puck often gains the centre ice or neutral area and then tosses the puck into the opponent's end; naturally, the defenceman is most often first to the puck and gains control. That will happen at least 50 times a game, guaranteed. But it's what happens next that often largely decides who wins or loses the game. How well your defenceman can safely negotiate the puck out of danger, and out of your end, without giving it away to the opposition often decides the outcome of the night. Count on it.

In any era, 10 or 15 players in the league excel at either moving the puck themselves or making a safe pass to the teammate with the best chance to get into the neutral zone. Another 10 use the boards or glass to dump the puck out effectively. Some are silent and steady, others hold more flash and pizzazz.

One player comes to mind as a perfect example. Late in the 1998–99 regular season, I watched Dallas beat L.A., 2–1. One name kept popping up all night long for Dallas. "Craig Ludwig picks up the puck, short pass, and away they go . . . Ludwig behind the net, moves with the puck to the face-off spot, against the glass and out . . . the Kings are on the power play, they shoot the puck. Belfour kicks it aside, Ludwig picks it up and backhands it the length of the ice.

Every year Ludwig plays and plays and plays, on every kind of shift but the power play. Couldn't score a goal to save his mother from burning at the stake but leapin' lizards, can the man play well on the blueline.

Now I don't know or care who the goof was as general manager of the Montreal Canadiens in June 1990, but two trades killed them and they haven't recovered yet. One of them saw Craig Ludwig shipped to the New York Islanders for whoever.

Ludwig had joined Montreal in the 1982–83 season and left at the end of 1990, having played eight years. While he was there, Montreal was 117 games over .500 and 399 goals+, and I'll bet you they won more than a few games due to good defence. Even if he'd been only the "fifth" defenceman and played part-time (not the case), you still can't let that kind of talent go. Geeze, he's a Gold Visa Card on skates. He's solid in his end, hits well and hard, clears the net with authority, never gets too fancy, and he's probably the best shot blocker in the league. Opposition players do not relax when he's in the area — he's mean. On offence, Craig had scored just 26 times, about three a year, and had 111 assists. Craig enjoyed his finest moment as an athlete in the final game of the 1999 Stanley Cup against Buffalo. That's when he set up the first goal in the 2–1 Stars' Cup-winning game.

Like good wine, Ludwig keeps getting better every year, even as he approaches 40. I love to watch him play defence.

MIKE KEENAN

Some like him, some put up with him, some just plain hate him. Mike Keenan is a controversial guy.

I'm not exactly sure where I stand regarding his coaching ability because I don't know enough facts, but from a distance I grade him somewhere between good and very good. I do know from personal experience, however: Mike Keenan is a super person.

We worked 15 games or so together as TSN broadcast crew members while he was temporarily unemployed a few years back. I really enjoyed the outings. Golly gee — in the airport, in the plane, at our 9 a.m. working breakfast the day of the game, lunches, and particularly during a cold one after the game in a bar or lounge with the gang, he's just a great guy to spend time with. I found him a remarkable fellow. His knowledge regarding the game, management, owners, and players is exceptional. He's funny, has some great stories, and is very generous with his time. I think his questionable moves and philosophy have mostly been successful. Shortly after being traded from Vancouver to St. Louis (where Keenan was coaching), Geoff Courtnall was 20 games into the season with only a couple of goals and five or six assists. After the morning skate I asked him how things were with Keenan. "Fine. He should be mad as hell at me, Howie, maybe even sit me out, but I've found out that he gives a guy three shifts to prove he's ready to play. If you do, you play. If you don't, you sit. If you sit through two games then you're on his shit list, and believe me, that's where your trouble starts.

"But if you work and check, you'll get your chances to play. I've had two or three chances to score a game, every game, and I've got just two goals. However, I've been around long enough to know that if I check hard and consistently, and I play, plus, I'll get chances and sooner or later the puck will start to go in. Mike knows it too, heck he preaches it. Keenan has been good for me."

Other players, wisely, are closemouthed when asked what Keenan is like. It's common knowledge he has two, maybe three, different personalities — one in the world outside hockey, the second his business face, and a third for dealing with the press. Obviously he handles the problem of underachieving, overpaid players, in a manner most unsettling to the hockey players, but he has a tremendous loyalty to the guy who consistently puts his heart and soul into every shift.

Mike knows what it takes to win, from ownership, management, and players. When any of the three don't measure up, they're gone or Mike's gone. Keenan has told me more than once that some owners don't want to pay the price to win it all.

In the mid-'90s, GM Pat Quinn's Vancouver Canucks were in big trouble (what's new?) so the owners fired a couple of coaches and then eventually Quinn. Next the owners hired Mike Keenan to try and get them out of trouble, but at that time you'd have had to been able to walk on water (the non-frozen kind) to make that team competitive. Mike made a few moves, apples for apples stuff, missed the playoffs, and the next summer the U.S. owners hired Brian Burke as new general manager.

It didn't help. Vancouver finished third from the bottom in 1999. Burke fired Keenan half-way through the season and hired former Colorado coach Mark Crawford to get them moving. That didn't help either.

The Canucks' future going in to the start of the next millennium looks dim. Alexander Mogilny seems to want out and they won't get much for him after his 1998–99 performance. Kevin Weekes, the minor league goaltending phenom, is 0 for 15 tries in the NHL and so far couldn't stop a beach ball in the NHL. He will someday, if he gets a chance to develop. In fairness you could take the best coaching group in the NHL and put them in Vancouver and the team couldn't play .500. Yep, it's that bad. Crawford? Like Keenan and Quinn, he walked into a situation that under any circumstances wouldn't work.

How much influence does the owner's representative have? How many of Quinn's, and now Burke's decisions, are made by a bean counter? We will officially never know, but you can bet your bottom dollar even though he is way out of his depth in this caper, the bean counter is making many hockey decisions and the Canucks will go deeper and deeper and deeper into the mud. Mike Keenan deserved his rewards in Philadelphia and Chicago, and then won New York its first Cup in a zillion years. Good for him.

Skills Come in Many Sizes

■ ■ ■

Geeze, folks, whenever I leave home I consider myself fair game for talking hockey, signing autographs, doing interviews, and such. I'll talk hockey with anyone, any time, anywhere, and it's amazing how many times I still hear, "Naw, so and so won't make it, he's too small."

I always come back with, "It's not the size of the body that counts. It's the size of the heart and skills." Half the reason people lament lack of skill in NHL today is because scouts and GMs focus on size.

If they have a clue who I am, I've usually got them by the short hairs because I'm lucky enough to be living proof. I hold four Stanley Cup rings and the Calder Memorial Trophy — yet I was not a greatly skilled, gifted, or big NHL player. I had to work my ass off, play as best I could within my skills, and please the coach by completing my evening's assignment.

Over the years there have been a number of smaller, "plumber"-type players such as myself, "feeders" and "bleeders" who've contributed well in the league. They generally survived by playing a tenacious role mingled with some skills. Some also possessed the unique ability to motivate and inspire both teammates and opponents — but in different ways. Players such as Johnny McKenzie, Stan Smyl, Rejean Houle, and Tie Domi certainly affected the game and others in it although most of them are small by today's standards.

Greatly skilled but slight of size players of the past include Yvan Cournoyer, Denis Savard, Ron Ellis, Camille Henry, André Boudrias, Marcel Dionne, Danny Gare, the Pocket Rocket, and Cliff Ronning. Today there are at least 30 players in the league 5'8" or 5'9" and in the region of 170 pounds who are excellent performers. If you're small of frame but have skills, a big heart, and want it badly enough, playing in the NHL is easy.

Three current stars are prime examples of small players with conflicting styles but impressive results: Paul Kariya, Theoren Fleury, and goalie Ed Belfour. The two forwards were within the top 12 scorers in the league in 1998–99 and both are considered among the leaders of their respective clubs. Belfour, of course, is an outstanding netminder with Dallas.

Last season Kariya scored 39 goals and 101 points while Fleury, traded from Calgary to Colorado later in the year, scooped 40 pucks into the net and tallied 93 points. Belfour won the Cup!

Kariya shines in the league purely as a natural sniper and playmaker. His skating, change of pace and acceleration, stickhandling, puck control (including passing and shooting), and his ability to see and feel the game are amazing. With Gretzky retired from the NHL, Kariya might be one of those superstars to step up and help fill the arena seats. Hopefully, his history of serious concussions will not hurt him or his playing career any further. It was wonderful to see him play all 82 games in the 1998–99 season after a lot of time out from the game.

Most little guys in the game today are very mean and tough, and play a bit like rattlesnakes. Fleury is one who takes the number of a player he's mad at, no matter what size the attacker, and sooner or later that fella's going to get chopped but good.

Fleury is a game-breaker, the go-to guy at game's end, and he is a nasty, obnoxious, little son-of-a-bitch all the time he's on the ice. Because of that, Fleury gets much more room accorded him while on the ice than a lot of other guys his size. The opposition finally caught up to him in the third round of the 1998–99 Stanley Cup playoffs against Dallas. He just couldn't fight through the size and strength of the Dallas checkers.

Another small boy who plays huge is goalie Eddie "the Eagle" Belfour. He plays like a giant with very big pads. Belfour also has very quick hands and great mobility on skates. My oh my, he gave Chicago seven years of excellent goaltending and in the 1998–99 season was sensational in Dallas. Belfour's been flirting with 2.00 goals against and under since day one and should have won the Vezina in 1998–99.

I've always liked Eddie's goaltending. He usually stands up, challenges well with the stick, and makes the big saves when it counts. He's very durable and he's got balls. Belfour has no qualms about dropping his gloves or giving someone deserving a whack with his goalie stick.

Goalies need to be very tough and patient mentally — like Fleury. Eddie goes to the attack when the situation calls for it, but he's also very smart and very cunning and has great anticipation. Belfour plays the game so easily he reminds me of Johnny Bower and Terry Sawchuk.

After years of hard work, Eddie finally silenced the critics in June of 1999, winning the Stanley Cup. Brett Hull, Mike Modano, and others had faced many comments by the media regarding their inability to "do the job." Led by Belfour, the Stars outshone the Sabres, and stamped their names on Lord Stanley's faceplate.

SEVENTY YEARS OF
HAVING FUN

■ ■ ■

My oh my, how the years go by.

When I sit back and think about my 70-plus years of being involved in the greatest game in the world, I marvel at how life moves along. I lean back in my cozy chair in the Sea Room, and the memories flood in — flicking and stickhandling frozen horse buns to and from school, scrub hockey on the pond, backyard rinks, frozen rivers, lakes, or dams used as the local natural ice rink. Games where rubber boots and toques were used as goal posts and skating, puck control, and passing assured every kid their fair time with the puck.

The score? Who cared?

We had fun, deked the odd opponent, out-skated one or two guys, and made passes that we imagined Primeau, Conacher, and Jackson made in the NHL. We even lost and found a puck or two in the snow bank.

When darkness sneaked upon us, we plunked ourselves on the same snow bank, took off our skates, and headed home for supper

— all the time planning a place to play that evening after doing our homework. My, oh my, those days were fun.

Despite a wide variance of skills, everyone got to handle the puck, score a goal, and enjoy the thrills of making offensive moves. Defence, extreme checking, or caring who won would only spoil the enjoyment.

Then came organized hockey: junior B, then junior A, senior A hockey, . . . and then the war. When it ended, I had eight glorious but scared years with the Toronto Maple Leafs, followed by four years of professional coaching before I was fired.

I moved to Newfoundland and spent 18 years in amateur hockey, some playing, most coaching, running hockey schools, and doing TV broadcasting. In the process I discovered lotusland Parksville, Vancouver Island, and 24 years ago moved there. Super boating, the best fishing — unbelievable. The hockey schools were very successful, and the weather? Golfing during the winter months on the ocean's edge, skiing at Mount Washington . . . super!

Hockey has been great to me and hopefully I have been good to hockey. I consider myself incredibly fortunate to have been able to spend the better part of my life playing or being involved in this wonderful game.

Hockey is the greatest sport of all for combining individual physical and mental skills with teamwork. By far it is the most exciting game to both watch and play, and I am thankful to have had the chance to share it with so many Canadians and Americans.

I have never ceased to be amazed at the hospitality and friendship shown to me over the years by most hockey fans and people involved in the game. The number of wonderful people I've met because of the game, not just in Canada and the United States, but also parts of Europe, is boggling.

I have given a lot to the game over the years, but I have been rewarded in spades. The game has given so much back to me.

Best of all, the game gave me some amazing friends in the form of teammates. When I look back, I see a huge number of great friends and amazing, or unique characters. These are people who I spent so many hours of my life with in dingy, stinky dressing rooms, or on a sheet of ice somewhere in North America. The long road trips, bus rides, airplane rides, and endless hotel rooms shared with comrades in the game. Sometimes we laughed together, sometimes we fought, and there were a few times when some of us actually cried. Winning and losing — together.

It is hard to put into words what that kind of camaraderie is really about, to express how much a part of you it becomes. The only feeling that comes close is the special bond between a man and woman, or that bond shared by active soldiers, together, facing the greatest loss of all. The difference is that in hockey there is much more time for laughter. War is hell. Hockey can be hell too, but it is always just a game.

Next to life, it's the greatest game of all.

In both, I feel like I've been lucky enough to be a winner.